Safe In The Shadow

Heather M. Marshall

Heather M. Marshall

Brown Star Publications

Safe In The Shadow

By Heather M. Marshall

1949 –

© Copyright Heather M. Marshall

Brown Star Publications 2006

www.brownstar-publications.co.uk

Heather M. Marshall asserts the moral right to be identified as the author of this work.

All rights reserved.

No part of this publication may be reproduced, stored in a retrieval system, or transmitted in any form or by any means – electronic, mechanical, photocopy, recording, or any other – except for brief quotations in printed reviews, without prior permission of the publisher.

Printed by: ProPrint

ISBN 13: 978-0-9553989-0-8

ISBN 10: 0-9553983-0-4

Sources of Reference

Extracts from the Authorised Version of the Bible [The King James Bible], the rights in which are vested in the Crown, are reproduced by permission of the Crown's Patentee, Cambridge University Press.

Revised Standard Version of the Bible, copyright 1952 [2nd edition, 1971] by the Division of Christian Education of the National Council of the Churches of Christ in the United States of America. Used by permission. All rights reserved.

'Helping Others' G. E. Childs, 'A Parson's Thoughts On Pain'
A. R. Mowbray 1949 [An Imprint of Continuum as publisher and the author].

'A Lay-By' A Religious Of The Community Of St. Mary The Virgin, 'A Light In The Night' S.C.M. Press 1958.

Hymn - 'Safe In The Shadow Of The Lord'
Timothy Dudley-Smith. Hope Publishing Company.

'How, Not Why' The Most Revd. Donald Coggan
'Thought For The Day' BBC Publications 1974.

'Becoming A Christian' J. R. W. Stott M.A.
The Inter-Varsity Fellowship.

Acknowledgements

I would like to thank my long-suffering family for their loving support. I am deeply grateful to my children, for their blessing on my writing.

I am indebted to my husband John: for tirelessly enduring hours of tedious dictation, for painstakingly word-processing my hand-written manuscript. Above all I am thankful for his encouragement and unwavering belief in this work.

My mother Marjorie Spencer (now in her late eighties) continues to be my life-long listener, staunch ally and friend. Her contribution to my life is immeasurable.

I am profoundly grateful for all the prayers offered for my healing; especially those of people unknown to me. I am humbled by the continuing concern for my health.

Finally, I would like to thank everyone mentioned in this work for their contribution to my life and who have consented to being referred to by name. In addition, I am grateful to those who are not specifically named but nonetheless played a vital part. This of course includes the staff of the Oral and E.N.T. departments of Pilgrim Hospital, Boston.

Heather M. Marshall
July 2006

Foreword

Safe in the Shadow is a remarkable book, the fruit of the meticulously kept diary of Heather Marshall's life. Heather recounts, with complete honesty, the significant events of her life, from student to teacher and wife and mother. One feels privileged to be allowed to journey with her and her family, sharing the highs and lows and being humbled by the courage and determination which has enabled her to overcome many difficulties and setbacks.

The title of the book comes from a hymn based on the opening words of Psalm 91:

He that dwelleth in the secret place of the most High
shall abide under the shadow of the Almighty.
I will say of the Lord, He is my refuge and my fortress:
my God; in him will I trust.

In the words of the hymn, and of the psalm which inspired Timothy Dudley-Smith to write them, is found the key to Heather's approach to life. Her faith in God and in Jesus Christ has been the rock which has been the foundation upon which her life has been built. I first met Heather, John, Charlotte and Thomas when they appeared in my congregation at St Mary's Church, Frampton. We became friends as together we explored faith and worked together to discover what God wanted them to do in His service.

Heather, as she describes in the book, developed more confidence in her abilities and gifts and was soon using them in the church and the community.

Then came the shock: she was diagnosed with cancer of the tongue. From that point her faith was tested to the full. Much of the book describes this traumatic time for Heather and her family but their faith remained strong and the love, prayers and support of family and friends enabled them to maintain hope throughout.

Many reading this book will identify with some of Heather's experiences. I hope they will also be inspired by her faith and receive the assurance that they, too, are *safe in the shadow of the Lord.*

The Revd Canon Neil Russell
Stamford

In loving memory of

Albert Edward Spencer

1914 – 1968

CONTENTS

PART 1

Chapter 1	Wednesday 14th October 1992	12
Chapter 2	A Network Of Support	21
Chapter 3	Preparation	30
Chapter 4	Tuesday 27th October - Ward 2B	38

PART 2

Chapter 5	The Pearl Of Great Price	46
Chapter 6	College	57
Chapter 7	Sunday 3rd November 1968	65
Chapter 8	Teaching	74
Chapter 9	Meeting John	81
Chapter 10	Early Married Life	88
Chapter 11	Parenthood	94
Chapter 12	Unsettled Times	103
Chapter 13	Boston Again!	111
Chapter 14	St. Mary's	119
Chapter 15	Mission and Ministry	128
Chapter 16	Romania	135
Chapter 17	Difficult Years	143
Chapter 18	Problems	153
Chapter 19	'It's Nothing Sinister'	157

PART 3

Chapter 20	I.C.U.	166
Chapter 21	Back On 2B	173
Chapter 22	New Experiences	181
Chapter 23	Hospital Routine	188
Chapter 24	Human At last!	197
Chapter 25	Real Food!	206
Chapter 26	Home	214

Chapter 27	Normality?	221
Chapter 28	Picking Up The Pieces	231
Chapter 29	The Way Forward	240
Chapter 30	Unexpected Healing	250
Chapter 31	A Minor Setback	255
Chapter 32	Obstacles!	262
Chapter 33	The Wheelchair Push	273
Chapter 34	One Year On	278
Chapter 35	2B Or Not To Be?	286
Chapter 36	The Commissioning	291

EPILOGUE

| The Lost Chain | 296 |
| Tuesday 26th July 1994 | 299 |

APPENDICES

Appendix 1	Major Surgery	302
Appendix 2	Minor Surgery	305
Appendix 3	Removal Of Metal Arch Bar	306

POSTSCRIPT 307

PART 1

Chapter 1
Wednesday 14th October 1992

Rushing along the corridor of the Oral Department at Pilgrim Hospital; I glanced back, calling out to John, 'You don't have to come with me you know'(hoping that he would take the hint and wait in reception)! In true Marshall fashion I was at least two metres ahead of him, I always walk as if on a route march!

Two days earlier on Monday 12th October, I had undergone a biopsy on my tongue. When my husband John had informed me that he would accompany me for the result, before work at 3pm; I was initially very pleased. At least I would be spared the hassle of parking the car. Now, I really thought that it was a bit 'over the top' for him to be with me. I could see no earthly reason for that. I felt like a child whose parent insisted on accompanying her to the dentist.

At 1.30pm, Val Thompson the nurse who had assisted at the biopsy, ushered us both into the consulting room. John sat in the chair next to the door, whilst I sat in the patient's chair. Mr. Glendinning the Consultant Oral Surgeon entered the room. I remember distinctly thinking that he did not look surprised to see my husband. Without smiling, he quietly greeted me by name and then acknowledged John. **'We've analysed the biopsy and it's a malignant tumour.'** Words that I had never, ever expected to hear, not even in my darkest and wildest imaginings. There had been no warning. Mr. Glendinning just dropped the bombshell!

Although numb with shock and disbelief, something suddenly registered: the instant realisation of why John had been led to come with me, coupled with the enormous relief that he was there. I sat petrified with fear. My thoughts were racing in utter turmoil. *This isn't happening! How can God let this happen to me? Aren't I special to him? He's kept me from harm before. So what on earth's He doing now?*

As my dazed inner questioning was continuing; I became aware that Mr. Glendinning was still talking. He was commenting on it being a very slow growing tumour in its early stages, which could be most effectively dealt with by surgery. He stated that the Consultant Ear, Nose and Throat Surgeon, who specialised in this type of surgery, would be joining us.

Mercifully, I was unable to see John. He said afterwards how dreadful it was for him not to have been sat with me. I am sure that I would have reacted differently if I had seen how devastated he was by the news. Even though tears were welling up in my eyes, I was determined not to break down in front of the consultant.

I partially heard Mr. Glendinning's explanation but was incapable of absorbing it, because my mind was still reeling in frantic denial. The word **Cancer** had not even been mentioned. I knew that I had to voice that dreaded word. I stated, **'You mean I've got cancer!'** There was a pause before Mr. Glendinning replied very solemnly, 'Yes I'm sorry you have.'

By now I had managed to gather my composure sufficiently to be able to ask further questions. John seemed to be coping; in that he also joined in this strained conversation. I still had my back turned to him, so was unable to see how he was reacting.

Then the Consultant E.N.T. Surgeon joined us. He gently reiterated what Mr. Glendinning had said; adding that there was a fifty per cent chance that the tumour had either been caused by a tooth chafing on the tongue; or just bad luck! He had considerable experience in dealing with this type of tumour. It was apparently a very rare occurrence in someone so young, who neither smoked nor drank, other then the occasional glass of wine. He explained that although radiotherapy was an option; in my case he preferred immediate surgery: to give the best chance of a successful outcome. Having explained this in further detail, he told me that obviously it was my choice. I immediately said, 'I haven't really got a choice have I!' He seemed to agree.

He then examined my neck. It appeared to be quite swollen, which indicated that the cancer cells could have spread. He appeared most concerned about my enlarged right lymph node and thyroid gland. He explained that the swelling could be a reaction to the biopsy, or that the cancer had spread even further via the lymph system. This would be established during surgery, by taking a frozen section for immediate analysis in the Pathology Laboratory. If this had occurred, more extensive surgery would have to be carried out. He obviously hoped that this would be unnecessary but it was a definite possibility.

The consultants then discussed a date for theatre. The Consultant E.N.T. Surgeon stated, 'I'll have you in a week on Monday, to operate on the Wednesday.' I retorted, 'Oh that's half-term, can't you make it the week after?' Here, John immediately piped up, 'Don't be silly, it wants doing as soon as possible!' The Consultant E.N.T. Surgeon commented, 'I think this time you must come first.'

He repeated that it was a slow growing tumour and not immediately life threatening, otherwise emergency surgery would have been arranged. One week would not make any real difference; nevertheless, it needed dealing with promptly. To try and lighten the situation I then added, 'Oh well, you've sorted out my plans for half-term then!' I asked how long I would be in hospital and I am sure that he said five days *(I recall thinking, so I'll be out in time for the Sunday service)*!

They enquired whether we had children and seemed relieved that at the ages of thirteen and ten, they were not very young children. John informed them that we would have support from our family to help with the situation. The Consultant E.N.T. Surgeon arranged to see us at 12 o'clock after his Friday clinic, so that he could give us as much time as we needed. By then we would have had time for the shock to sink in and to reflect on what we wanted to ask him.

As Val escorted us into the corridor she asked, 'Are you alright?' I suppose that she felt completely helpless, for she could obviously see that we were not. By this time I was crying very softly. Fortunately, it was lunch-time and everywhere was deserted. Val added, 'If you've any problems just ring ward 2B.' This meant nothing to us. It would have been helpful if there had been someone there 'to pick us up off the floor' and to offer some immediate counselling and support. We now felt completely on our own.

It was a long silent walk back to the car. What words could adequately express the depth of our despair. Once in the car, we clung to each other and sobbed. How John managed to drive home, I do not know. We were both numb with shock, utterly devastated and very frightened. Ahead of us lay the grim task of telling our two children, the rest of our family and friends. I felt as if my whole world had fallen apart and I was a very tiny broken piece.

As we unlocked the front door, our friend Carole Hampson drove round the corner. She had obviously come to find out how I had got on at the hospital. Dismayed at having to face someone else so soon; I scuttled into the house, whilst John told her the bad news. Moments later I reappeared very red-eyed. Carole and I just hugged. Words were totally inadequate. John made us some tea and though still feeling very traumatised, we did manage to say a little about the situation. After Carole had gone, we knew that she would inform Neil Russell our vicar and other friends from church. At least John would be spared that task. He now had the unenviable task of telling Charlotte and Thomas. Prior to Thomas' arrival from school, I purposely disappeared upstairs. It was heart-rending to later witness my son's distress. He was only ten.

About half an hour later I was sitting at the kitchen table when Charlotte breezed in. **'Well, have you got cancer then?'** Immediately her bright face crumpled and she burst into tears. After we had hugged and she had stopped crying, quite amazingly Charlotte became very strong as she said, 'You'll be alright Mum, you've got to think positively.' She was the very first person to say this to me. Then rather scathingly she added, 'It's no good, there's no one up there (she rolled her eyes up sceptically). There's no God to help you. It's no good you asking Him up there to help you.' She concluded angrily, 'So He can't help you!' How I longed to hug her and tell her that without having trust in God to help me, I had nothing. My faith in God was all that I had to hold on to. Yet I said nothing. She was no longer on that wavelength. A few years ago I could have shared that with her; though not in her present state of unbelief.

Later, whilst John was talking to Charlotte, I was preparing our evening meal in the kitchen with Thomas, who by now seemed his normal self. I remember acting very brightly, organising him to make an instant chocolate mousse. He enjoyed doing that. We chatted away about everyday things and I distinctly recollect thinking, *this is all so unreal, here am I carrying out my normal tea-time routine, with this dreadful scenario in the background.*

As soon as we had eaten, John dashed off to Pilgrim Hospital to see Dr. Adrian Cozma, our friend from Romania. The timing of our bad news could not have come at a worst moment for Adrian. We knew that he was going out for a farewell dinner. Adrian was due to return to Romania the following Monday. John then intended to visit my mother and his parents.

Busily washing up, I just hoped that he would speak to Mum before she rang. I was in dread of all the painful memories it would awaken in her; especially since we were approaching the anniversary of my father's death. He had also suffered from cancer. When the phone rang, Charlotte (already primed) was quick to answer. It was Neil Russell asking for John. Shortly after, it rang again. This time it was Mum. Charlotte wanted to tell her that I was in the bath but I would not avoid speaking to her. 'Mum you had better sit down... John's on his way to tell you.' By this she knew that her worst fears had been confirmed, for at the mention of the word biopsy the previous day, Mum had known. When I told her what the consultants had said, she just remarked, 'Thank God they've caught it in time.' We then both became emotional.

At 8pm, during Thomas' bath time, there was another call; this time from my old school friend Kathleen Cockerill. She had been in my thoughts earlier that day, when I had posted her birthday card. Her usual cheery greeting of, 'Hello how are you?' was soon shattered. All I could answer was, 'I've had some very bad news today, you'll have to bear with me as I might get upset.' Very conscious of my quivering voice, I informed her. I really felt for her because she must have been at a loss as to how best to respond. We then managed a long chat: for by then, I was in control of my emotions. At one point Kathleen, quite in amazement said, 'You're very calm, I'm sure I wouldn't be.' All I could think of saying was, 'Well, Thomas is in the bath, he's probably listening.'

John was not late back that evening. He was absolutely shattered. It must have been a terrible ordeal telling his parents, who had no inkling whatsoever of anything wrong. He had also seen Neil and Kathy Russell. We were late to bed that evening. How could we settle to a night's rest knowing what we did? We cried and held each other tightly. Though it had often been discussed as something that we ought to do; John and I had never prayed together except as part of a group. Tonight we did. John prayed for God to help us. I only managed a few words before dissolving into tears of utter helplessness.

Remarkably I slept until about 3am. I awoke conscious that John was in a very restless state. Apparently he had not slept but had been churning it all over. He went downstairs to make some tea. Mentally alert, my mind in overdrive, I once again but now much more intensely, began bombarding God with questions that I desperately needed answering. *Why...? What's the purpose of this tumour? How can this be happening to me? I just don't understand. It's all a nightmare! Oh God, tell me it's not true... Why God?*

One moment I was lying in bed, pleading with God: the next moment I had shot bolt-upright, as if I had just received an electric shock. It was as if I heard God replying, 'Now you know what it is, this good hard shock that Charlotte needs!' In one of my recent talks with John's mother she had surprised me by saying that Charlotte needed a good hard shock to bring her to her senses. I had given it no further deliberation. I so badly wanted the relationship between Charlotte and me to improve. Was this how it could happen? Had I got to endure something so horrendous, for this reason? Oh yes, I believed that God had answered me but what a response! I certainly, did not think much to His way of doing things and told Him so. Yet if it had to be... then...? Implausible as it sounds, I was filled with a strange sensation of excitement.

On his return with the tea, John understandably did not share my new mood of incredible elation. After all, he had not experienced my personal revelation. He listened but made no real comment. I could no longer sleep. My mind was far too preoccupied. I was aware of being extremely keyed up. The adrenaline was certainly flowing! Firmly believing that I had been given an answer; I had to accept it, trusting that God had got it right and that He knew what He was doing in all of this mess. I had no choice but to accept the dreadful situation and simply get on with it!

After breakfast, John rang Ann Pilbeam, who was a teacher at Kirton Primary School and also a member of our church. He informed her of the situation, so that the school would be aware in case of any adverse reaction from Thomas. Most specifically, he needed to cancel the remainder of my supply teaching commitment for that term and the following one. He also contacted Charlotte's school. He then went to sort things out at work.

I was pleased to have time on my own, to do my daily Bible reading and to pray. Believing that God had given me a reason for the tumour, helped me to start coping. Still feeling somewhat dazed and floundering in what seemed a most unreal situation; I knew that God's answer, though very hard, had to be accepted and worked through. That morning I could not concentrate on my usual Bible reading notes but the final verse of the previous day's reading spoke to me so much that I noted it down. I found it very helpful to me that day:

'And whatever you ask in prayer, you will receive it if you have faith.'

Matthew chapter 21. verse 22 R.S.V.

Afterwards, I tried to resume my normal morning clearing up routine: albeit in a very slow and dazed state of mind. Happening to glance out of an upstairs window at about 9.30am I noticed someone sitting in a white car at the front of our house. It looked like Neil but no one rang the bell. Later I discovered from Carole Hampson that he had called and had even checked the back to see if I was in the kitchen. He had not rung the bell in case I was catching up on some sleep.

I decided to walk into Kirton to see Glynne Goringe, the treasurer of the Scout and Guide Joint Management Committee, of which I was secretary. I now felt that I had to resign (for which in all honesty I was not sorry). For the past year Thomas no longer went to Cub Scouts. I only kept the post out of duty, I had no real interest in it.

Thursday 15th October, was a beautiful sunny, autumnal day. As I hurried along I prayed that I would not meet anyone I knew. Usually I meet so many people, that it takes me ages to shop locally. Glynne was the first and only person to whom I had to impart my bad news, face to face. What an ordeal that was! Fortunately I had done all the photocopying after our last committee meeting, so it was only a matter of tidying up the paperwork. Strangely enough I had decided in early September, to withdraw from Kirton Primary School

Parent Teachers' Association: even though Thomas still had another year at the school. That only left the Middlecott School P.T.A. of which I was also a member (that in fact folded up shortly after my hospitalisation).

On my arrival home, I found some chrysanthemums on the front doorstep, without a note. However there was a heartening letter from Carol Meeds, the secretary of Kirton Band. It was the first encouraging written word that I received. I later discovered that the flowers were from Jane Hales.

Meanwhile, John had a most upsetting time. On that first day he found it impossible to talk to people without becoming tearful. During the morning he had called in at Boston Police Station to speak to colleagues. Then he wandered over the footbridge and into St. Botolph's Church, where sat quietly, he met Canon Peter Fluck. He poured it all out to Peter.

Neil came round after lunch. He said that everyone was absolutely devastated. John asked if I wanted to speak to Neil on my own but I declined. Though, when John was making the coffee, I showed Neil the helpful verse of Scripture that I had found that morning. I was pleased that Neil said a prayer for us all before he left.

Later in the afternoon John returned my library books which were one day overdue. The librarian joked, 'I hope you've got a good excuse?' John blurted out, 'I didn't bring them back yesterday because I'd just heard my wife's got cancer.' Afterwards, he felt awful at how he had come straight out with it. The librarian looked shocked, refusing to accept any payment for overdue fines.

Mid-afternoon, my sister-in-law Carol came round, bringing me some flowers. Not long after Thomas arrived home, Ann Pilbeam brought more flowers and a card from the staff at school. Ann referred to Val Wilkinson (a dinner lady at the school whom I vaguely knew) who was at present undergoing chemotherapy. I recalled that I had wondered about Val's health in the summer, since I had noticed her hair loss. Ann told me how concerned Val was to hear about me and that she would call round to see me. During this conversation poor Mum was in the kitchen trying to pacify Thomas. He was cross that school knew about our situation. He could not understand why people were making a fuss, or why we wanted people to know.

When Mum had arrived earlier, she came in as if everything was normal and chatted matter-of-factly, in her usual manner. It did not seem right and after a few seconds I could stand the pretence no longer. I broke the ice by hugging her. The Spencer family have never behaved very demonstratively towards each other. I was soon to discover that a hug and sometimes even a kiss, was the common reaction of people seeing me for the first time since my diagnosis: amazingly even from those I did not know very well. A hug seemed to express something that could not be verbalised.

Being an extremely shy and undemonstrative person, as John so charmingly phrased, 'a real cold fish'; this physical contact was initially quite overwhelming and I did feel ill at ease. However, I soon found it to be a most comforting and important gesture of support.

Each time we faced someone new, tears bubbled over. Obviously it was most distressing for the people we were closest to. Since the diagnosis, our home had suddenly become quieter and much calmer. There had been no unpleasant words or arguments. After months of daily raised voices and frequent shouting, it was most uncanny. Charlotte quite subdued, was unusually helpful and extremely careful about what she said and did.

Thursday was a long sleepless night as we contemplated our next meeting with the Consultant E.N.T. Surgeon. The situation seemed so totally unreal and we were still very much numbed by the shock of it all. Surely we would wake up soon? What a tremendous relief it would be to wake up and realise that it had only been a bad dream! I could vividly recall nightmares that I had experienced and... oh the indescribable relief, upon awaking.

Only it was not to be...cancer was now our reality!

Chapter 2
A Network Of Support

Friday being pay day: we decided to shop prior to the hospital appointment. I was consciously trying to stock up for the family, so a larger amount of groceries were piled high into two trolleys. I handed over my bank card but it was rejected for the first time ever! A telephone call revealed that I had insufficient funds in my current account. The amount transferred from John's salary had not cleared. Fortunately, John had his card with him, therefore he settled up. Instead of feeling most embarrassed; somehow I managed to sit there calmly waiting, while the cashier and manager sorted it out. As John pointed out, 'It's nothing to get het up about; this is trivial compared to what we are up against.' It certainly was. I could see the funny side of it, because I thought of how I would have reacted in normal circumstances. Likewise, being the world's worst worrier, I always anticipated problems before they existed! Yet ironically, the discovery of my nasty ulcerated tongue back in August, had not triggered off the usual reaction in me.

Sat in the hospital car park, John informed me that he would ask the surgeon to let him know what we were up against, even if there was more bad news to come. He told me that he had never deceived me before and could not contemplate keeping anything from me now (John later admitted having considered the possibility that the cancer could have spread to other parts of my body, in addition to the already suspected right lymph node and thyroid gland). This was a very sobering and new line of thinking for me. It was too shocking to grasp the implication that I might be terminally ill! Numbly, I told John that I would want to know...whatever! What were we saying? How could we be talking about such things? It was ridiculous! A week ago I was happily teaching and looking forward to a weekend in Bicester. How could things change so dramatically?

Dr. Adrian Cozma met us at the entrance to out-patients. I was pleased to have his support but did not realise until we were waiting very apprehensively outside the consulting room, that John intended him to accompany us. The surgeon greeted us warmly and had no objection to Adrian's presence. At the beginning John did most of the talking. I sat very quietly, quite overawed by the situation. John mentioned our concern about how much we would be told about matters and whether anything would be kept from us. The surgeon assured us that he would not keep anything from either of us. He would be totally honest and he added, 'Better to fight what you know, than to be in the dark.' On that we agreed: even though the thought of receiving worse news was too dreadful to actually contemplate! John informed him that we both had a very strong Christian faith and had very supportive family and friends.

The surgeon reassured us that he had been doing similar surgery of the type that I would need, for the past ten years. The easy part of the operation would be the removal of about one-third of the tongue. This would take approximately a third of the time. The reconstructive work was the more complicated surgery and would take up most of the time. The entire operation would probably last about five hours. As it was major surgery, I would need to stay in the Intensive Care Unit for the first day after the operation. This was standard procedure and nothing to be alarmed about. He would explain the operation in detail, the evening before surgery.

He emphasised the importance of building myself up as much as possible, because I would subsequently lose weight after the operation. Drinking Guinness was suggested; but he did not think I looked like a Guinness drinker! I have always been very underweight for my height, whereas John and Adrian could have happily done with less weight on them! We laughed that it should have been one of them to lose weight so drastically and not one who was already lean enough.

The surgeon commented that obviously the post-operative appearance of a young female was an important consideration: that in my case there would be no real difference to my looks. I would not find the operation on my tongue painful and he added, 'I don't expect you'll believe that.' I was quick to respond, 'No I certainly don't.' He stressed that my mental state was of paramount importance and crucial to the success of the operation. 'Together, we would get in there and fight.' Above all, I had to be positive.

Then he mentioned that my speech would be affected. I was utterly appalled, in spite of him saying that it would improve with speech therapy. I felt absolutely gutted. This was the cruellest blow of all and as dreadful a shock as having the cancer diagnosis. It was for me the most distressing aspect; far more upsetting to contemplate than if he had said that my appearance was going to be greatly affected. I had never been an oil painting. The concern that I had shown over my rather plain appearance in my twenties had long gone. Other things were far more important. I had always prided myself on being articulate. As a French teacher, a clear voice had been essential. Since our move to Kirton almost five years earlier, I knew that clarity of speech was more important to me now, especially with regard to my reading lessons or leading prayers in church. So much so, that it had made me realise that perhaps after all, even I had a talent that God intended me to use. Now, my world was disintegrating rapidly. Was even this gift to be taken from me?

When we stood up to leave, the surgeon mentioned being on holiday the following week, so that he would be well prepared for the operation. He made his hands shake, joking, 'You wouldn't want me to operate now.' We left the room, faintly amused at this welcome touch of humour.

Adrian discussed the speech implications with me as we returned to the car. He reassured me that surgery to the side of the tongue was the least detrimental to speech. If the tip of my tongue had been affected, then it would be far worse.

Our second meeting with the surgeon, marked the turning point in what up to now had been the most harrowing two days of our married life. Although I had begun to feel positive after my 'revelation', it had still been extremely traumatic, trying to reconcile the shocking news of last Wednesday. In contrast, John had been really broken in spirit, because he had felt so utterly helpless. Now, he too, began to feel positive. The surgeon had inspired us with the utmost confidence. He had reassured us that everything was really in my favour.

Adrian encouraged us enormously: by informing us of the surgeon's excellent reputation in his specialist area (Head and Neck

Surgery). Adrian had been busy asking questions of the surgeon's colleagues. They all spoke of him in glowing terms.

Both John and I felt that we could really trust the surgeon. He came across as a very caring human being. Thank goodness he had a pleasant, unassuming and most approachable manner. (How unlike the consultant whom I had seen many years before, concerning an eye problem. He had behaved in an arrogant and condescending manner)! After our in-depth consultation, we were more at ease. We left the hospital feeling brighter than when we had entered it. In spite of the sobering and totally unacceptable possibility of the clarity of my speech being ended; my mood was primarily very optimistic. What a startling contrast it was, to two days earlier.

Arriving home, we had all the shopping to unload, before having a very late lunch. A neighbour brought round some red roses for me. She thought that I was already in hospital. By now, it was school-leaving time. When Thomas arrived home, he was livid. Apparently, one of the teachers had asked about me in the middle of a lesson. I wished that she had been more sensitive and spoken to him on his own. He became even angrier when Val Wilkinson called round. While we talked in the lounge, Thomas who was supposedly cleaning out his rabbit hutch, was banging and crashing about outside the window. We could hear him talking very loudly to his rabbit - Popcorn, as he vented his anger. He hated people coming round.

Val was simply amazing. Her first words to us being, 'Here am I, look at me and I've got cancer!' We were so impressed by her strong, very positive attitude. Val loaned us some literature from 'BACUP' (British Association of Cancer United Patients - later to become 'CancerBACUP'), a registered charity, providing advice and information about all aspects of cancer, as well as a counselling service, offering emotional support for cancer patients and their families. A friend who was a nurse, had put her in touch with BACUP. Nothing had been offered her at the hospital, as we had found. We discussed the need for some sort of immediate support to be available at the time of diagnosis. From our own personal experience, we acknowledged that it might have helped cushion some of the initial shock.

Later on, John was able to use the general booklet on cancer: with its simple diagram of good and bad cells, to explain the disease in greater detail to the children. Thomas especially, was really confused. He was frightened that he might catch it from me. So, in the early days he was very reluctant to come near me and refused to give me his usual kiss. In his mind, disease, whether it be cancer or aids, was all the same. It must have been dreadful for John, trying to answer their questions honestly; yet all the time mindful of his own doubts and fears. As I have already mentioned, it is heart-rending to witness the distress of your own children. You can put up with a great deal yourself. It tore me apart to hear Thomas ask, 'My friends' Mums don't have cancer, why has my Mum got it?'

Mum was assisting me to prepare our evening meal, when John's parents arrived. They had been too upset to come the day before. In fact, like Adrian, John's Dad had spent a sleepless night on the Wednesday. They spoke very positively and we knew how fortunate that we were to have their support, together with that of my Mum's. A few practical details were discussed. John's sister Jane, had offered to look after Thomas at half-term. That evening John called round to see the parents of Charlotte's best friend. It was arranged that she would stay with them for half-term; thus leaving John free to be at the hospital whenever he wanted.

The strange calm in our home came to an end that Friday tea-time. By then I was feeling exhausted, after the week's events and the sudden influx of visitors, over such a short time. I was soon niggling irritably at Charlotte, who was now back to her normal infuriating ways!

That evening, Jayne Featherstone, a friend from the ex-Bishop's Course Group, telephoned. She had something really lovely to say. In the summer, she had visited the Iona Community and had bought some wooden brooches; carved in the shape of a dove, for herself, two friends and her sister-in-law, from a little gift shop. Strangely, Jayne had felt compelled to revisit the shop at least twice, for she had a very strong conviction that she must purchase another dove brooch. Yet, she had no idea whom it was for. On her third return visit, she bought an extra brooch. As soon as she heard the news of my tumour, she realised that the brooch was for me. Jayne said that she would see me on Sunday at the Confirmation Service at St. Mary's. How touched I was, by this tangible show of God's love for me.

Saturday 17th October, was the Annual Police Federation Dinner Dance, at the Golf Hotel in Woodhall Spa. This date had been arranged months earlier and we saw no reason to change our plans. Our original intention had been to drive over in the morning but in reality we did not leave home until the afternoon. By now, we were beginning to look forward to the weekend, especially as we really did feel much brighter.

Since Wednesday, John seemed to have been constantly on the phone. I had a few very good friends, from school and college days, in various parts of the country. We wanted them to know, because we badly needed their prayer support. By Saturday, most people that we wished informed, were aware of the situation. I was content to let John do the talking. However, I did speak to my oldest friend Angela Steven. At one point during our conversation, I said something to her about why this had happened to me. She immediately retorted, 'Why not? After all, we each know someone who has suffered, or is suffering from cancer?' I later read that cancer affects one in three people in the western world. Angela seemed very heartened by how positive I sounded.

We departed for Woodhall Spa after lunch. It was a glorious autumnal day. After a few miles, I decided to drive. It would help to occupy my thoughts. On arrival, John and I ambled through the woods. They were breathtakingly beautiful in their autumn colours. It was a lovely peaceful walk, during which we hardly spoke. John wanted to call on Jack Kirk, a retired policeman and a member of the Christian Police Association. I had heard what a lovely couple Jack and his wife Edna were and it was true. After the initial pleasantries, John broke our news and they were so concerned. Before we left, we had a short time of prayer and Jack laid hands on my head and prayed for my healing. I had never experienced this before. It was very moving and so beautiful.

We strolled a different way back through the woods. I was enjoying the walk but beginning to shiver as the day was losing its warmth. John, suddenly made the comment, 'Now I know why I became a Christian. I'd have just gone to pieces if I hadn't got a faith.' In my mind, I echoed his sentiments. We paused to admire the goodies in a baker's shop and I took ages to select six Belgian chocolates and some Viennese Whirls. I promptly made short work of the chocolates! I think John had one of them. I have always been rather a pig concerning chocolate. I was enjoying this occasion of self-indulgence.

Margaret Brown, the Police Welfare Officer, had contacted John as soon as the news of my tumour was out. She had arranged to meet us before the dinner. We chatted over tea in our hotel room. Margaret was such a warm motherly person and I found her easy to talk to. I had been quite overcome when she handed me a huge basket of flowers. They were lovely. I think the Police Welfare Department, sent me at least three beautiful floral arrangements. I have always loved flowers and I treasured all of them. They certainly boosted my spirits.

The dinner was unimpressive but we thoroughly enjoyed the music. We had anticipated that under the circumstances, the evening would merely be a diversion and that after dining and a few dances, we would retire early. Incredibly, it was a superb evening. We were both so relaxed and able to join in a variety of dances until 1am. We really let our hair down. It was a tremendous release of tension after the past few days. John's colleagues showed great concern. It was very heartening to have support from people whom I hardly knew. I was on a 'spiritual high'. It was quite remarkable that I should experience such strong positive feelings, under the circumstances. One particular song, 'I will survive' sung by Gloria Gaynor, really made the adrenaline flow. As we danced to this song, I suddenly thought, ***this bloody cancer's not getting the better of me. No way!*** My stubborn streak had finally surfaced.

On Sunday morning we sped back for the Confirmation Service at St. Mary's. I was extremely apprehensive about people's reactions. We did not want this special service to be marred in any way. The church was full by the time we arrived. Carole Hampson's daughter Katie was being confirmed and we had been invited to a buffet lunch afterwards. We sat near the back of the church with the rest of Carole's family group. Jayne had quietly slipped a package into my hand. The simple carving of a dove, that Christian symbol of peace, was most appropriate. As the time drew nearer to take Holy Communion, I was finding it hard to compose myself. In my determination not to show that I was upset, I raced up the aisle, only to almost dissolve in tears as I knelt at the altar. John was also apparently close to tears.

We had both regained our composure by the time coffee was served. Once more feeling very bright and positive, I enjoyed a lively chat with my three friends from the ex-Bishop's Course Group: Jayne Featherstone, Val Marriott and Judy Williams, who were all wearing their dove brooches.

Judy Williams handed me a small parcel with the terse instructions, 'Don't open it until you're at home!' On opening it in the privacy of home, I found the book 'Somebody Loves You' by Helen Steiner Rice. Inside the cover Judy had written 'To my friend, at a time when she needs to know we care.' How relieved I was, that I had taken Judy's advice. All the love being shown to me was so overwhelming. I was in tears - again!

I spoke to Val Smith who had recently moved away to another church but had returned for the Confirmation Service. When Val brightly said, 'Hello how are you?' I realised that she did not know. I did not want to spoil the occasion for her, so I said nothing about how I really was.

The next time that I saw Val was the following January at Neil Russell's farewell service in Frampton. She had found out about my tumour much later. Indeed, the card from her and her husband Colin, was the last one that I received, out of well over a hundred. Quite amazingly, although Val did not know about my state of health in October, she had been praying for me, without realising it! Her friend Annie who owned a delicatessen shop in Red Lion Street, had asked her to pray for someone called Heather. Later she discovered that the unknown Heather, was in fact me.

After a pleasant lunch, we had a few hours to spare, before going to St. Thomas' Church in Boston. The C.P.A. (Christian Police Association) of which John is a member, were to take the evening service. I knew that I would be included in the prayers and thought that I ought to attend. A very subdued Adrian, joined us. It was to be his last evening with us, as he was returning to Romania the following day.

Before the service actually began; a member of the congregation, whom I vaguely knew, blurted out to me, 'How on earth do you get cancer of the tongue?' I cannot remember my response. I was gutted. It was a reaction that I could not handle. Though I realised that the person was extremely concerned and had no notion how those words impacted on me.

John led the service. I sat with Adrian near the front of the church. I watched as John introduced the C.P.A. team. I marvelled at the way God had transformed him: three days earlier he would not have been able to take part in a service, let alone lead one. It was amazing that he too, now felt so positive. The service was very inspiring. Paul Elliott sang two songs. He informed us afterwards, that they had been chosen especially for me; certainly he sang them in a way that was extremely poignant. One entitled 'I'll never let go of your hand' by Don Francisco, was most appropriate in my time of need.

Over coffee after the service, there was much concern from the congregation. I had never met John Moore, the vicar of St. Thomas' but he held my hands as he spoke very warmly, assuring me of their prayers. I knew that Margaret Barsley, a deacon at St. Thomas' and our good friend, would keep them closely informed. One lady spoke to me, saying that she had suffered from cancer many years earlier. It was during her recovery that she had found a faith. I found meeting someone who had previously suffered cancer and was now cured, the most reassuring message that I could possibly receive.

Very sadly we said au revoir to Adrian Cozma. We had grown so fond of him during his five month attachment at Pilgrim Hospital. He had become almost one of the family. We knew how much he wanted to stay, especially with the change in our circumstances. As we hugged and he said, 'See you next spring,' I could only murmur, 'I'll be better then.'

Chapter 3

Preparation

John rose early the next day, to drive Adrian to Stansted Airport. Val Wilkinson came after school. The card she brought me, was especially meaningful. It depicted a frog in a pond and a cat reaching out with its paw. We have a small wild area in the corner of our back garden: a scaled down version of the beautiful woods and large pond that we had directly behind our home when we lived at Sudbrooke near Lincoln. Many delightful hours were spent in those woods, with Charlotte and Thomas when they were small. I shall always treasure those memories of our happy family life. How things change! Since John introduced frogs into our garden pond, four years ago: every spring we have observed tadpoles turning into tiny frogs. The pond had become a magnet to the neighbours' cats, as they had previously devoured all the goldfish! Hence the appeal of the card.

On her way out, Val suddenly remembered that she had just spoken to a friend whose relative had endured cancer of the tongue, some twenty years earlier. Val thought that the tongue had been reconstructed with some sort of synthetic material. I was most surprised to hear this. I honestly had not got as far as thinking about how the reconstruction would be done. I was still coming to terms with the diagnosis and its implications. Val laughed, 'Well they can't do a graft can they, there's nothing on you!' I laughed, indicating the largest part of me, which was my rear and gave no more thought to that conversation. That week, I was to hear of at least two other 'successful cancer stories' which made me believe that God was using other people to get His message across to me.

My oldest friend Angela Steven wrote to say how pleased she was that I sounded in such good heart, during our telephone conversation. She shared some thoughts with me from the book of Job, which they had recently been studying at their church: 'Like Job, it is better to conclude that God knows best and to accept his Sovereignty; better to continue in faith and perseverance than turn to bitterness and resentment in the face of suffering we cannot understand. What

really cheers me and I trust will cheer you and John, is that our suffering will only be in vain if we let it. That is not God's purpose.'
'But he knows the way that I take; when he has tried me I shall come forth as gold.'
Job chapter 23 verse 10 R.S.V.
That verse conveyed something to me. Although I could not fully comprehend; I felt deeply comforted and strangely upheld by those words.

During the week a few cards began arriving. Many contained helpful verses and thoughts. On that Monday evening, Kathy Russell took me along to the M.U. (Mothers' Union) Holland West Deanery meeting. It was with very mixed feelings that I attended. Everyone seemed to be rushing around busily before the meeting. I had expected to be included in the prayers so it came as a considerable blow to hear the prayers delivered in such a general way and without any mention of sick people. I took this very much to heart.

Being responsible for the M.U. prayers at the Frampton meetings; whenever there was a joint meeting I always tried to check up beforehand with the other groups, in case of specific prayer needs. I experienced such deep pain at this apparent lack of communication. It seemed that my family and I were being denied something vital. We needed all support possible, in order to get through this terrible ordeal.

Afterwards over coffee, one of our members came to chat to me about her family, just as she would normally do. She obviously was not aware of my situation and I could not bring myself to tell her there and then. I answered her quite mechanically, wishing that she would hurry up and leave me alone. It had been a mistake to come. I had not found the support that I needed. It was evident that most people at the meeting were unaware of the nightmare that I was living under. My whole world lay shattered in pieces, yet everyone else was carrying on as normal!

However, one member who was aware did come to talk quietly to me. I appreciated that enormously. Joan Deane very kindly invited me to go round for coffee later in the week. She thought that I would have time to kill and I really valued her thoughtfulness. In reality, I had to decline. With all the unexpected visitors, things were not getting done.

At home John had to bear with my hurt and bitter disappointment. How I wished that I had stayed at home. Instead of being boosted up, I had been knocked down. It doubly hurt because I knew how much care and thought that I put into the prayers that I prepared. Although deep down, I knew that it would have been too upsetting for me to have been mentioned. It was a no win situation and I felt so very, very sorry for myself.

The following morning, Neil gave me a lift to St. Michael's Church for the short service of Morning Prayer, which he, Val Marriott and I usually attended. As he was unable to stay for the service he had arranged for Val to come along slightly earlier, so that I would not have to wait around in the cold.

It turned out to be a very special service that morning. On a small table Val had lit a big candle and placed it near the large open Bible. Also on the table, lay a small grey, tan and white stone, approximately seven centimetres long. Immediately, I knew the significance of this stone because Val had spoken about it on more than one occasion. Apparently at a M.U. conference, members had been asked to focus all their thoughts and prayers on to a given stone. Val had told us how meaningful this prayer activity had been. Consequently her stone which mattered so much to her, lay on her kitchen shelf where she could always see it. Before our short service started, Val told me that she wanted me to have the stone... How could I have thought last night that nobody cared? I felt deeply ashamed and utterly humbled. I was in awe at the way God had put me in my place but in the most gentle and gracious way possible. He really did understand!

The week before my scheduled admission, time dragged terribly. I filled up one morning by shopping with Mum. She indulged me, by treating me to coffee and gâteau mid-morning and later to lunch. I bought a couple of pretty nighties for hospital, some smart black velour slippers, a new photo-frame for my family picture and a few other oddments.

One morning Joan Mills the P.C.C. (Parochial Church Council) Secretary, invited me round for coffee. Joan really made a fuss of me, making sure that I drank plenty of milky coffee with some delicious biscuits. It made me realise that my friends were also coming to terms with the shock of my illness and showing their concern in various ways.

Of course, I was endeavouring to build myself up physically: so I pampered myself by bingeing on my favourite foods, specifically prawns and chocolate, although not at the same time! My weight did not increase and I was still only eight stone when I went into hospital. Understandably, my appetite was not that good, anticipating what was looming ahead. Fortunately, the soreness of the earlier biopsy on my tongue, was now less painful. Mr. Glendinning had prescribed painkillers for me but I chose not to take them if avoidable. I was now well accustomed to eating and drinking on the left side of my mouth. Most importantly I prepared myself spiritually for what was to come. My daily quiet time of prayer and Bible reading, became even more essential to me. I tried to fit this in, as soon as the children had gone to school. Once I had spent this valuable time, I was content to continue with whatever needed doing.

By now, Charlotte was her 'usual self'. It was evident that she was not going to change drastically, so once again there was renewed tension. I had expected her to be more co-operative and considerate. There was an occasional little gesture but nothing very much. Thomas was his usual thoughtful and helpful self.

Mid-week I realised how much I wanted my two very dear old college friends to know about me, because I badly needed their prayer support. I rang Trudy Elliott (we share the same birthday), tearfully blurting out my bad news. After I had talked, Trudy shared something far worse with me. Her friend Brenda had cancer of the colon; her operation was to be the day after mine. Her three children were aged from ten months to eleven years. It shook me; that even though I was up against it, here was someone else in a more serious situation. From that night, Brenda, husband Olly, their children and Trudy who was supporting them, were all very much in our prayers. When I rang Sandra O'Toole, I was more composed. Sandra promised to pray for me and asked if I minded if she included me on the prayer list of their group. Of course, I did not object.

Fortunately during this week, John was around most of the time. A few people seemed critical of this, implying that he should be at work, keeping busy until my hospitalisation. John could not bear to leave me at all. He knew that he could not possibly concentrate on anything else. I was so thankful to have his strong support.

The Police were extremely caring and most understanding of our needs at this time. After John's initial three days of compassionate leave; his boss suggested that he should see his doctor because things would obviously take time to resolve. John clearly had enough to contend with at home, without the additional stresses of a demanding job. The G.P. signed him off work suffering from 'effective disorder' (stress related). John felt guilty about having what turned out to be seven weeks off work. On being given another 'sick note', he expressed concern because he knew that his colleagues were having to cover his duties. The doctor simply stated, 'There's not one of them who would want to swop with your situation is there!' That put it into perspective for him.

Towards the end of that final week, John was busy preparing for the service that he was due to take at St. Mary's on October 25th. This helped to occupy him. I perceived that this would be a very memorable service for us: an occasion to draw on the strength that we would need to face our future, which after the dragging interval of the earlier part of that week, was now getting too close for comfort and we were scared.

John had roped my friend Judy Williams in, to do a reading at the service. I knew that this was to be my very last chance to read properly in church, prior to major surgery. I was determined to go out defiantly on a high note. Who knew what was in store for me? John wanted me to read out a prayer before he did the prayers of intercession. He understood how appropriate the prayer was in my situation. One particular line being immensely poignant:

'Lord, Hold my Hand, when I'm sick with fear and anxious.'

Initially, I had doubted whether I could read out something so profoundly moving, without becoming tearful. Later, I sensed that it would be alright. It had to be; after all, it was my prayer. It said everything that I needed to say to God. Mercifully, my voice was able to keep free from emotion; yet I was aware that it might be distressing to other people, especially Mum. Understandably, there were some emotional moments after the service. Fortunately, most people slipped away quietly. They did not seem able to speak to me.

Monday of half-term finally arrived. I did a final wash load and other oddments, before going to see Neil for coffee. I had not spoken to him on my own since the diagnosis and I needed to speak to him, as my priest. For once, there was a cosy fire in his study and we had a good talk. There were also things that I wished to impart, regarding how much John and I valued his friendship, especially with regard to his move to Stamford. I had no idea, how surgery would affect my speech. For that reason these things had to be said now.

Originally, we had understood that my admission day was to be Monday. When the letter arrived, it stated Tuesday 27th October at 10am. This suited us better. It meant that we could attend the Morning Prayer service at St. Michael's Church, Frampton West, before going into hospital.

John's Mum and my sister-in-law Jane, came to collect Thomas mid-afternoon. He enjoyed playing with his two cousins and we thought that it would be better if he was kept fully occupied with them. Thomas departed, very matter-of-factly, far better than him being upset. Somehow, I managed to conceal my distress until after he had gone. It still all seemed so totally unreal and yet the nightmare would not go away.

After our evening meal, John took Charlotte round to her best friend's house, to stay for the week. Charlotte, was her usual bright self as we hugged. She still did not let me kiss her; that was nothing to do with my tumour, it was simply not the done thing in her eyes. I found her positive outlook, a great help to me as we said our goodbyes.

Later that evening, her boyfriend called. In some surprise, I informed him where she was. He was well aware of that and had simply called to say how he hoped everything would go alright for me. I was really touched by this concern. How relieved I was, that Charlotte had such a caring and thoughtful friend, to whom I hoped she would be able to confide in, even if she could not talk to us and I said as much to him.

That night I lay in bed, gripped by a dreadful foreboding of what lay ahead of me. An icy coldness seemed to pervade my whole being. I lay immobile on my side of the bed, while John very still and equally as silent, lay on his side of the bed. There was nothing to say to one another. It was as if we were both absorbed in our own thoughts. Was this what it felt like to be a condemned man on the eve of his execution? There was to be no escape... time was running out.

On Tuesday 27th October, John and I joined Neil as arranged, for the short service at St. Michael's. Val Marriott had previously phoned, to say how sorry she was at being unable to join us; but assured us that she would be with us in spirit. She would be praying for me, as she and her husband were driving down to Bournemouth, the following day.

The short service was geared up for us. I read the lesson, acutely aware that it might well be the last time that I was able to read in church. Instead of the customary said psalm, we sang '*Safe In The Shadow Of The Lord*' based on Psalm 91. The sung version was new to me. I was only able to partially join in because by then I was fighting back the tears. Nevertheless, I found the words tremendously comforting. Little did I realise that I was to use this very psalm a great deal, while in hospital. At especially traumatic times, the words of the refrain - '*I trust in Him, I trust in Him,*' would run through my mind, or would be hummed very softly (I am not one for singing out loud).

'Safe In The Shadow Of The Lord'

By Timothy Dudley-Smith

1. Safe in the shadow of the Lord
   Beneath His hand and power,
   I trust in Him, I trust in Him,
   My fortress and my tower.
2. My hope is set on God alone
   Though Satan spreads his snare,
   I trust in Him, I trust in Him,
   To keep me in his care.
3. From fears and phantoms of the night,
   From foes about my way,
   I trust in Him, I trust in Him,
   By darkness as by day.
4. His holy angels keep my feet
   Secure from every stone;
   I trust in Him, I trust in Him,
   And unafraid go on.
5. Strong in the Everlasting Name,
   And in my Father's care,
   I trust in Him, I trust in Him,
   Who hears and answers prayer.
6. Safe in the shadow of the Lord,
   Possessed by love divine,
   I trust in Him, I trust in Him,
   And meet His love with mine.

Chapter 4
Tuesday 27th October - Ward 2B

My anxiety level increased as we drove nearer and nearer to Pilgrim Hospital. On arrival, I was experiencing such an awful nauseous feeling and it seemed as if there were hundreds of butterflies inside my churning stomach. Although, I was confident (based on my previous experience of going into hospital for routine eye surgery) that once I was amongst the hustle and bustle of ward 2B: I would be pre-occupied with having tests, answering questions and be more relaxed.

Apart from the occasional little twinges of fear and anxiety, I had overall, experienced a remarkable sense of peace. I believed without any doubt that God was with me in my trial. So what was there to be afraid of? I was really on a 'spiritual high'. I do not mean this irreverently, but it seemed to me that God had bent over backwards to prove His love and provision for me. This had been shown in many tangible ways: by the cards, flowers, gifts and visits by well-wishers. It was humbling to realise that so many people really cared about me.

I was shown into room 5: a single room overlooking the main entrance and visitors' car park. I was greatly relieved because the thought of being kept awake by snoring patients had not exactly thrilled me! John immediately tried out the television (another plus) and sussed out the radio. The ward was so quiet. Nothing appeared to be happening. We sat there for a very long hour before Staff Nurse Rachel Frecklington came. She seemed pleasant but reserved as she took my admission details. I still did not feel very relaxed. In response to a question from John, she astonished us by saying that the surgeon would remove muscle from my chest to graft onto my tongue! So, it was not to be a synthetic patch as Val Wilkinson had thought! Nevertheless, I gave it no real thought. I had to go along with it now. I was here.

When the staff nurse had gone, we glanced at my notes. By the side of the heading 'Emotional State,' were the words: *seems a little anxious*. I thought indignantly, I think I'm entitled to, under the circumstances. By the side of the heading 'Spiritual,' were the words: *has a friend who is a vicar*. I saw the funny side of this and remarked to John, 'It's a good job my faith goes a lot deeper than that, or I'd be in the ... by now!'

Nothing much more happened that morning. John went to see the Chaplain the Revd. Michael Johnson, before leaving the hospital. He arranged to return during the early evening when we expected to see the surgeon. I busied myself arranging the flowers and cards, which started to arrive as I was settling in. My sister-in-law briefly popped in with another bunch of flowers. Jane Hales followed with a huge basket of dried flowers and a card from the churchwardens, vicar, P.C.C. and all at St. Mary's Church. Out of all the cards I received, this said very simply all that I needed to know: ***'May remembering all the times the Lord's been with you through the years help you to trust that He's with you now during this difficult time.'*** I received another copy of that card but amazingly from over a hundred, I received only two cards that were duplicated.

On my bedside locker, I placed my 'treasures': the photo of John and the children, taken outside our balcony in Portugal on our lovely August holiday, the long purple haired troll that Charlotte had given me for 'good luck', the stone from Val Marriott, the cuddly rabbit that Val Halgarth had sent to keep me company, a selection of special cards and my Daily Light book. Bearing in mind how immobile I would be after surgery, I pinned up the rest of my cards on a notice-board which faced the bed. At least I would be able to focus on something cheerful.

Busy concentrating on eating my last cooked meal before surgery, I was feeling almost like a condemned prisoner eating her final meal; only I had no choice what I ate. I had to have what the previous bed occupant had ordered: creamed potatoes, steamed fish with parsley sauce and peas...yuk! I found the rather dishy young doctor who had turned up while I was eating, far more appealing! He came to introduce himself and examine my neck. He was the surgeon's registrar. He said something about inserting a needle into a suspect lump (right lymph node), to take a sample for examination. He could not find any lump. I mentioned that my right breast felt quite sore. He said that he would return at 2 o'clock to examine this.

I was just starting to eat my congealed rice pudding, when the speech and language therapist Christine Ash arrived. I liked her immediately. She chatted to me, ascertaining what the surgeon had told me about the intended surgery and its effect on my speech. I asked her directly the question that was uppermost in my mind, 'Will I be able to communicate?' Christine reassured me that because the tumour was on the right side of my tongue, the left side of the tongue, would compensate for any defect. She amused me by saying that immediately after surgery, my mouth would be very swollen and my speech would sound very slushy. I would probably think it sounded as if I had a mouth full of gob-stoppers but this was quite normal. After her departure, I abandoned further attempts to eat lunch, for it was time to get changed.

I was busy putting things away in my locker, when the surgeon suddenly appeared. This was the first time that I had seen him since my admission. He too examined my neck and could not find a lump or anything suspicious. He seemed surprised at this hopeful sign and informed me that there would be no need for his registrar to take a sample for analysis. He ascertained when John would be returning to the ward and told me that he would come back to see us during the early evening, to discuss the operation. When the registrar returned, he examined my right breast but found nothing irregular. I did not realise the significance of this examination, because I had not grasped what the nurse had said earlier. I had no inkling that even this part of my anatomy was to come under the surgeon's scalpel!

In the afternoon I was taken for X-rays and a blood test. 2B had arranged a visit to the Intensive Care Unit: to see where I would be after surgery. Hopefully, it would prepare me mentally. The sight and sound of so many machines could otherwise come as a tremendous shock. The I.C.U. nurse was very friendly and most reassuring. She pointed out that I would be closely monitored. I was really relieved to hear that. Yet to me, the I.C.U. held no terrors. Again, it had not really sunk in, that I was to be in such a position, as to need intensive care.

I have included the following incident, although I have no personal recollection of its occurrence. Apparently that afternoon, a young and very pretty student nurse, came and introduced herself as Joanna Townend. She asked if I would mind her observing my operation, if the surgeon gave permission. I agreed. Many months later, Jo informed me of how wary she had been about entering my room to speak to me, in case I was upset. She told me that I did not seem frightened; only very detached, as if I were in another world.

Late afternoon, the hospital chaplain Michael Johnson visited me, in response to a message that John had left. They knew each other slightly but I could not recall meeting him before. I had though, because he had conducted the Revd. John Duckett's marriage service in February. Michael was a lovely warm person, whom I found very easy to talk to.

The surgeon arrived at 5pm; earlier than expected. He appeared almost disconcerted that John was not present and rather brusquely said, 'There's nothing wrong with your memory, you can pass the information on to your husband.' He restated that the easy part of the operation was the removal of the tumour. Having spoken about this aspect, he then said, 'Now there's one question you must want to ask?' He paused to await a comment but I stared at him blankly. I could think of nothing. My mind did not seem to be functioning properly. I was dumbstruck. The surgeon continued very patiently, 'Having got rid of the tumour, how am I going to repair the tongue?' Here, I managed to recover my thoughts quickly enough to blurt out that a nurse had mentioned something about muscle being taken from my chest. I added that I had vaguely imagined that a synthetic substance would perhaps be used! He seemed rather exasperated, as he remarked that he wished others would leave it to the surgeon, to inform the patient correctly.

He then gave a fairly detailed account of the reconstruction work that would take up about two thirds of the surgery time; it being an incredibly complicated process. Awful though this all sounded, I simply could not grasp the implications of indeed anything he was telling me. He might just as well have told me that he was going to decapitate me! At this point, details were irrelevant. I was unable to absorb them. As much as I thought that I wanted to know what was going to happen to me; in reality, all that I was concerned with, was surviving major surgery! John later received the sketchiest outline: something about a muscle being brought out in a long sausage, which would be discarded two weeks later *(See Appendix 1)*. What did register, was the information that if the cancer had spread into the suspect right lymph node and thyroid, the subsequent removal of the former, would mean a permanently dropped shoulder.

Tea that night (my last supper!) consisted of corn beef sandwiches and carrot cake. I quickly scoffed them and could easily have demolished the same again. Two friends, Bob and Linda Hiron (ex-Bishop's Course Group) came with some chrysanthemums. By then, I had a room full of flowers and we were now putting vases on the floor. They had very kindly brought me some books and cassette tapes.

At 6.30pm John arrived and as arranged we joined the hospital chaplain Michael Johnson , for a special service of 'Anointing and laying on of hands.' He had invited Penny Church, a Midwife teacher to join us. John and I were both anointed with oil, in this lovely and most moving service. In spite of becoming very emotional: I experienced an inner assurance, of being prepared for what lay ahead. Afterwards we talked for ages with Michael. Jenny Dumat the assistant chaplain and my mother then entered the chapel. My mother had come to find us, having been waiting in my room.

That evening when the night staff came on duty, I was busy watching television. I knew that I would have a problem sleeping in hospital. Pauline Telford the nurse in charge, said that I could have my sleeping tablets with my drink when I was ready to settle and not at the early time of 9.30pm, as the other patients normally did. So, at about eleven o'clock I settled for the night.

To my amazement, on awakening the next morning, I realised that I had enjoyed a really good night's sleep. The notice 'NIL BY MOUTH' was now fixed to my door and above my bed. I heard the clatter of the breakfast trolley pass by and knew that I had a long drag ahead of me. John came for about an hour. It was a real wrench parting with him that morning. He went along to the twelve o' clock communion service in the hospital chapel. He then intended to leave the car at the hospital and walk into town, to help friend Annie at her delicatessen shop in Red Lion Street. He wanted to keep busy during the period of my operation. Indeed, John spent the entire afternoon washing up, while being reassured by Annie, that everything would be fine! He would then return to the hospital for about 6 o' clock.

I busied myself sorting yet more flowers and cards, arranging the most attractive cards where I would be able to see them. Another lovely basket of flowers had come from Alan Kemp, Reader at Frampton Church and his wife June.

Dr. Chalmers the anaesthetist, came to see me. He was extremely pleasant and explained the necessary procedures. The consent form was filled in and other details taken. I started to read one of the paperbacks that Neil Russell had loaned me and remember being somewhat surprised at his choice of romantic novel.

By one o' clock I had changed into my glamorous hospital gown. My hat was on my bed. An extra hospital identity band was on my right ankle. I had already had a pre-med. injection and all details had been carefully checked with me. I knew that I was the only one on the surgeon's list that afternoon. At 1.30pm the porter collected me. A young student nurse helped wheel me down; she was at my head. I had no recollection of her being Joanna Townend who had introduced herself to me the previous day. I remained silent en route to theatre. I was incredibly calm; very relaxed and in complete acceptance of whatever lay ahead. My mind was totally absorbed, as I sang in my head, the refrain of yesterday's psalm: **'*I trust in Him, I trust in Him.*'**

I suddenly recalled how excited I had been, at the novel experience of being wheeled along for eye surgery at Lincoln County Hospital. Then, I had to travel a long way from the ward, including going in the lift before reaching the operating theatre. The feeling this time was not one of excitement but of deep inner serenity. To my disappointment and great surprise; I travelled only a few metres from ward 2B, before arriving at the entrance to theatre. I had not realised their close proximity.

Inside, the receiving theatre nurse met us. My hat was donned. My name, date of birth, the absence of jewellery and any artificial bits were checked off. My wedding ring was securely taped. The six crowned teeth were carefully noted. My wrist and ankle bands were examined. Then two male Operating Department Assistants in dark green, joined us. Another set of doors opened to reveal a long corridor with intensely dazzling lights overhead. It seemed a long way down before we turned into a small room on the right (the anaesthetic room). Long wooden poles were inserted into the canvas on my bed and I was lifted across onto a trolley. I then had to roll over to my side before being transferred gently by hand, back to the bed.

I remember how peaceful I felt. I was vaguely aware of many masked faces all smiling kindly down at me. I recall recognising Dr. Chalmers and thinking how different he looked in his green gear. One of the nurses held my hand. Joanna told me afterwards, that it was her. I was unaware of the pointed trocar with cannula being inserted into my left wrist (trocar, a pointed instrument with cannula: a hollow tube for introduction of fluids into body). Nor do I recall asking, 'Will the anaesthetic take long to work?' I apparently commented, 'You'll make sure I'm out first!' All I remember is that everything and everyone was blotted out, as I intently fixed on the ceiling beam. It was T shaped, not quite in the shape of the Cross: but it had to be as far as I was concerned. My entire being concentrated on that Cross, which I just had to focus on. Nothing else mattered... except Jesus.

PART 2

'Again, the kingdom of heaven is like unto a merchant man, seeking goodly pearls: Who when he had found one pearl of great price, went and sold all that he had and bought it.'

Matthew chapter 13 verses 45-46 Authorised K.J.V.

Chapter 5
The Pearl Of Great Price

Completely oblivious to anything; other than of being in a most blissful state of mind, I cycled along Boston High Street. It was about ten o' clock at night. 'Oi stop!' The sudden shout from a policeman, standing opposite the junction of Bridge Street; made me realise that I was cycling along in the dark, without lights. Hastily stopping to switch them on, I pedalled furiously away, now feeling extremely foolish. Little, did I realise, that this was to be the first of many encounters with the law!

The reason for my unusually reckless behaviour? After months of thinking and mulling over how much I wanted to become a Christian: I had finally made an important commitment. A couple of friends and I had attended a meeting at Boston Baptist Church, to see yet another Billy Graham film. By then I had viewed many of them and had heard a great deal about the American evangelist. He was scheduled to begin his second crusade in London that June and many local churches were preparing for this important evangelistic mission.

It was 3rd March 1966 (two months before my seventeenth birthday). At the end of the meeting, people were invited to go to the front of the hall, if they wanted to publicly acknowledge that they were committing their lives to Christ. I did not go forward (that was not my way) but quietly and sincerely I asked Jesus into my life.

My parents were not churchgoers, although as young people in their home town of Doncaster, they had regularly attended Sunday School and church. I had the impression that churchgoing was something that had been the norm amongst their generation. It was something you did, more as a duty than because of a deep personal commitment.

In February 1956, when I was nearly seven; a new family moved down Blackthorn Lane, a few doors away from us. John and Audrey Cole, were very involved with youth work at Holy Trinity Church, on Spilsby Road. Our parents soon became acquainted. I started playing with their daughter Judy, who was a year younger.

I remember how thrilled I was when they first invited me along to Sunday School. Soon, my younger brother Alan and I were attending regularly. Once a month, Mum would take us along to the family service. At first, the complicated Anglican service, was a real mystery to us. However, there was always someone ready to help us to find the appropriate page. I was not impressed with church but enjoyed Sunday School. I believed in God and Jesus in a simple childlike way.

At eleven I moved up to Covenanter Bible Class. Mrs. Cole led the junior group which met on a Sunday afternoon. During my second year at Boston High School, I decided that I really could no longer be bothered with church and Bible Class. Once I had missed a couple of classes, it became harder and harder to return. Instead of going out on a Sunday afternoon with my two close friends, Angela Fiddling and Jennifer Simpson (who also lived down Blackthorn Lane); I would be at home doing school work, inwardly wishing that I had gone. After about three months' absence, I realised that I was missing something important and returned to the Bible Class. The leaders had assumed that I would not be returning and were very surprised to see me.

Ever since I was of junior school age, I had longed to learn French and German. I read avidly and my choices usually involved travel and adventure stories. I loved war films, where I would listen attentively for any German phrases. My ambition was to be an air hostess. Foreign lands fascinated me: Geography being my favourite subject. Indeed, the only reason that I wanted to go to Boston High School and not Kitwood Girls, was so that I could learn French. In 1960, a foreign language was not part of the latter's school curriculum.

Three of us from Tower Road School, had a joint interview with Miss Thomas, the headmistress at the High School. The other two girls trotted out the boring and probably the most expected responses. They wanted to be teachers. I was the one who was different! That was the last thing I wanted to be. I proudly told Miss Thomas that I wanted to be an air hostess. (In reality, they left school at fifteen, whilst I stayed on to take A-levels and go to college).

I thoroughly enjoyed learning French. We had a fairly young teacher whom I liked very much and I made good progress during that first year.

(However, by the start of the second form, an eye problem had reoccurred. For when aged about seven and a half, I was dressing in front of my bedroom mirror. How excited I was at seeing two images of myself, as I pulled on a red jumper and combed my hair. The double vision persisted but its novelty value soon wore off! My G.P. referred me to an eye specialist. The Ophthalmic Surgeon immediately ruled out surgery for correction of the squint in my left eye. He maintained, that although my left eye muscles were extremely lazy: they could be corrected by exercises.

I regularly attended the orthoptic clinic, an out-patients' clinic then held in Wide Bargate, Boston. I worked with Miss Ghest, the orthoptist, on various eye exercises, which were all designed to stimulate the muscles of my lazy left eye: thus reducing the difficulties in focusing and to improve and maintain binocular vision. Happily, the squint was corrected once I had begun the exercises. So as a young child, I was not bothered with the problem for long. Occasionally, the left eye would start to drift into the inner corner, when I became over-tired. Fortunately, it always cleared up after about a week. I simply became accustomed to this slight inconvenience.

During those junior school years, I had an annual hospital check-up with the Ophthalmic Surgeon. One day a letter arrived completely out of the blue: it was admitting me into hospital for an eye operation. I was absolutely petrified at the thought of surgery. Dad and I cycled to Boston General Hospital to discuss the matter. It turned out to be an administrative error. Annoyingly, the surgeon dismissed the matter far too lightly. He did not realise what real terror it had caused.)

The squint, which reoccurred when I was twelve, just would not go away. Indeed, the problem of my awful squint was not addressed, until spectacles were finally prescribed for me about ten months later. Until the problem was resolved, things were very difficult for me at school.

After my first year at Boston High school, I was moved into the A form. I had badly wanted this because I wished to take Latin, which was only on offer in that class. How pleased I was to study that and be able to drop loathsome Needlework. Nor did I mind missing out on Domestic Science either. Besides, I reckoned that in the normal course of life's events, I would spend plenty of time cooking. This was in spite of the firm views I now held: to remain single and pursue a career. Marriage and children were not for me. I much preferred learning a foreign language (even a dead one) to anything remotely practical. I knew that once in the A form, I would be eligible to study German in my third year.

Much to my delight, I was placed in the top set for French. Unfortunately the teacher was renowned for her strictness and as a timid twelve-year-old I was scared of her. I was moreover, distinctly ill at ease having to function with a squint. I could not cope with her fierce manner. I was soon made to feel hopelessly foolish and I was downgraded to the B set. I was far happier there. I was with the teacher whom I had worked well with during my first year. I stayed in the B set for the next four years. Sadly, only those in the top French set were assigned to study German; a fact that I have always bitterly regretted.

In 1964, at the age of fifteen, a group of us attended confirmation classes, led by the vicar of Holy Trinity, the Revd. Frank Hines. In due course, we were confirmed. Even my father attended this special service. Since the war he had become very sceptical about Christianity.

By then, I had experienced a few years of Christian teaching. I felt in awe of the way some of the leaders would speak so openly about their faith. They spoke of having a personal relationship with God, through their belief in Christ. I could see that they had something very precious. How I longed to share this but judged that it was far out of my grasp.

A year after I had automatically gone through confirmation, I suddenly realised that I was seeing and understanding matters of faith in a very different way. It was as if a light had been switched on and I could see clearly, after years of being in the dark or semi-light. Jesus' life and death now made real sense to me. His sacrifice on the cross, was to bring me back into fellowship with God. At last I understood the implications of everything that had up to now all been accepted unquestioningly. God loved me and wanted me to respond by allowing Him to be involved in my life. It was electrifying. I had, at long last, recognised Jesus knocking at the door of my life. The verse which made this point very clearly was from Revelation chapter 3 verse 20 R.S.V.

'Behold, I stand at the door and knock; if any one hears my voice and opens the door, I will come in to him and eat with him, and he with me.'

I had heard and puzzled over this verse for a long time. Acknowledging that I wanted to become a Christian was one thing but knowing how to, was another matter. The verse implied that I should simply invite Jesus into my life. This I did. For some inexplicable reason I chose the privacy of the bathroom, no one else being at home at the time. I was on my knees, praying hard, willing something extraordinary to happen (a sign, may be I expected a rushing wind or fire?) so that I would feel different and thus know that I had become a Christian. Yet, nothing happened. Nor, did I become a kind, loving person, that I thought I should automatically become. My quest continued...

I happened to read a booklet 'Becoming a Christian' by John Stott. He outlined three necessary steps for me to take:

1. *'I must acknowledge myself to be in God's sight a helpless sinner...No amount of good deeds on my part can win God's favour...I need a Saviour to bring me back to God.'*
2. *'I must believe that Jesus Christ died on the cross to be the very Saviour I have just admitted I need.'*
3. *'I must come to Christ and claim my personal share in what He did for everybody...I must ask Him to take my sins away.'*

The booklet stressed further implications. There is a price to be paid at the time of accepting Him and indeed afterwards:

1. *'The faith which receives Christ must be accompanied by the repentance which rejects sin.'*

To be sorry for our past and present wrongs is not enough. We must turn away from every thought, word, action and habit that we know to be wrong.

2. *'He wants to be my Lord as well as my Saviour.'*

This means actively involving Him in every aspect of life: both in the ordinary routines of day to day, as well as the more serious and important issues. We must seek to discover His will for our lives: to become Christ-centred instead of self-centred.

3. *'I must confess Christ before men.'*

If I open the door of my life to Him, *'I cannot be a secret disciple.'* At the end there was a prayer of commitment and this I made for myself. Also, were the following helpful words: *'Do not be in any doubt that the Lord Jesus has come into your life. Do not worry if you do not feel any different. His sure promise, not your fluctuating feelings, is to be the ground of your certainty. Read Revelation chapter 3 verse 20: R.S.V.'*
"Behold, I stand at the door and knock; if any one hears my voice and opens the door, I will come in to him and eat with him and he with me." 'and John chapter 6 verse 37: R.S.V.'
"All that the Father gives me will come to me; and him who comes to me I will not cast out." 'Believe His word. He will not break it.'
My search was finally over.

A few weeks later, when I watched the Billy Graham film; the decision I made that night, merely confirmed the one which had already been made. Yet, the date I saw the film (3rd March 1966) somehow stuck in my mind, as the date of my conversion. Is there any wonder that experiencing such exalted feelings, all common sense had alluded me on my cycle ride home?

These intensely powerful feelings stayed with me for some time. I felt so wonderfully happy and at peace, knowing that God was involved in my life and that I was no longer meant to drift along pleasing myself. My life had at last gained purpose. Every afternoon on arriving home from school, I spent at least half an hour in prayer and Bible reading. I followed the Scripture Union Bible Reading notes. This 'quiet time' was my priority before I tackled homework.

I received a great deal of guidance and encouragement from Miss Anne Hancock, the Senior Girls' Covenanter Leader. Miss Hancock, a speech therapist, also lived down Blackthorn Lane and was nearby, whenever I wanted to discuss my developing faith.

She asked me to share my experience of becoming a Christian. For me to talk to a group of about twenty teenagers, on how I became a Christian, was something that in my wildest dreams I could never have envisaged doing. I was always the quiet, timid one; who never volunteered for anything. I never spoke up in Bible Class. In fact, it took all my courage just to say anything in lessons at school. I was so painfully shy and lacking in confidence. I was also dreadfully self-conscious and blushed very easily. How I hated being like that. I really envied my friends who seemed to be far surer of themselves. School reports used to upset me terribly. They always spoke very highly of my academic achievements. However, all the favourable comments were negated drastically by the reoccurring comment, *Heather is far too quiet in class*. I cringed inwardly when I read such statements.

My short talk went very well. I felt God gave me the necessary courage to speak. I knew that I had achieved something worthwhile and that I had made a small but significant breakthrough in the struggle to overcome my shyness. From then on I found it much easier to contribute in class. I also became more involved in church activities. On one occasion I even read the lesson in church. I am sure that I was trembling visibly as the time approached to do the reading, I was so nervous. Amazingly, once I stood at the lectern; a great calm came over me, my voice was steady and I was able to read confidently.

As well as attending the Senior Covenanter Saturday Youth Club, a new club started on a Friday evening. Many of my close friends went to this 'Over 17's Club' (of which I was the treasurer). We had a great time participating in a variety of fun activities, as well as the more serious issues. Saturdays were often spent hill walking in Derbyshire, or messing about (supposedly punting) on the river Cam at Cambridge. Those were my favourite outings. How pleased I was, that at last I had other things to think about; other than working hard at school.

In June 1966, a coach-load from Holy Trinity travelled to London to see Billy Graham. I recall how I prayed like mad, that Mum would go forward but she did not. One of the young men in our group, went out to the front. It was a most impressive occasion.

Every year, Covenanters always took part in a Christmas concert. Until then, I had never shown any interest in participating. I decided that this year I would. It was to be a traditional Nativity play. My friend Maureen Parker, declined to be Mary, on account of too much A -level work (mock exams were looming ahead in February). So, I was asked to be Mary. Since primary school, I had never taken part in any production. I was always overlooked, in favour of the more confident members of my peer group. I thoroughly enjoyed the challenge. I know that I surprised quite a few people by my performance; in spite of nearly falling flat on my face and almost dropping 'Jesus' as I descended the steps onto the stage, as if I were literally flying.

From quite early on at Boston High School, I had been corresponding with a French girl of the same age. By the summer term of my fourth year, I started to consider the possibility of a French exchange visit. These were usually arranged during the Easter holidays and were of three weeks' duration, prior to taking French G.C.E. exams the following term. My parents raised no objections. Dad informed me that he would pay a small amount towards the trip but that I had to fund most of the money.

So, I spent most of the 1964 summer holidays doing land work, notably bean pulling. I hated such physical work but was sufficiently motivated to stick at it! The following holiday, I spent time working in the chicken factory, on Willoughby Road, Boston. What an eye-opener that was!

The exchange scheme which the school followed, was to link pupils who were totally unknown to each other. I was able to use this scheme for the administration and transport in order to visit my established pen-friend.

It was a memorable three weeks. I undoubtedly found it quite a strain: being a very quiet person, having to speak in French all the time; but I managed it. My oral French improved considerably. My French friend and her family lived in Herblay, a peaceful village a few kilometres south-west of Paris. I was introduced to a lively group of her friends and we all went around Paris sightseeing together. I found it most amusing that no one could pronounce Heather properly, the 'th' sound caused great problems. My best friend, Kathleen Anderson, in a letter to me, even sent me some good British soil, in case I was homesick! At times it did feel strange and uncomfortable in a non-English speaking environment. It was the first time that I had ever been away from my family. Yet, on the whole, I thoroughly enjoyed the experience. Everything considered, it was an excellent introduction to France and her people. Easter was such a lovely time of the year to be viewing the French countryside. I was very impressed by what I saw and was eager for further visits.

I had worked extremely hard for my G.C.E. exams. I achieved grade 1 in 5 subjects, grade 3 for French and English Language. Mathematics as expected, was a hopeless failure the first time round. I hated the subject. I had always wanted to take French at A-level and had simply assumed that I would. However, there seemed to be a few obstacles. Nothing ever seemed to come easy for me! One day the Biology teacher, Miss Ruth Painter, actually asked me if I would consider studying Biology as one of my A-level subjects. I was flabbergasted: certain aspects of Biology were alright but I was really not interested in the subject. Besides, I was so squeamish. When we had been set the delightful task of dissecting eyeballs, I had been in the minority group who had chickened out!

The teacher for that year's French A-level course, was the very same teacher who had humiliated me at the start of the second form. She was adamant, **'Heather Spencer cannot possibly study French A-level! She has only been in the B set for French and her French is not good enough!'**

I was gutted. All these years I had set my heart on studying the language as fully as I could. I was desperately upset. I remember clearly, tearfully begging God, over and over again, to let me take French. I felt so passionately about it, that I implored Him to let me be a success at French and I would be happy not to have any boyfriends. This was a frequently sought request! I found it very hard, especially when even some of my more studious friends started dating. I felt that I must be an oddity and that no one would ever ask me out! Yet, in desperation, I made this bargain with God.

Surprisingly, I almost settled for the three subjects that the headmistress Miss Thomas suggested: those being English, Geography and Religious Education. The latter I had never ever remotely considered! Her additional comment to me about this choice was, 'Besides, French and Geography cannot be accommodated on our timetable.' She was a most persuasive lady and I cycled home in total acceptance of what she had said. I was even beginning to see myself as an R.E. teacher!

Dad, an established clerk, worked in the Treasurer's Department at County Hall. He dealt with the education accounts and was well acquainted with and highly respected by all the Boston headteachers. He intervened.

I took English, French and Geography. I did the minimum work for English. I worked hard at my Geography and extremely hard at French. I had the challenge of proving to myself, the rest of the French group and especially to the teacher, that I could do it. My best result was in French. I did better than some of her more favoured pupils. How delighted I was with my grade B. I recall how satisfying it was to hear the teacher's words of congratulations and most importantly to feel that she really meant it.

It is only years later that the bitterness towards her (for giving me such a hard time) has been replaced by gratitude. I learnt a very valuable lesson in life: in that even when circumstances are very difficult, they can still be overcome.

My ambition to be an airhostess had long since passed. For years I had no notion of what I wanted to do. Of one thing I was certain, I was not going to teach. At the beginning of my lower sixth year, Dad and I had a long discussion about my future. I still had no specific career in mind. Dad suggested a teaching course. Initially I was dead set against it. However, as we talked over the pros and cons of becoming a teacher; the idea became slightly more appealing. I sent away for all the information I could and began to think, that it was not such a bad suggestion after all. Some of my friends were choosing colleges of education and two were keen to go to university. The latter never appealed to me, although my grades would have enabled me to. Having decided that I would train to be a teacher, I thought that a three year teaching course was what I wanted to do; rather than university.

As I gained in confidence, a different side to my character, was also emerging. I was not the 'goody-two-shoes' that I mostly portrayed. In August 1966, a Convenanter house party was held in Dolgellau, North Wales. I and another equally quiet friend, soon involved ourselves in playing all sorts of harmless pranks on the boys' dormitory. It was hilarious because no one suspected that we could possibly be the perpetrators. We were much too quiet and boring for that! The girls who were far more extrovert were the obvious targets for revenge. From then on, every subsequent house party gave a wonderful opportunity to scheme and wreak havoc on the opposite sex (all good clean fun of course)! My close friends: Kathleen Anderson, Catherine (Kate) Church and Maureen Parker, were usually involved. They say that the quiet ones are always the worst!

I believed that God was very much involved in all these changes to my life. As the prospect of leaving home and starting college (scary events in a young person's life) loomed ahead, I felt inwardly at peace and very content. I had made the best preparation that I could ever do. I no longer had to face the future alone. I had become a Christian.

Chapter 6
College

The summer of 1967 was an exciting time for me, as I was busily preparing to go to Bishop Lonsdale College Of Education. I had chosen a Church of England college because the emphasis was on training teachers who held a Christian faith. This, I believed was vital to the welfare of the children, whom I would eventually be teaching. The college at Derby appealed: for by then, I had grown to love the beautiful Derbyshire countryside, having over the past two years enjoyed regular trips to the Peak District, with Covenanters.

That summer we had our last family holiday. We travelled by local bus to Skegness. It was typical British holiday weather, cold, wet and very windy. For the first time ever, I had my own bathroom. At the age of eighteen, I used to spend hours in front of a mirror! Somehow, I managed to lose the bathroom door key. Dad searched every antique and furniture shop in Skegness, to find a replacement. He obtained a similar sized key and then sat for hours, huddled on the sand, patiently filing it to the required pattern. This sort of action was typical of him. He never seemed to be put off by anything and would always persevere in completing a task, however time-consuming and impossible, it seemed to me. He was a very skilful and resourceful person, especially when it came to practical matters.

Although my father had left school at fourteen, he had studied hard at evening class and had also followed postal courses; both to improve on his basic secondary education and to equip himself with the necessary skills (book-keeping and shorthand) for working in local government. He had an alert, mathematical mind and he used to spend hours trying to help me with my awful Maths and Physics homework. I must have tried even Dad's patience, because I used to get so uptight and frustrated, arguing with him when he was only trying to help me.

Dad was very much a family man, who rarely socialised. He was content to do things with and for the family, rather than having his own separate interests outside the home. He was a deep thinking, very private sort of person.

Up until 1967, family holidays had been spent in a variety of British holiday resorts further afield than Skegness. We had always travelled there by train, that being very much part of the holiday for us. However in 1967, Dad had been unwell. He began to experience pain in his lower abdomen especially when urinating. He often had to lie down at lunch-time before cycling back to work. Indeed for a number of years, he had experienced problems with low blood pressure. He took a number of tablets daily, often joking that he must rattle inside. I have a very distinct memory, as a young child of three or four, sobbing inconsolably because Daddy had to go away for a few days (into Boston General Hospital, for tests).

In 1965 during our holiday in Blackpool; at the ripe old age of sixteen I finally learnt to roller-skate. My brother Alan had done this as one of the usual young children's activities but for some reason I had never even attempted it. I thoroughly enjoyed this and Dad joined Alan and me on the rink. We spent a wonderful time skating. Poor Mum spent much of her time that holiday, watching the three of us whizz round. Dad had to have another short stay in hospital a few weeks later, because he became dizzy and breathless with low blood pressure again. I blamed the skating for this. After that, his blood pressure was stabilised. He settled down and apart from having to take tablets, continued to lead a normal life.

Although Dad had driven during the war, we had never owned a car. As a family, we depended upon public transport, our bikes and our legs. I have many fond memories of our Sunday outings: family bike-rides and picnics. We often spent Sundays at Freiston Shore, or along the Witham, inland past the Sluice Bridge. These were very simple but very enjoyable family pleasures. Needless to say, friends and neighbours were very good and if we needed a lift, there was always someone to oblige.

That year Dad decided to start driving lessons. I was thrilled, as it would make life so much easier for us. I had no inclination to learn myself: yet I could see that once Dad had his own car, I would no doubt be the navigator and more than likely would eventually learn to drive. It was planned that Dad would drive me to college, accompanied by the driving instructor, when I started there in September. As it transpired, Dad was not well enough. Mr. Tom Maddison, his driving instructor (also a neighbour for years, in Blackthorn Lane) very kindly drove Mum and me to Bishop Lonsdale College Of Education, on Friday 22nd September 1967.

Once away at college, I was in a totally different world. My Christian faith really gave me the confidence, to settle among strangers, away from home. Wonderfully, before I had even started there, I had been contacted by a Christian couple. Trish was about to start her third year at Derby and her fiancé who lived in Boston, had just finished his course. They visited me at home during the summer. Knowing that I would have a Christian contact at college, was most reassuring. I believed very strongly that God had prepared the way ahead for me, by establishing this new friendship. Furthermore, on being shown into my college accommodation on arrival, a surprise letter awaited me. One of Trish's friends, Jill, who lived in Lonsdale Hall (my hall of residence) was inviting me round for a chat. So as soon as I had waved goodbye to Mum and Mr. Maddison, I went to find Jill's room. She made me feel very much at ease and we talked for a long time. My first afternoon in a strange place miles from home, turned out to be far more pleasant than I had envisaged. Meeting another Christian, was a wonderful start to my first day.

That night as prearranged, Trish met me after the welcome meeting for new students. She introduced me to some other Christians with whom she shared a flat. They invited me to go along to a Crusaders' Bible class, which they helped with on a Sunday afternoon. I was only too pleased to go along. I thought that it would help me to settle in.

At the Saturday introductory lecture for the first year students, I happened to be sitting next to someone, who recognised my Scripture Union Badge (a lamp). Immediately, Sandra Morris and I found that we had much in common. We were in the same group for our education lectures and the associated curriculum subjects, as well as our Christian faith. So even on that first weekend, I felt very heartened that I had already met up with people, with whom I could identify.

I wrote a glowing letter to my friend Kathleen Anderson. She shared it with many of my friends at the 'Over 17's Club.' As I was the first out of my group of friends to start college, I knew how apprehensive they would be feeling and I was eager to encourage them.

Trish had told me about the college Christian Union and I was keen to join. Sue Marlow, another student in the same education group as Sandra and I, also joined. At the start of our first year, there were about nine of us who initially joined C.U.

I found adapting to a much less structured approach to learning: with the emphasis on the student's initiative, rather than on a very rigid form of teaching (as at the High School) quite difficult. In addition, the more relaxed, free and easy atmosphere of a mixed college community was initially hard for me to handle. Nevertheless, I settled in straight away. I was certainly not at all homesick. On the whole I was very happy in my new life. As we were not on the telephone, Mum, Dad and I corresponded regularly by letter.

During that first year I spent a considerable amount of time with the third year group whom Trish lived with. I attended the missionary prayer group held at their flat. On Sundays, after going along to Crusaders with them, I often stayed for tea. I felt closer to many of the third years, than I did towards those of my own year. This turned out to be somewhat of a disadvantage, for as the year progressed; I realised that my third year friends would soon be leaving. Towards the end of our first year, we had to sort out our accommodation for the following year. First year students were expected to move out of the supervised halls of residence into lodgings. Groups of friends were considering where to live together. As I had not formed any close friendships amongst the first years, I was rather worried about what to do. The people I had most to do with, were in my education group and in C.U. In desperation I asked Sandra and Sue about sharing with them and their two friends. Very kindly they agreed. In practice, our planned group of five, did not materialise. Sue and her friend stayed on in a hall of residence; whilst Sandra Morris, Trudy Elliott and I went into unsupervised lodgings.

Mum kept the details of my Dad's developing illness from me. Over the Christmas holidays, I noticed that he was not his usual self. He had to spend a great deal of time lying down. Like most small girls, I had been a real 'Daddy's girl'. Yet in adolescence, I became very difficult and our relationship suffered. Dad was old-fashioned in outlook and quite strict. We clashed over many issues. I would frequently lose my temper and say some very nasty things. Much of this, I now believe, stemmed from the deep frustration that I felt over being so quiet and timid outside the home. Only my family saw my quick fiery temper. I hid my real feelings from friends and acquaintances: masking any displeasure or disappointment under occasional moodiness.

I worked at the Post Office that Christmas, as did many of my friends. I found it physically hard work but most enjoyable. The postman, on whose area I was working, introduced me to his family. I used to call there daily for a welcome hot drink. His wife and young family were lovely. I had a soft spot for their son, Ian, aged six. I marked his birthday down in my diary, fully intending to send him a card. Ironically, I was to remember 3rd November for a very different reason.

Early in the spring of 1968, Dad's illness had developed to such an extent that the consultant had arranged for him to be admitted into St. George's Hospital Lincoln, for radiotherapy treatment. I had no inkling whatsoever what that entailed, or might indicate, nor did I (as far as I can recall) try to find out. I know that I was slightly concerned but it never entered my head that things were becoming serious. I was selfishly absorbed in my new exciting life at college, which I was thoroughly enjoying. For most of the time, home life was not a concern. I switched off from what was really happening at home. Dad had three-weekly sessions of radiotherapy and came home at weekends.

Although, this is written twenty-five years afterwards: I can vividly recall the tremendous joy that I experienced on arriving at Boston Railway Station for the Easter holidays; to find Dad waiting. He looked so much better, so much brighter, more like his old self, as he helped me with my luggage. Radiotherapy had certainly helped him.

During the summer, my younger brother Alan (then sixteen) travelled to his annual scout camp. After years of family holidays, my parents went away on their own. They spent a week at Paignton in Devon, followed by a few days in Doncaster (their birthplace) visiting our relations. They stayed with my paternal grandmother, who at the age of eighty-seven, was still living alone in her own home.

For the first time in my life, I went camping. Eight of us stayed in North Wales for a week. Four of us were close friends from Boston High School. The four lads were from the Covenanter Youth Club. As individuals we were all fairly quiet. Once the initial shyness and awkwardness had worn off, we settled down and had a reasonable time. Certainly by the end of the week, we were all quite sociable!

I amused everyone by managing to flush my watch down the toilet, instead of an apple-core, that had been in my pocket! Of all the stupid things to do. I was very upset, though naturally I had to hide it. I had treasured this first watch since childhood. It was in gold plate and had a delicate spider's web drawn on the face. For some inexplicable reason, I chose a small travelling alarm clock, as a replacement for my lost wrist-watch. I recall how Dad was trying to set the mechanism, to show me how the alarm worked. He was obviously in discomfort and was breathing very heavily. This always used to irritate me. I became quite short-tempered because he was taking so long.

One of the cards that I had received on my nineteenth birthday in May, was from my close college friend, Trudy Elliott, with whom I shared the same birthday. It was a copy of the famous 'Praying Hands' portrait by Albrecht Dürer. I found the picture very striking and more so, when I read the background to it: an account of true sacrificial friendship. Albrecht Dürer and Franz Knigstein were artists but had to work part-time as labourers to finance their studies. They decided to draw lots to decide, which of them should find full-time employment to support them both; whilst the winner would devote all his energies to studying. Albrecht won and agreed that after qualifying; he would return to finance his friend's studies. After Albrecht had become very successful, he discovered that the sacrifice Franz had made, was far greater than either of them had foreseen.

Through hard labour, Franz's fingers had become twisted and bent. They could never control an artist's brushes. Yet Franz showed no bitterness. He was glad to have played his part in his friend's success. One day, Albrecht found Franz at prayer. He was so struck by his praying hands that he sketched them and later completed one of the great masterpieces of the early Renaissance. As I liked the picture so much, Dad offered to make a frame for me. It took him such a long time to complete it. More than once, I asked Mum very impatiently, if the frame was ready. Finally, Dad completed it, so that I could take it back with me for the start of my second year at college.

A few days before college started; the four of us who had gone camping together (Kathleen Anderson, Kate Church and Maureen Parker) attended Valerie Foster's wedding. Val was the only one of my friends who had not gone away to college or university. Afterwards, Kathleen gave us all a lift home. It had been a lovely happy occasion shared with many of my close friends. Unexplainably, while sat in her car, I suddenly became upset at having to return to my other life at college.

Once back at college, I quickly settled down, without any further regrets. This year I had moved out of Lonsdale Hall of residence, into unsupervised lodgings, which I shared with Sandra Morris and two third year students. Trudy Elliott, my other friend from our education group, was supposed to be sharing with Sandra. Unfortunately, Trudy had been ill in the summer holidays, so had not yet returned. Although I missed her, it did give Sandra and me the opportunity to get to know each other better. I had often felt excluded, when the three of us were together.

I had a double room to myself, with my own kitchen and bathroom. It was absolute bliss. As a quiet, introverted person, I had always needed to spend a great deal of time on my own, for my own sanity! Last year I had shared a room with someone, who although quite pleasant, was far too sociable for my liking and often invited her friends to our room. I had found this almost total lack of privacy, extremely trying, especially when I wanted to have my 'quiet time'. Happily, I had found an isolated corner, tucked away in the attic, where I took my Bible and escaped! No one ever discovered me and

I was so thankful that God had given me some much needed breathing space.

Chapter 7

Sunday 3rd November 1968

That October, we were frantically preparing for our second year teaching practice. On our first year practice, there had been five students working together in one class. This time we were to be in charge of our own class. Teaching practice was due to commence after half-term, on Thursday 7th November. Therefore all our thoughts, efforts and prayers were focusing on that.

I had visited my school twice. Some of my friends were attached to inner-city schools but I was fortunate in going to a large primary school at Etwall, an extremely pleasant village, a few miles south-west of Derby. Imagine my delight, when on being introduced to the headmaster, he immediately commented on my Scripture Union badge. It helped knowing that the head was a practising Christian, someone on my wavelength. The teacher whose class I was to take, was also a lovely, warm person and so helpful. After some of the horror stories that my friends had related; I was relieved to be in a school I liked and where I had been made to feel most welcome. Of course, I knew that it would be really hard work. Having a class of nine and ten-year-olds for a solid five weeks, was quite an ordeal to contemplate!

On Wednesday 30th October, on a beautiful autumn day, I travelled home by train with Judith Cole. Judy, the friend with whom I had first gone along to Sunday School all those years ago, had started at Bishop Lonsdale College in September. This meant that from then on we could travel together, usually in her father's car; thus solving all my transport problems. As that famous landmark of Boston Stump loomed nearer (such a welcome sight on arriving home), I felt quite excited about my longed for half-term break, after the hectic build-up to teaching practice.

Back home, I was shocked to find that Dad looked so poorly. He was in bed because he was in considerable pain. Mum informed me that even up to this time, he had grimly persisted in going to work; although at times he just could not manage it. He had long since stopped cycling there and would either catch the bus or have a lift from a neighbour. They were very understanding at work. His former brisk walk had now become excruciatingly slow. I spoke to him about college and my forthcoming teaching practice. I was so disappointed that Dad was unable to show the interest that he would undoubtedly have shown, had he not been so ill. He seemed to sense my disappointment at his lack of attention. Sighing deeply, he said, 'I suppose I'll be all right one day...'

Apparently life was continuing as normal. Mum did not like leaving Dad, in case he needed the bathroom. On that Thursday when she biked to the local shop, (after refusing my offer to go) Dad had declined my help, preferring to wait for her return. Very late that Thursday evening, I awoke to hear my father in dreadful pain. It was heart-rending listening to him, crying out in such agony: while Mum tried to comfort him. How I prayed that Dad would be spared further distress. I could not bear to think of him suffering; in the way that I had accidentally overheard. I kept this incident totally to myself. In my shocked state, I just could not admit to Mum what I now knew.

On the Friday I cycled along to one of the Alms' Houses on Freiston Road. I had been visiting an old lady there for the past two years. On my return, Mum informed me that when Dad had been taken by ambulance for his outpatient's appointment: the consultant had decided to admit him straightaway. I was filled with such tremendous relief. At last his suffering had been recognised and his pain would finally be dealt with.

On Saturday afternoon, Mum and I went to visit Dad in Boston General Hospital. He was sat up in bed. We only stayed about ten minutes, because he looked in such a very dreamy state (presumably from the effects of morphine for his pain relief). He told me that our vicar from Holy Trinity, the Revd. Frank Hines, had visited him during the morning. That meant so much to me. Inwardly, I was really overjoyed, to hear that a Christian minister had spoken to my father; hopefully in a way that I was unable to. I took heart from this visit, especially because I felt sure that the vicar would have prayed for my father. It did not seem fair to tire Dad further. We left him, still trying to eat the pink blancmange, that he had been eating when we arrived. He really did look as if he would fall asleep in the process. We had to laugh. We told Dad that we would be back the next day. Glancing back at him from the corridor, we waved and left him.

That night I attended Covenanter Youth Club. As it was half-term, a few of my old school friends were home from college. I had a good talk with Kate Church, my very oldest friend, for our mothers were in hospital together; Kate being born three days after me. We had been friends at Tower Road School and then at Boston High School (sadly, the only one of my close friends with whom I am no longer in real contact). I shared with Kate my feelings of relief and thankfulness. I firmly believed that God was working in the situation. He had shown me that by the Revd. Frank Hines' visit. I remember that I had a great deal to tell Kate. I felt so optimistic: my prayers for Dad's healing were being answered.

On Sunday 3rd November, I went along as usual to the morning service. I thanked the vicar for visiting my father. I said that I hoped that he had not found Dad too doped up. He told me that they had been able to have a good talk. I found this extremely reassuring. That afternoon my brother Alan went off to his Covenanter Bible Class. At about 2.15pm, I was busy getting ready to visit the hospital (visiting hours were from 3pm and Mum and I were to cycle there). Mrs. Doreen Sutton, our next-door neighbour came round. As we were not on the telephone, the hospital had contacted the Police, who in turn had visited Mrs. Sutton.

In some distress, Mum went off with Mrs. Sutton; merely telling me that the hospital had sent for her. I was left alone. I recall being in my bedroom, on my knees, my Bible open searching for some words of solace. In tears I begged God not to let it be true, not to let my Dad be dead. I prayed like this... but it did not feel right. I cannot explain... I just knew that my prayers were futile.

Not long afterwards (though to me it seemed an absolute age), Mum and Mrs. Sutton returned. 'Your Dad's dead.' Mum's words met me as she came in through the door; before she broke down. Mrs. Sutton sat with us both for some time. I felt so shocked that this could have happened. I wept in disbelief. Dad had died at 2pm. Stubbornly he had taken himself to the toilet and died of a heart attack. Mum had agreed to a post-mortem, she obviously suspected something else. How we got through that dreadful afternoon I do not know. It was the worst day of my life. After Mrs. Sutton had gone we just sat there, totally devastated and very tearful. As mother and daughter, we had never been very demonstrative. We were a caring family but in a quiet, very reserved way. I put my arm round her. How utterly hopeless and helpless I felt.

Sometime later, my brother Alan could be heard whistling loudly, as he cycled up the garden path: totally unaware of the awful news awaiting him. On seeing our distraught faces, he quite casually asked, 'What's the matter?' His immediate reaction was one of silent withdrawal from our company and to shut himself in his bedroom. At tea-time he reappeared, looking very red-eyed.

We went through the motions of having tea. I could not eat anything but drank my first cup of tea in years (I had gone over to only drinking coffee in my late teens, just to be different)! It sounds so ridiculous now but I recall considering the pros and cons of having a cup of tea: finally deciding that the occasion merited it! You would not believe that such trivial thoughts could have occupied me, but they did! Alan surprised us by saying that he was going to the evening service. I thought that was very brave of him. It would have been far too upsetting for me.

My friend Jennifer Simpson, stopped by in her car to collect me for church. I went outside to briefly tell her. Jennifer obviously did not know what to say. I felt pleased when she said that she would come round in a few days' time. Shortly after, Kate, the friend with whom I had spoken so positively the previous evening, arrived. Mum showed her in. I blurted it out. Kate just hugged me.

Alan told us that prayers had been said for our family that evening. How glad I was that I had stayed away. Nevertheless I was very touched by this. A long sleepless night followed, as I tried to sort my shattered thoughts out. *Why hadn't God healed my Dad? Why had he taken him from us?* Dad was only fifty-three and he died twelve days before his fifty-fourth birthday. For once in my life I had been really organised. I had already bought his present, a new toilet bag.

The following morning Alan went out. I had to write a few letters for Mum and she had telegrams to send to our relatives. That very day, I received a letter from my friend Kathleen Anderson, who had not come home for half-term. It was a very encouraging letter. The things that she had written about all seemed to help me in the awful situation that I was now facing. I dropped her the briefest note, knowing how concerned she would be.

We knew how bad the news was for us to cope with but we really felt that it was the cruellest of blows, for Dad's elderly mother, aged eighty-seven, to bear. As the younger of two children, Dad had been her blue-eyed boy. We knew that his sister, my Aunty Dorothy, would have a very difficult time. Poor Grandma became very bitter. She survived my father by almost five years.

Aunty Dora (Mum's cousin) came over from Peterborough, accompanied by her husband Archie. She stayed with us, whilst Uncle Archie went home; until the day of the funeral. I had to inform college that I would not be returning straight away. Instead of going back on Wednesday 6th November, ready for my teaching practice on the Thursday; we were in the throes of funeral arrangements.

The post-mortem revealed extensive cancer of the bladder. Apparently Mum had long suspected cancer to be the cause of Dad's illness. She had kept it completely away from the family. Our G.P. had never mentioned this possibility to her and I know that she felt quite bitter about his handling of it. Mum admitted to me, that while she had never spoken about her suspicions to my father: she was sure that he had known. In spite of the fact, when learning that he was to have radiotherapy, he had told her quite bluntly, 'Radiotherapy's not just for cancer you know!' Mum told me how Dad had simply carried on with normal life, as best he could, without complaining or making a fuss. At times he had experienced excruciating pain: often pacing the bedroom floor when it was at its worst. Dad had put a very brave face on his suffering. There had been no self-pity: instead he had shown real dignity and a great strength of character throughout his illness.

Once the post-mortem results were known; Mum started to feel that it was a blessing that he had been spared far more pain and distress. For me, the feelings of despair and of being let down by God, also changed. Instead of feeling angry and embittered towards God, for not healing Dad physically in the way that I had asked: I experienced inner peace, an acceptance of what had happened. I was so thankful to God for His perfect timing; that it had happened at half-term, when I was at home. How could I have coped if I had been away at college? Above all, I was so glad that I had been able to see Dad before he died. How thankful I was, that at least I could remember him: still looking like my Dad (albeit a paler, weaker version) and with all his faculties, before the ravages of cancer had done their worst.

Although my father had been a very quiet, reserved sort of person; he was extremely well-liked and respected by those who knew him. To work colleagues and friends, he was known as 'Ted' (Edward being his middle name): whereas Mum, her relations and family friends all called him 'Aby' (pronounced *Abbey* -from his first name - Albert). His office at County Hall, overlooked Boston Stump. He had considerable contact with teachers and headteachers, who all held him in high regard. So much so, that the joint teachers' organisations held an appeal and a cheque was sent to Mum. The letters of condolence that Mum received said some lovely things about him as a person. Someone had written that he was 'one of life's little gentlemen'. Many regarded him as a personal friend.

Numerous colleagues and friends were present at his funeral service. It was the first one that Alan and I had ever attended (I was nineteen and Alan seventeen). My faith was certainly tested on that day. The Revd. Frank Hines took the service at Boston Crematorium. Remarkably, I was in complete control throughout. I was able to take part in all the singing, without any trace of emotion, even during the final hymn, 'Abide With Me.' Instead of being grief-stricken, an incredible feeling of thankfulness seemed to flow right through me. I could really thank God that He had removed Dad from further agony. Strangely enough, ever since then funerals have caused me varying degrees of emotion, even of people I was not particularly close to. Much stranger, I am never able to hear, let alone try and sing 'Abide With Me' without some distress.

Before returning to college, I went round to see Mrs. Audrey Cole, the neighbour who had first introduced me to Sunday School. I found it very helpful to talk to her about what had happened. She shared with me something that my father had told the vicar. Apparently Dad had said, 'She'll be a blessing to her Mum.' It was a great consolation, to hear what Dad had said about me, the day before he died. This, rightly or wrongly, I kept to myself.

I suppose I should have shared more with Mum. We found it hard to talk on a deep level. I could express my feelings more openly by letter, or in the notes that I left for her to find, after my return to college. It was even harder to communicate with Alan. Although he had become a Christian in the summer of 1967, we were not able to talk about our faith without mutual embarrassment. Yet we could write to each other about spiritual issues. I remember how Alan wrote a very special letter to me during one of my low periods, shortly after Dad's death. It is amongst my collection of 'precious keepsakes', along with Dad's letters.

The watch Dad had worn, now became mine. There certainly had been a reason for me not to have bought a replacement watch for the one that I had thrown down the toilet! Somehow it was very comforting to wear Dad's watch. The 'Praying Hands' portrait that Dad had framed for me, during the last few months of his life; became my dearest and most treasured possession. A deeply poignant dimension was added to the inspirational story of sacrificial love, shown by the artist's friend: the pain my father must have experienced as he struggled to keep to his word in framing the picture.

I returned to college, having missed the first week of teaching practice. The headmaster was very supportive and invited me to spend Sunday afternoon with his family. I never accepted his hospitality because I always helped with the Crusaders' Bible Class with Sandra Morris. Thankfully, I was fully occupied for most of those early weeks. Obviously there were moments of sadness, times when I wept. Again, God's timing seemed perfect. Teaching practice could not have come at a better time. It certainly absorbed most of my day and night!

It must have been far worse for Alan: then in the lower sixth at Boston Grammar School, on his own with Mum, having to be the man of the family; surrounded by such painful memories. In contrast, I could forget about harsh reality for most of my time.

I received considerable support (especially prayer) from my old school friends, with whom I regularly corresponded. More direct help came from my friends in the Christian Union. I knew that I was not alone. Again, God's timing worked out best. Trudy Elliott, my other close college friend, did not start her second year until the spring term. So during those early weeks of bereavement, I had Sandra's undivided attention (school preparation permitting)!

At times my mind reeled in the total shock of it all: I still could not grasp the finality of what had actually happened. My emotions were a confusion of sorrow, thankfulness and guilt. I tried to squeeze out the sadness; by focusing on all our happy family memories. Many never experience the love and care of a good father. How much I had to thank God for; even though Dad's life on earth had been cut short.

The guilt was much harder to bear. I spoke about this only to Sandra. I was so fortunate that she was a good listener and extremely supportive. I felt guilt-stricken over some of the nasty scenes and words of the last few years. It was horrible knowing that my unpleasant behaviour, could never be undone. It made me feel dreadfully guilty. Dwelling on it all, became much too painful and for the most part at college, I managed to shut it away. College work and life were completely absorbing and enabled me to 'escape'. Time enough to face 'grim reality' when I went home.

In spite of coping extremely well after Dad's death; that first year, especially Christmas and holidays, were such difficult times for us, as we tried to adjust to the huge void in our family life. Mum at fifty-one, was a relatively young widow. Fortunately, she had some very good friends and a few outside interests. The way she appeared to be, showed a remarkable strength of character. She was not the sort of person to wallow in any kind of self-pity. Like my father, she was a very private sort of person. Her innermost thoughts were kept to herself.

Occasionally, she would come and spend a day shopping with me in Derby, or we would meet in Nottingham. One Saturday, the Coles were visiting Judy and they offered to bring Mum over. I put her off, as I was bogged down with college work. Fortunately, she ignored me and turned up, saying that she would go and shop on her own. Of course, I realised my mistake and spent the day with her. Now, in retrospect, I cannot believe that I could have been so selfish and uncaring.

For years after, intense feelings of sadness and grief would come flooding back. Oh, what might have been...? The sorrow of not having Dad around, to share my adult life. Early on, the hardest time for Mum and me would be in the autumn, from late-October to Christmas, as the events were relived. Even years later, this awareness of great loss can still sweep over me and not always at the appropriate season.

Chapter 8

Teaching

It had always been my intention to qualify as a teacher and remain in the Derby area. Even when Dad died I still stuck to this idea. During my final year, I vaguely contemplated staying on for a fourth year to do the degree course (Batchelor of Education). I found the thought of leaving college, a very daunting prospect, after having enjoyed three years of close community life. However, I soon realised that to stay for the extra year, was not for me. On one occasion, Trudy and I were discussing our plans for the future. She intended to go home to teach. As I told Trudy that I intended to stay in Derby, the words suddenly sounded so wrong. From then on, I knew that I would go home. Timing again worked out perfectly. My course finished in the summer of 1970. My brother Alan started at Scraptoft College of Education near Leicester, in September of that year.

All newly qualified teachers had to apply to the local education authority of where they wished to teach, rather than for a specific post. Initially, a couple of teaching posts in tiny village schools were mentioned. It would have meant early bus journeys, as I had no other means of transport. At that time, I still had no desire whatsoever to learn to drive. Before I left college, I was quite certain that I was destined for Algarkirk. My neighbours had even driven Mum and me there, to view the school.

I was not thrilled at the prospect of being in a small rural school, without my own transport. Imagine my utter delight, when quite unexpectedly, I received the offer of a post at Woad Farm County Junior School. This large town school, situated on the Woad Farm council estate; being a mere fifteen minute walk away from my home in Blackthorn Lane.

My initial meeting with the headmaster Mr. Frank Naylor, went far better than I had envisaged. For his first words were to express his condolences at my father's death and to explain how well he had got on with him. This was very comforting and put me completely at ease. Mr. Naylor's decision to offer me the post, was partly influenced by the fact that on my application form, I had stated that I was extremely interested in teaching French. Although Geography had been my main subject at college, I had done a short course on Primary School French. Mr. Naylor needed someone capable of teaching French to his or her own class and to the parallel class.

My first class were somewhat 'guinea-pigs', with regard to my French teaching. I loved that aspect of teaching and I think they did! We spent our time in role-play and playing games. The concentration was purely oral and great fun. The scheme we followed was 'En Avant,' a Nuffield course. I was really happy at Woad Farm. In fact all my energies went into teaching. School became my entire life. How I loved my class of nine and ten-year-olds. Mr. Naylor was such a warm fatherly figure and the staff were extremely friendly and helpful. It was just what I needed at the start of my teaching career.

At some point in the summer term of 1971 (as the end of my probationary year approached), Mr. Naylor was diagnosed as being terminally ill with cancer. His death followed quite rapidly. As a school, we were all shocked and saddened by the loss of our dear headmaster. It brought back terrible memories for me, as well as for my friend Jennifer Neal (who taught in the adjacent classroom). Mr. Naylor's death came less than four years after my father's death. Jennifer's mother died from cancer on 2nd November 1968, the day before my father died. These details only came out years after we had taught at Woad Farm. In 1971, Jennifer and I had no idea that we had both experienced the loss of a parent at the same time.

My second class at Woad Farm were to become even dearer to me. I became so attached to them and found it hard not to have favourites. I still attended church but there was less desire to be involved with other activities. Indeed, out of school, I was quite lonely. My closest friends were now teaching elsewhere or still at college. The one old friend from Holy Trinity days, with whom I had the most contact, was Diana (Di) Pettifer. She taught at the old annexe at Park Board School. Di thought that I had become far too involved in school and needed some social life. I had just begun to enjoy socialising (or man-hunting!) with Di, when she met someone. So, I was once more on my own.

One evening I made up a foursome with Di, her boyfriend and his friend Dick, who was home from an R.A.F. camp in Yorkshire. Dick and I got on very well. It made me realise that even for me, there were other things in life! When he broke off the friendship, a couple of months later, I was broken-hearted. Di and her boyfriend had split up the previous weekend and the way Dick had become rather evasive, had made me fear the worst. Sure enough, he and Di started dating.

I had a very difficult time coping. My friendship with Di cooled considerably. However, on one particular Saturday, Di and I had arranged to go out together. I was really looking forward to a night out again. Then, that Saturday morning, I received a note cancelling our arrangement. Dick had decided to come home. How I ranted and raved, as I came up with the nastiest names for Di that I could think of. For a time I think I almost hated her. I was so hurt.

Every New Year's Eve, I often used to half-heartedly make New Year Resolutions: the sort to do with my character, to be less quick-tempered at home and not to be so shy. Before the onset of the leap year 1972, I actually wrote my list of resolutions down. I had never done this before. It was done out of sheer desperation. I knew that I was getting nowhere in Boston. I was in a rut! Teaching and the children, seemed all that I had. I had no social life whatsoever. Moreover the chances of meeting any new 'interesting' people were nigh impossible. Things badly needed to change. I listed five resolutions at the back of my diary:

1. Learn to drive
2. Get a car
3. New job
4. Move from Boston
5. Man!

I began driving lessons in the autumn of 1971. I was absolutely hopeless and spent a fortune on lessons. My first test was a complete fiasco. My second test was on 29th February 1972. This time everything went differently. The examiner was so pleasant and immediately put me at ease. Amazingly, we actually followed the route that Mr. Tom Maddison, my driving instructor, had taken me on only minutes earlier. It was with whoops of joy, that I returned to school. My class all cheered.

Not long afterwards, I was able to buy my friend Kathleen Anderson's Austin 1100, that she had driven from new. I bought it at a bargain price. It was in excellent condition, a lovely Air Force blue. I called her Heidi.

Mum bless her, in her usual unselfish manner, had never made any demands on me. Though, she had obviously been pleased that I had initially come home to teach. She had been a great help to me, especially in preparing practical things. She was gifted at art and craft; whereas my efforts were always very crude. If something went wrong on my first attempt, I had very little patience to persevere. Mum helped me: by making models and puppets, sorting out Science experiments and covering work cards.

Mum agreed that it was right for me to move on. She told me to ignore unhelpful comments, from people who felt that I should stay at home with her. So, I applied for a few posts. One seemed quite a challenge. It was a Scale Two Post, to be responsible for French in a large junior school near Watford. Having sent off the application, it seemed to me that I did not stand a chance: it was way out of my league. I was thus panic-stricken, when Mum came along to my classroom, with the letter inviting me for interview in Watford.

Jim Medley, my father's former colleague and very good friend, drove me to the school. He, his wife Jessie and my Mum went into Watford, leaving me to my fate! Jim and Jessie had been a staunch support to our family ever since that sad November.

There were three of us being interviewed. On discovering that one lady was French I thought, w*ell, that's it then!* Besides, as the youngest there, I had the least teaching experience. Yet, I was the successful applicant. The headmaster, on account of my inexperience of teaching French: offered me the post as a Scale One; saying that he would review this at a later stage. I was more than happy to accept. I would have a new job, and a new life. These were the challenges I needed, not an increase in salary. That would have been a bonus; but I was after all, just nearing the end of my second year of teaching. The items on my New Year's list were gradually being resolved.

It was such a painfully sad day for me, when I had to say goodbye to Woad Farm. It was like saying goodbye to my family. My class had become so special to me. I was never to enjoy such a close rapport with any class again. At the final assembly two of my girls were sobbing. A group of the boys hung around for ages afterwards; they seemed so reluctant to leave. One of my pupils had said his goodbye to me the week before. (He was a very bright, likeable lad. Indeed on two occasions, he and another boy in the class, had come round to clean my car at home). He produced three red roses for me (which I treasure and still have as pressed flowers in an ornament) and tried to be as matter-of-fact about it as he presented them. Two pupils whom I was extremely fond of were Caroline Whitehead and Christopher Cook. They corresponded with me in Watford and Caroline even visited me once at Blackthorn Lane.

In September 1972, I moved down to Watford. The Meriden Junior Mixed School, was on the edge of the Meriden estate, in Garston, a suburb of Watford. I had managed to get lodgings in Garston, about two miles away from the high-rise block of flats which overlooked the school. Life was so very different (absolutely no home comforts)! The family were only in it for the money, with the minimum being done and at times rather grudgingly. Meals were usually convenience type: either frozen or tinned. Nothing was freshly cooked. How I missed Mum's good home cooking. Fortunately, school lunches were on offer. All the staff were entitled to a free lunch, as they had to do 'dinner duty'. Something else I had to get used to. I enjoyed the meals but not the duty! The staff were a hard, rather odd bunch. Such a contrast to the staffrooms that I had been in. A couple of young female teachers, did show some concern about me being new to the area, away from all my family and friends but they moved away shortly after I started. They probably would have helped me to settle in. No one else bothered.

Since beginning teaching in 1970, my daily Bible reading and prayer times had long since stopped. Now it took me all my time to even think about God. By the time I moved to Watford, I was still attending Holy Trinity Church fairly regularly but I had no other Christian involvement; apart from keeping in touch with all my old Christian friends.

I had noticed a Congregational Church in Garston when Mum and I had been over in the summer. So one September morning I decided to go along. It was a modern church and I enjoyed the more informal type of service. A few people gave me a friendly welcome. One of the church wardens, Mr. Ron Jordan, invited me round the following week to meet his wife. On that Tuesday evening, the thirteen-year-old boy of the house where I lodged, was being especially annoying. He had long since started to pester and tease and I was relieved to be going out. Ron and Eileen Jordon were a lovely Christian couple and made me feel so welcome. I found that I could talk openly to them: of the problems of being in digs and the teenage boy. They had accommodated students in the past and told me that if ever I were in difficulties, to contact them.

I fully intended to return to the church but somehow I cannot recall ever going back. As a way of trying to meet people, I had joined a badminton and also a German evening class. My landlady's elder son introduced me to a few of his friends and so slowly I began to make a few social contacts.

Just before Christmas I started to go out with Clive who lived in London. At the same time my landlady, quite out of the blue, decided that she could not be bothered with a lodger any more and gave me a week's notice! As it was literally a week before Christmas, there was not much time to sort out new accommodation and I was soon to go home for the holidays. In desperation, I rang the Jordans to explain my predicament. They responded wonderfully, by offering me a room, short- term, until I could sort something else out. I moved my things and then travelled home for Christmas.

It was quite staggering: everything on my list of resolutions had been achieved. I remember how upsetting it had been, watching all my close friends gradually pair up. In 1971 and 1972, my four oldest friends were married, whilst I remained feeling unwanted and unloved. I had been quite convinced that once at college, I would meet that 'special person'. There had been someone in the Christian Union who had shown an interest. In my usual shy, very naïve way, I had not recognised the signs and had consequently put him off in 'true Spencer fashion'! How lonely and dreadfully unhappy I had been: unable to attract a member of the opposite sex. Now, it seemed that even this was changing. In Watford, I had finally begun to enjoy more of a social life and at last I had met someone!

Bitterly puzzling over why I had been so old (almost twenty-two) before Dick, my first boyfriend came on the scene: it dawned on me that I had probably been my own worst enemy. Being acutely shy in male company, I tended to feel awkward and self-conscious. I would attempt to hide this, by giving out unfriendly, defensive vibes as a way of protecting my vulnerability. Suddenly ... and it came as such a terrific shock: I remembered my tearful bargaining with God at the age of sixteen. Had I not told God that I would be willing not to have a boyfriend, if only I could do French A-level? In great shame I realised that I had completely forgotten my side of the bargain. God had truly honoured His. I had not only done French but had done well in it. Had I not also begged God to let me be successful in French? Even more remarkable, was the fact that in spite of not studying French at college: it was because of my willingness to teach French, which had very much influenced my first two teaching appointments. God had given me far more than I had asked. If only I had remembered 'that bargain' I might have been spared all the wallowing in self-pity, loneliness and despair, when things did not happen as I thought they should.

Chapter 9

Meeting John

Life in Boston over Christmas was pleasant and relaxing. By now Di and I had long resolved our differences. I no longer harboured anger towards her and Dick. Besides meeting Di, I enjoyed seeing other old friends who were likewise, home for the holidays.

Another friend who had been previously concerned about my lack of social life in Boston, was Carole Forinton. Carole always seemed to mother me, even though she was a year younger. We had started off by not liking one another. This was especially when she started to go out with my younger brother Alan. I was very jealous that my brother had a girlfriend, when he was only sixteen. They went out for nearly three years. By the time their friendship had ended, Carole and I had become good friends.

On Boxing Day evening, I accompanied Carole, her boyfriend and her parents to Norprint Social Club. Carole, who was a friendly, outgoing person, started talking to a young police constable, whom she had met the year before. She was always ready to play cupid and invited him to join our group, mentioning that there were two 'spare females'. For some reason, he sat beside me. John was tall, dark and very good-looking and most importantly, so easy to talk to. From that moment, the evening passed very pleasantly. We seemed to hit it off straight away. I was more than pleased when John wanted to take me home. The goodnight kiss was a little longer than the quick peck that I had anticipated. In my usual tactless way I said, 'You don't waste any time do you!' Fortunately, he did not appear to be offended and arranged to see me the following day.

By the time I returned to Watford, John and I were getting on well. Once back in Watford, I continued to see Clive. We met once or twice a week. John was ringing me up and we were also writing to each other. I felt in a very strange position: as if I were leading a double life.

I was now living with the Jordans. What a contrast to my last term in lodgings. I really appreciated being in a warm, Christian home. They were so kind to me. Mrs. Jordan really mothered me, at a time when personal problems were tremendous.

I had to make the choice in February, when an arranged visit by John, clashed with something that Clive wanted to do. John received a last minute call saying 'not to come.' Then I wrote to explain about Clive. I knew how hurt John would be, but I put it out of my mind. After all, establishing myself in my new life was all that mattered.

Before the end of the spring term, Mrs. Jordan helped me to find a bed-sit. I had enjoyed staying with them but they had only agreed to help me out short-term and I really wanted my independence. I think my social life had caused them a few headaches, for I am sure that they regarded my welfare, as if I were their own daughter.

I was no longer happy with Clive. We were so different in outlook. Things were starting to become difficult and I saw the dangers of further involvement. I decided to contact John. He, of course spoke in a very cool manner, as I grovelled. Much later he admitted how pleased that he had been, to hear from me but had deliberately adopted a 'couldn't care less' attitude. To my surprise he suggested that I ring him when I arrived home for Easter. I sensed that there was some hope.

Our first date was a lovely meal at Hagnaby Lock on Monday 9th April 1973, a few hours after my return from Watford. From that time, our relationship developed very quickly. On 31st May John proposed. My immediate reaction among my tears, was to blurt out, 'I thought you'd never ask!' Things were happening to me that I thought never would. For so long I had dreamed of meeting someone and of getting married. It seemed that my dearest wishes had finally come true. I could hardly believe my good fortune. I was so happy. I was in love! When we met, I was twenty-three and John was a mere nineteen!

We celebrated our engagement on Christmas Eve, 1973 (two days before the first anniversary of our meeting). We returned to Hagnaby Lock: John a true romantic, bought me red roses and we drank champagne. I wore a royal blue velvet evening gown. I looked glamorous, in spite of having to get up from my sick bed because I had tonsillitis! Of course, we had been unofficially engaged since John's proposal in the May. From then on, all I wanted to do, was to return to Boston to teach. Typical of the way events seemed to happen in my life. As I have previously mentioned, nothing ever comes easily to me. I moved away to make a new life for myself and end up meeting someone from home, after only a term away!

Furthermore, I had never really been happy teaching in Watford. My energies had been spent in developing my social life and at great cost to my teaching performance. Instead of putting everything into school life (as at Woad Farm) I had done very little once I was away from the classroom. I was never given the Scale Two Post. After two terms there I had enquired about this. The headmaster dismissed this curtly, saying he did not think so. I had not injected anything new into the school, so I could not expect more money. At my interview he had mentioned the possibility of my running a French club. So, I started a weekly club, after school. By then we were planning a French trip to St. Aignan (Loire region) in June 1973, so there was a good response. I really enjoyed running the club. It was the first time that I had organised an extra-curricular activity. It of course, made no difference whatsoever. The headmaster had no intention of upgrading my post to a Scale Two.

It no longer mattered. The development of my personal life, was far more important to me than my teaching career in Watford. I was head over heels in love! I was going to get married and then I would be looking for another job. It turned out to be sooner rather than later. The prospect of sticking it out in Watford, for another full academic year, was too grim to contemplate. As we planned to marry in the summer of 1974, there were many practical details to be arranged. It would be far simpler if I moved back home. January 1974 was the earliest date that I could hope for; so during the autumn of 1973 I applied for whatever job was available in the Boston area.

In October, I had an interview at Frithville County Primary School, for a Tuesday. The head had agreed to let me have that day off to attend. During the weekend, another possible interview came up for the Monday afternoon, at Donington. The head refused to let me have the Monday off as well. Feeling rather aggrieved, I planned to travel home after school on the Monday. John was due to travel back home on that Monday morning. It was a horrible foggy day. He wanted me to travel home with him. I felt in a dilemma. I hated the prospect of a long journey alone in the fog. The headmaster was unavailable, so I left a message for him! We drove home in convoy. A most irate headmaster rang my mother to put her in the picture and I had to face his wrath on my return. I did not care. In my opinion he had been totally unreasonable and I was desperate to sort out a teaching post for January 1974. To be able to do this, I had to give in my notice to Hertfordshire County Council by the end of October. Hence my panic!

In reality, my new life in Watford only lasted four terms. In January 1974, I was on permanent supply teaching for two terms at Frithville School. It was a tiny village school with approximately sixty pupils. I taught the first class, which was family-grouped and had pupils aged from four to seven. This certainly came as a challenge compared to my previous teaching experience. I enjoyed trying to teach the younger children! Most welcome, was the warm friendly atmosphere. The headmaster Mr. Brian Neall, was very approachable and most helpful; such a stark contrast to my previous 'boss' whom I had nicknamed Hitler and not just because of his moustache!

As John worked in Lincoln, I began applying for posts there. My first interview at a large middle school on Monks Road, was an ordeal. For the first time ever, I had to face a panel of six people. Needless to say, I was unsuccessful. Later on, the post of French Consultant, a Scale Two Post, at Manor Leas Middle School came up. Again, it seemed far too ambitious for the likes of me but I applied. Shortly after my application, Mr. Neall my headmaster at Frithville, informed me that the headmaster of Manor Leas had spoken to him about me and was favourably impressed by Mr. Neall's recommendation.

John accompanied me to the interview. We sat in a huge staff room, where everyone was so friendly towards each other and to the six interviewees. Again, there was a native French teacher. So to my way of thinking, she was the firm favourite.

This time, there was only the headmaster and his deputy, for the interview. Mr. Duncan Logan, a Scotsman, was extremely pleasant and very easy to talk to. The interview went so much easier than the previous one. Most of the time was spent discussing the French trip that I had been on, while teaching in Watford. To my amazement, I was called back and offered the Scale Two Post. Mr. Logan stated his interest in my experiences of taking children to France and of my enthusiastic approach to teaching French. He was fully in favour of introducing children to French before secondary school age.

The school had been teaching French for a few years and had an annual trip to Paris. I was chosen instead of the native French teacher because as well as spending approximately half my time teaching French to various classes: I would have my own class of third years (ten to eleven year-olds) to do ordinary class teaching. After four years of teaching, I had achieved a Scale Two Post. I was to be the French Consultant of a large middle school in Lincoln. Quite a daunting prospect, for it was the largest school that I had ever been in, let alone worked in. There were four or five parallel classes per year group with a staff of over twenty.

When I met John, my Christian faith was no longer very important to me. I had far more vital concerns to occupy my time. John did not have a faith. As we began to discuss marriage: I realised that although my faith had been pushed firmly into the background of my life; it still meant enough to insist to John, that I could only get married in church. John agreed out of respect for my wishes. Though, it caused him a difficult inward struggle; being married in a place where he did not feel comfortable.

By then, the Revd. Frank Hines had left Holy Trinity Church. He had been replaced by a much younger man, who was on holiday at the time of our marriage. The Revd. Tom Sharp took our service. I had met Tom before in my Covenanter days, because he took services at Holy Trinity during the interregnum. He was the vicar of Leverton.

Both John and I were very impressed by Tom. He was a lovely, gentle minister. He conducted a beautiful service. As John and I knelt at the altar steps; Tom quoted a verse from Scripture, which really spoke to me:

'And we know that all things work together for good to them that love God, to them who are the called according to his purpose.'
　　　　　　　　　　　　Romans chapter 8 verse 28 Authorised K.J.V.

I really felt a princess on that day. I knew that I looked just as a bride should look. How glad I was that I had embarked on wearing contact lenses: in spite of the panic that I experienced the day before my wedding, when I accidentally rubbed my left eye and the lens disappeared behind the eyeball! I had always been squeamish with regard to doing anything with my eyes (the fact that I had been able to insert lenses was almost a miracle) and I became almost hysterical. Fortunately, brother Alan calmed me down so that he could retrieve the wretched lens. Of course, he had to refer to this mini-drama in his wedding speech!

The day before my wedding, was memorable for another reason. Alan had accidentally shut his cat in the dining room, where our sixteen-year-old budgerigar was. I entered to find the cat on top of the cage, Ricky dead on the cage floor. I was inconsolable. As everyone was out doing the flowers in church, I went round to Mum's very good friends, George and May Oglesbee, for comfort. I think much of my reaction was due to the deep sadness within me; that my father was not around to share my happiness. My brother Alan would be giving me away and not my dear Dad.

My wedding photographs really did look good. August 10th 1974 was indeed the happiest day of my life so far. I was surrounded by my family and most of my close friends. Trudy Elliot and Liz Williams from my college days, even managed to attend.

Life from then on became very demanding. As well as having to adjust to married life (made even more complicated by John's unsociable shift work) I had full-time teaching in a new post, to get used to. Life was very hectic and quite fraught in those early months. By then, there was no time whatsoever in my life for God. I no longer attended church. Sunday became just an ordinary day. My faith had ceased to exist in a meaningful way. Teaching and running a home, totally absorbed me. I would look back in disbelief to the way I had once been: when everyone and everything that mattered to me, revolved around my Christian faith. My present life was totally different to the life that I had once had. Occasionally, I felt that something was missing but I did nothing about it. I did go along once to a Methodist Church with my elderly neighbour Mrs. Brown but that feeble attempt was the only one that I made. However busy and fulfilled my life appeared to be; deep down I was not truly at peace with myself. I knew that I was denying a vital part of my being. Yet, I continued to take the easy, uncomplicated way out, merely pacifying myself with the thought... *I'll have to sort myself out sometime...*

On the whole, I was enjoying my new school; especially teaching French, which after all was the subject that I really loved teaching. However, introducing the first year pupils (aged eight) to French was very wearing, because there had to be so much repetition of such basic material. Most afternoons, I taught four different beginner groups, for approximately thirty minutes each, virtually doing the same thing. The continuous oral work was very tiring. My voice certainly felt the strain!

For me, the main adjustment was fitting in the domestic chores! I had never done much of this, even when in my bed-sit and I really resented having to come in from a hard but very satisfying day's teaching, to have to prepare a meal. How I loathed ironing all those police shirts. There were a few instances of near hysteria when I had to tackle them. Eventually, I learned to adapt to the more boring aspects of married life! Nevertheless, we were very happy. We had an old draughty, rented house on Long Leys Road, Lincoln. Our house overlooked the West Common and at the back, there were fields, where horses grazed. It was a beautiful location.

Chapter 10

Early Married Life

Initially when Mr. Logan invited John to accompany the French trip, I thought that he was joking. I was so excited at the prospect of returning to Paris: this time with my husband. It was not quite a second honeymoon because eighty children were travelling with us! I spent a considerable time preparing for this visit. I was expecting difficulties even before we set off; being the world's worst worrier!

At the end of June, we left Lincoln at 6.30am and arrived at Les Lilas on the outskirts of Paris, at 10.30pm. By the time the children were settled into their dormitories, it had turned midnight and I realised that I was in for trouble. The squint had returned to my left eye. Just as well that I had wisely worn spectacles for the long journey.

As I have previously mentioned; the weakness in my left eye first manifested itself at the age of seven and a half and then again at the age of twelve. Once I had started to wear spectacles permanently, the squint had been kept in check. Occasionally when I was overtired, my left eye drifted inwards slightly but after a night's sleep everything was alright.

The last time the squint reappeared, I was twenty. It was the summer following Dad's death. Mum, Alan, his girlfriend Carole Forinton and I, holidayed in Great Yarmouth. After years without any eye trouble, I was distraught that the problem had reoccurred. The Ophthalmic Surgeon told me nastily, that it was up to me to control it. If I wanted, I could bring myself out of it! I was reduced to tears in the hospital loo. He had upset Mum as well. Nevertheless, it had the desired effect. The following day, normal vision was resumed.

So there I was, in that most romantic of cities, with a squint! For over five years, my eye problems had been completely forgotten: until that late evening in Paris, when with horror, I realised that the past was repeating itself. After all, had I not had a stressful year combining marriage with a new job? John, of course, had had no inkling of my previous eye history.

In many cases of fatigue, in the past, I found that I could restrain the squint by focusing on some print. After concentrating hard on that morning's Daily Light reading (this tiny book of daily readings always accompanied me wherever I went; despite the fact that I rarely bothered to use it) the squint disappeared. By the time we went on our first visit, everything was alright. I even wore my contact lenses. Furthermore, I had my portrait done in the Place du Tertre, Montmartre, always one of my favourite places in Paris. The portrait bore no resemblance to me, but I was so thrilled knowing that I was sitting there, binocular vision restored once again!

As the week progressed, the squint became much harder to keep in check. On our return journey, I had to wear my sunglasses to hide it. I felt so miserable, having to pretend that everything was as normal. It had been a wonderful week in many ways but now it had turned sour for me.

After the weekend, John informed school of my eye condition. I saw my G.P. and was subsequently referred to the Consultant Ophthalmologist at Lincoln County Hospital. He very brusquely informed me that surgery should have been done years ago. Furthermore, he became extremely irate about the fact that I had gone ahead and worn contact lenses, without first consulting my doctor. He stated that there was a very long wait for this routine operation. I also saw the orthoptist and did the various eye exercises and eye tests that I had done in childhood. I did not return to work until September. By then we had moved into our own two bedroomed bungalow at North Greetwell. Throughout that really hot summer of 1975, I had a permanent squint!

It was very difficult for me, trying to teach with this handicap. Fortunately, I had a taped patch over the left lens of my spectacles, which meant that the squint was obscured from the children's view; so I did not look such a freak. I was therefore totally relying on my right eye. A couple of near misses, driving to work, made me realise that I had impaired vision. From then on, I travelled to work by bus. Instead of twenty minutes in the car, I had two different bus journeys to get to school. I had not used a bus since college days. It was a real nuisance and so time-consuming.

In early October, the orthoptist invited me to attend her clinic: for some reason a few people were extremely interested in my case. I explained how difficult it was coping with full-time teaching, with my eye-patch. She placed a special tape over my left lens, which negated the squint effect. I could now see properly. To all intents and purposes both eyes appeared normal. This made me feel so much better. Most importantly, she promised me that she would urge the consultant to make me a higher priority. I was duly informed that my name had been placed higher on his list but that I might still have a six-month wait.

My surgery date came earlier than expected. My operation was scheduled for 26th January 1976. The special tape had made such a vast improvement to my quality of life and state of mind; so the waiting was not as bad as it might have been. I had no fear whatsoever about having an operation. By then, I had grown so apart from God, that it never crossed my mind to pray about having surgery. So, when John admitted on his first post-op. visit, that he had actually said a prayer for me, I was so ashamed of myself.

I had become friendly with another lady in my ward. I remember feeling profoundly disturbed, when her priest came to see her. There was no one like that to visit me. I had cut myself off from everything connected with church. In fact, apart from John and my Mum, no one visited me. I had no real friends at work and socially the only people I mixed with were John's colleagues. All my close friends lived miles away. I got on well with the other patients and nurses. The eye ward was the only mixed ward in the hospital and I thoroughly enjoyed my stay there. Surgery was a complete success. I stayed off school until after half-term. By then, I was able to drive to work. My eye problems were now a thing of the past. Life carried on very much as before and I continued to ignore God.

I was in my third year of teaching at Manor Leas, when I decided that I ought to improve my own standard of French. Deeply regretting not having studied French as a main subject at college: I toyed with the idea of doing a degree. I embarked on a weekly evening class doing an 'Institute of Linguists' Course;' with the aim of working towards at least the intermediate level, which counted partly towards a degree.

Over the three or four years that I attended, my oral French (always my weakest point) developed fluently and I achieved a distinction at intermediate level in that aspect. Unfortunately, I kept failing the translation paper. This was a terrible blow to my pride, because I had never failed a French exam before. The first re-sit of the translation paper, was when I was six months pregnant and the second and last attempt was when our child was nine months old. I then decided that having reached the oral standard that I had always longed for I would stop there. By then, I was not sufficiently motivated for further study.

On the whole, teaching at Manor Leas Middle School was very fulfilling and I was immensely happy there. I had a tremendous feeling of achievement, regarding how my French teaching had developed: from those hesitant experimental days at Woad Farm, right up to my present post, as French Consultant. I often wished that my dreaded French teacher from Boston High School days, could have witnessed this success. I really appreciated my good fortune, in being able to teach a subject that I had always loved. The annual trips to Paris were a real bonus to me: thoroughly hard work but great fun!

It gave the children the opportunity to see their rather strict teacher, in a different light! I would encourage the girls to play pranks on the boys' dormitory or on the very popular male teacher. It was also an occasion to get to know staff better. For instead of socialising in the staff-room at lunch-breaks, I tended to stay in my classroom marking; therefore lightening the workload to be finished at home. Although, I had not formed any close friendships with anyone, the staff were extremely amiable, very helpful and full of life. Instead of the usual female predominance, here there was a good representation of male teachers. I valued this lively and most stimulating environment enormously; congratulated myself on how well my career was going and knew that I could not possibly give it up. Teaching French meant everything to me.

Before our marriage, John had talked about having children, saying the ideal time would be after about five years. He was very family orientated. I did not share his keenness. The longer that I taught other people's children, the less I wanted my own!

At the end of my fourth year at Manor Leas, I knew that I needed a change. My request for changing from the third year, to the top year, was refused. I felt rather peeved about this: especially after teaching some very pleasant classes, I was allocated the worst second year class for the following September. Out of four possible teachers, I was landed with a terrible class, who had run rings around their male teacher. Our year head told me quite bluntly that I was the 'lucky one' because Mr. Logan knew that I was the sort of teacher who would stand no nonsense and would do some good with them! It was not the change that I had in mind.

That August, John and I stayed at Cheddar Gorge for a few days. After nearly four years of marriage, the issue of children was very reluctantly (on my part) discussed. We were now in a position to live off John's salary. At times, in spite of my love of French, I did find general teaching, especially Maths, a real chore. After eight years in school, I did wonder about doing something else. That summer, I thought very seriously about what I really wanted. It was a most difficult decision. Finally, I came to the conclusion that I would not want to miss out on having my own children. Once my mind was made up, I was thus very impatient. Fortunately, I conceived straight away. I was thrilled.

I had a really hard task with my class. They certainly took some taming! They were such a challenge but I am pleased that they were my last class. Indeed, I became very fond of them. By the time I left in June, I had the satisfaction that I had transformed them into a pleasant, well-disciplined class. I did wonder sadly, if all my work would be undone by whoever replaced me for the last few weeks of term. I took my entitled maternity leave (eleven weeks before expected date of birth). By then, I was becoming increasingly tired.

The only black boy in the school, was in my class. Although very bright, he could be disruptive. Not surprisingly, he had caused me considerable anxiety. In spite of this, I knew that I had made headway in befriending him. I sensed that there was a bond between us. An unforeseen drama on my final afternoon in class was to strengthen this bond! During the last hour, I handed round some sweets. Suddenly there he was, gasping for breath! He was choking on a sweet! Instead of panicking, I just marched up, pushed him forward and gave him a hard slap on his back. A huge boiled sweet shot from his mouth! It left me feeling considerably shell-shocked. At the end of the afternoon, the boy came up to chat. He asked me what names I had chosen for the baby. I was touched that he was showing an interest. As we said goodbye, I noticed the tears in his eyes.

Becoming pregnant, marked the start of my search for the faith which had once been so important to me. At the beginning of 1979, expecting my first child, I began to think wistfully about the deep faith that I had once professed. I knew that I should want my baby to be baptised. How could I go along to a church if I were not practising my faith? I realised that it was time for me to sort myself out. I was at such an important stage in my life: about to become a parent. I needed a firm foundation for my life. I did not want to continue as I had done for the past five years, inwardly aware that something vital was missing.

Chapter 11
Parenthood

Ever since I had read the story 'Charlotte's Web' to my favourite class at Woad Farm, I had adored the name. I wanted my first child to be a girl, so that I could call her Charlotte. John, not keen at all on my choice, preferred Emma. In true 'school-marm' fashion and rather selfishly, I told him, 'I'm carrying this baby, I'll have first choice!' We finally agreed on Charlotte Emma. I knew that the baby would be a girl; I remember clearly saying to someone, 'When she's born... I'll do...'

After the first three months of feeling sick and vomiting frequently, I was fine. I was determined that my very slim figure, was not going to suffer and that is why I was sufficiently motivated to continue swimming regularly (even to the extent of getting up at 8am on a Sunday, to take advantage of a cheap swim at R.A.F. Scampton). Having read up on all the benefits of breast-feeding, I was determined to do this. No way was my baby going to be fed by bottle! Besides, I knew that it was the very best way of getting back to my pre-pregnant size. There was no way that I wanted to put on any weight. I had always been underweight for my height and that was the way I intended to stay!

In spite of attending parent-craft classes with John, I was totally unprepared for what happened. The expected date of birth was 1st September. Colleagues at work, had pointed out the possible disadvantages, in that the child would become one of the eldest in the class.

On Thursday 16th August 1979, John was due to work a 5pm to 1am shift. We went shopping in the morning. In the afternoon I began to feel strange, so I went to bed. As I did not feel up to cooking a meal before John went to work, he arranged to bring in fish and chips for supper. By early evening, feeling a bit better, I decided to clean our lounge venetian blinds. All the while I washed them, I had to keep sitting down, as a most uncomfortable feeling kept occurring in my stomach. In disbelief, I thumbed through to the relevant pages of my childbirth manual, wondering if I was experiencing labour pains. I really was none the wiser for reading it up either! It could not be happening yet: baby was not due for another two weeks. Somehow I managed to complete the blinds. I also ate supper. John returned to work, saying he would warn the Operations Room staff, that I might be phoning them.

By 11pm, I could not stand much more of the discomfort. At midnight I was admitted to Lincoln County Hospital. John was a wonderful support to me right throughout my labour. Indeed, if it had not been for him reminding me of the breathing exercises; I am sure that I would have gone to pieces. All the gentle airy-fairyness of those classes was very quickly shattered as with grim realisation came the shock that labour was bloody hard work! I could not cope. It was awful. I suffered excruciating backache throughout. I was offered the use of the gas and air analgesia machine but as I have always had a fear of face masks, (ever since a frightening ordeal at the dentist's as a child) I only held it to my face for a few seconds. I simply could not tolerate it. I was given some pethidine but it did not seem to work for me.

John was kept busy, massaging my back and reminding me of my breathing. I said some awful things in my fear and pain: at one point I screamed out to God, 'Let me die, I can't stand it!' By 6am I was in the second stage of labour and ready to push. Yet, I was absolutely exhausted and to avoid further distress: the decision was made to do a forceps delivery. Initially, I thought, *great, now for some help.* That feeling soon dissipated. What a dreadful ordeal it was! By now, I had a young doctor and a crowd of about half a dozen at the delivery end: while I gripped poor John's hand, for grim death. What a row I made, as if I were being tortured. No way was I enduring such pain quietly. I let everyone know how ghastly the whole experience was for me.

Then, on Friday 17th August at 8.09am an amazing calm descended; as a beautiful baby girl was handed to me. I put her to my breast and instinctively she suckled. What a marvellous feeling that was. John and I, were now the parents of a healthy baby girl. We shed tears of joy!

As she was two weeks early, she was taken to the Special Care Baby Unit for a few hours. How I fretted, I was so worried in case she was given a bottle of cows' milk. Fortunately, for my sanity, she was returned by early afternoon. I had never had much to do with babies. I was not the sort of person to drool over a baby longingly. Charlotte was like a beautiful doll. She settled well to breast-feeding. During one early morning feed, the nurse remarked on how well I was coping. She was very surprised to discover that it was my first child. Obviously, maternal feelings within me had surfaced.

I had first discovered St. Edward's Church at Sudbrooke, on a long walk with Mum, in early pregnancy. It was two miles from our home in North Greetwell. One Sunday morning I drove there. I was welcomed warmly. The Revd. Kenneth Jardin, was a very kind Irishman. I then attended church regularly. In those days, I would very often go along to R.A.F. Scampton for a swim and then, with my hair still wet, attend church.

Being so slim, you could hardly tell that I was pregnant. The vicar had no inkling of my condition, until Charlotte arrived. He was absolutely staggered, when his gardener (a relative of my hairdresser) told him my news. Unexpectedly, he came round to see us. What a shock for John and me: the first time a priest had been in our home! Fortunately, he went before it was time to breast-feed one squalling infant.

During those early months of parenthood, we sorted out some more life insurance. On one section, details of my father's death, had to be recorded. Our insurance agent commented, 'Don't worry, you know cancer's not hereditary.' In astonishment, I stared at him. It had never entered my head: that because my father had suffered cancer, so would I.

In character, I resembled my grandmother Spencer, who had been a difficult person to deal with. At times, I was certainly that! Poor John had his work cut out in those early days, to break through the protective barrier of shyness and cold reserve. I had though, related well to my grandmother, especially in talking about our faith. Grandma Spencer had lived until the age of ninety-two. I had often thought, that I should be like her - an awkward old lady living to a great age!

John did not want Charlotte to be baptised as a baby. He thought it far better to let the person make his or her own decision, as an adult. Nevertheless, he finally agreed to my wishes. In December, her baptism took place.

Spiritually, I was only at the beginning. My regular trips to church, being my only involvement. I was too busy with the demands of motherhood, to read my Bible, or to pray properly. At least I had made a start. It was so good to be worshipping as a member of a church again.

I really enjoyed bringing up Charlotte. It was a different sort of hard work but so rewarding. One day, while collecting my child allowance: the person behind the counter, casually asked if I had returned to teaching. I retorted sharply, 'I would not have had a child, if I was not going to bring her up myself!' I believed very strongly in that. I would not have missed those wonderful early years for anything.

In June 1981, we bought a newly-built three-bedroomed house, backing onto the beautiful wooded area of Sudbrooke. In the spring of that year, about to move into this lovely house of our choice, we were anxious to have another child. This time, conception did not occur immediately. I was really put out!

We had only been in our new home a short while, when rioting occurred in Toxteth, Liverpool. John at that time, was a member of the Police Support Unit (P.S.U.). On the Friday afternoon, after the previous weekend of riots: I received a telephone call to say that the PSU were being mobilised, to go to Liverpool that afternoon.

As a policeman's wife for over seven years; I had already endured endless hours of long sleepless nights, when John had worked overtime and had been unable to contact me. It was on such occasions, that I even indulged in a glass of sherry, in desperation, to try and calm myself down. I had occasionally rung the police station to enquire about him. John absolutely hated me doing that, saying that if anything happened, I would be the first to know! Usually I had to try and stick it out. Waiting and not knowing, was a nightmare. The first and the very worst instance of John being late: came a few weeks after our wedding. Mum was staying at the rented house with me, where we did not have a telephone. John was about two hours late. The doorbell rang. In relief, we opened the door, to find a strange policeman standing where we expected John to be. I literally froze and I am sure Mum did as well. John had only sent him round as messenger. He was to follow very soon. Men!!

John's trip to Toxteth reduced me to jelly. It was a dreadful weekend to get through. A born worrier, I had visions of all sorts happening. How relieved I was, to find out that they were being used as a peace-keeping force and were not in any conflict situations. Throughout those few troubled weekends, John was likewise occupied. Thus the opportunities to become pregnant were diminished!

John as before, had no preference regarding the sex of our second child. Again, his main concern, was that the child would be healthy. Of course, this was the only really important factor. Yet, I did so want our second child to be a boy, for I wanted to give him my father's second name, Edward. Neither of us, had any preference for the first name. Then we remembered our American friend Tom Larussa. John had met this young American student in London, during a visit to our old friends Angela and Alastair Steven. John being the friendly chap that he is, had spent ages chatting to Tom, whom he had met outside a fish and chip shop. He had even invited Tom to visit us in Lincoln, if his travels took him that far.

The following weekend, Tom arrived at Lincoln Police Station. Initially, I was very angry at being landed with an unwanted guest! I had preconceived ideas about Americans and felt far from hospitable. I was proved wrong. Tom was a lovely person and we throughly enjoyed the short time that he spent with us. Accordingly, we decided upon the name Thomas. I was hopeful that I was carrying a boy because the pregnancy was entirely different. I had a rough nine months, feeling nauseous throughout. There was no way that I could have gone swimming.

As the time grew nearer, I often used to think in disbelief, 'I'll never be able to love my second child, as I do my first,' for I regarded Charlotte as 'my treasure'. The second birth was a doddle. It was such a complete contrast to the difficult time that I had experienced with Charlotte. Although the memory of that unpleasant event had soon faded: the pleasures and demands of motherhood saw to that.

One week before the expected date of birth, I recognised the signs. This time I could handle the discomfort, because I was mentally prepared. I seemed to gain great comfort, from focusing hard on a light, as the pain washed over me. I spent most of my early hours in labour, from about 7pm, sat on the loo, concentrating on the light. Again, John was on an evening shift. Fortunately, Mum had stayed for the weekend and was not returning to Boston, until the following day, Tuesday 18th May, my thirty-third birthday. So she was there ready, to care for our toddler Charlotte, aged exactly two years nine months.

By the time we went to hospital at 11pm, I was on the verge of the second stage of labour. On this occasion, things were not going to be so long-winded. How relieved I was, knowing that I was not destined to lie in labour for hours on end. A few minutes before midnight, the midwife informed me: that if I wanted baby to share my birthday, I had better slow down a bit. I said, 'Let's get it over with!' At 11.46pm on 17th May 1982, just minutes before my birthday, Thomas Edward was born. Our happiness was complete. Although Thomas' birth was so easy, he was a more difficult baby. I had problems breast-feeding him in those early days in hospital. In addition, I was really very low, after his birth, in spite of being 'over the moon' that we now had a boy and a girl.

Thomas' birth was soured by the Falklands' War. I was listening to the news in hospital, weeping at the loss of young lives. How could I be happy? I was upset at all those British and Argentinian sons being killed. After all, babies grow up to be cannon fodder. I felt my G.P. was rather insensitive about the whole issue. I was prescribed tablets to help me relax and to sleep at night. I did not want to take anything, obviously I was concerned about the effects they might have on breast-feeding. I only took them for a short while. Things were extremely difficult for those first few weeks. Then, I seemed to get over it. Besides, there was not much time to have such sad thoughts, with the demands of a young baby and boisterous toddler to contend with. Once I had adjusted, I was more than happy, bringing up my two small children. The fears that I had felt about being unable to give as much love to the second child were dispersed, as soon as Thomas was born. He was immediately just as special. Good old maternal feelings!

When John was at work, Charlotte and Thomas came along to church with me. It was quite an outing. Unfortunately, there was no Sunday School at St. Edward's Church and by the time Thomas was a toddler, he was a handful to manage at the back of the church. With mixed feelings, I decided that Nettleham Methodist Church, with its large junior church, would be more suitable for us. This move coincided with the Revd. Kenneth Jardin, taking up an appointment in Monte Carlo.

Accordingly, in December of 1983, I went along with a neighbour, to their Christmas service. Gill and Howard Gelley and their two children were very involved with Nettleham Church. The warm, lively atmosphere overwhelmed us. There were so many families with a wide age range of children. We started attending regularly. Charlotte settled into one of the Sunday School groups and I would go out with Thomas to the crèche.

As a family we were very happy. I never missed teaching. Family life came first. I thoroughly enjoyed bringing up my two small children. I looked on this as my work now: a work of the most worthwhile kind. It was fascinating being involved in the development of Charlotte and Thomas. I tried to do a variety of different things with them. Shift work had its advantages: in that I often had John's company and help in the daytime. This meant that tasks, such as supermarket shopping, could be done on my own, whilst John looked after the children. I certainly did not feel that I was vegetating. The demands were obviously of a different nature to when I was teaching full-time, but I felt very fulfilled in the role that I now had.

Right from Charlotte being a baby, I had continued with my weekly evening class. I needed the stimulus of a night out. As I have previously indicated: after another fail at the wretched French translation paper; in 1980 I decided to switch languages. Having bitterly regretted not taking German at school: I had done one year at evening class, during my second year at Woad Farm. This had enabled me to communicate: albeit very simply, on two lovely trips to Austria in 1971 and 1972. My elementary German was now very rusty and I was keen to master the language properly.

This coincided with John's return to the Ruston Bucyrus Brass Band. He had played in a brass band for years prior to our meeting. It was only during our courtship that he stopped and he had not bothered since. Even though I had no musical ability, I thought that if he were to deny this interest that had once absorbed his life for so long; he might regret it bitterly later on. He did not take much persuading and was welcomed back by the band. His timing was perfect because plans were under way for their first exchange trip to Neustadt, Lincoln's twin city. I was thrilled about the possibility of going to West Germany. As Charlotte was still a baby, I reckoned that I would not be missed. (In contrast, the next time the band went to Neustadt, Thomas was almost two and there was no way that I would have left him).

It was wonderful to communicate in my very simple German and I thoroughly enjoyed the change from speaking French. For me, there would be no more school French trips. Now they had been replaced by trips to West Germany. We were very fortunate. It was wonderful how things had worked out.

There were plenty of extra church activities at Nettleham, but I thought it wise not to become further involved. John was quite happy for me to attend church with the children as long as they wanted to go. I could foresee problems in later years; when as teenagers, they would probably prefer to stay at home with their Dad.

Early in 1984, John had been working in the Community Affairs Department at Lincoln. He thoroughly enjoyed it there. John being an extremely extrovert person, oozing with self-confidence, loved meeting and talking to people. Whereas, I had none of these characteristics. John tended to say too much, whilst I tended to be far too quiet. They say opposites attract!

At the beginning of 1984, I was preparing myself mentally for Charlotte starting school, in the September following her fifth birthday. Early on in the spring, the guidelines for commencing school, were altered. Instead she became eligible to start after Easter, when she would be only four years and eight months old. I was dreadfully upset. I had dreaded the prospect of my first child starting school. Now it was even worse. It worked out for the best though. Thomas, at the age of almost two, could now have my undivided attention during school hours. Potty-training began in earnest!

Chapter 12
Unsettled Times

In September, Charlotte had just commenced her second term at school; when John was promoted to Sergeant at Grantham. For me personally, it could not have come at a worse time: I was happy at Nettleham Church, Charlotte was settled into school and I had joined 'The Friends Of Scothern School' committee. At last I was beginning to get more involved in the community. I hated the thought of moving.

The hardest wrench of all, would be to leave our lovely woods. They were my escape: my sanctuary from the monotony of daily life. In minutes we could be away from the housing estate, in a different world, with such tremendous variety of natural beauty. I loved the woods. From being a toddler, Charlotte had been used to going on almost daily walks. I would think nothing of going off with the children, to walk for an hour or so. It was an ideal adventure playground. All our family and friends were taken there.

The Police paid for John to be accommodated in lodgings for six months. In that time, no interest was shown in buying our house. When the six months were up, John had to travel daily at his own expense. Over the years, I had become accustomed to having long chunks of time on my own. Just as well that I was the sort of person who enjoyed a great deal of solitude. Understandably, having to cope alone with two small children, proved a terrific strain. I was thus far happier when John was travelling home daily. At least there was someone to talk to at the end of the day.

Throughout my teaching career, I was far too preoccupied to be concerned about world problems. While I taught, I put on a cold, quite strict exterior. Becoming a mother, made me far more sensitive to human suffering. I rarely watched the news: I found it too disturbing. I would shut myself in another room, when harrowing scenes were on the television.

One evening in 1984, I made the mistake of watching an update on the Ethiopian famine. The sight of a tiny boy, following some older children, each forlornly holding an empty food bowl, was heart-breaking. My son Thomas was probably of similar age. In bed, I could not forget what I had seen. I ranted angrily at God, for allowing such human tragedies to happen. I felt so guilty that my children should have so much.

I was half-dozing, still feeling very upset, when words seemed to speak to me, 'Hold a coffee morning.' That was it. I spent the next few hours, working out who to involve and how to organise it. My determination to do something practical, helped me cope with the guilt and anger that I felt towards this huge issue of famine. Friends and neighbours rallied round and two weeks later we raised £88, which was donated to Oxfam.

I thought that this would be the start of other such fund-raising. In time, it seemed almost futile to even try to help the third world; when so much donated aid was not getting through. For a while, my concern continued, until I became bogged down with our own problems and world issues just faded into the background. It really was a depressing time for us all: especially for John, with the added strain of travelling daily to Grantham. The children were not seeing much of their father. We were all really sick of the hopeless situation.

In the spring of 1985, John managed to get a transfer to the Police Headquarters Operations Room, at Nettleham. What an answer to my prayers. I could stay near my beloved woods and resume my interests with renewed vigour. I was so happy. Everything had worked out really well. Sadly, John having escaped the rigours of a long journey to work, detested working in an environment, which was so removed from direct contact with the public. The Operations Room was like working in an underground bunker, with no natural daylight. Additionally, Legionnaire's Disease was found in the air-conditioning system, which made several people ill!

Ever since leaving Boston, I had followed the fortunes of one of my favourite pupils from Woad Farm. Chris Cook's ambition had certainly materialised. Over the years he had worked his way up to the first team of Boston United, to become a very popular and talented striker. In May 1984, when the club made it to the F.A. Challenge Trophy final at Wembley; there was so much local excitement about this historic appearance, that I felt compelled to write to Chris and wish him well. He sent a lovely letter in reply, in which he included some photographs. As he lived very near to my mother, I took the children round to meet him and his wife, when we were next in Boston.

By now, I had joined the Sunday School team to teach the three to six-year- olds. Thomas always played up whenever I took the class. He was difficult. As he was reluctant to stay on his own, I usually stayed with him when someone else took the group.

Charlotte thoroughly enjoyed mixing with other children. She readily made friends, being very sociable like her Dad. From when she was tiny I had started to do simple prayers with her. After her nightly bedtime stories, we would always say prayers, either some from her favourite prayer books, or those we made up.

As Charlotte grew older, she used to question why her friends' Daddies all went to church but her Daddy did not. When she first asked me this, I was floored as to how I should reply. Quite close to tears, all I could think of saying was, 'We'll have to pray that one day he will.' Even though, deep down I wished John did share my faith; I never considered it a possibility. In spite of my words to Charlotte, I am ashamed to say that I do not recall ever consciously praying for John's conversion. It was just too way out.

When I had discussed the problems of being married to a non-Christian, (regarding bringing up children in the Christian faith) with my oldest friend Angela: she had merely stated, 'You knew what you were doing when you got married. That's why God says in the Bible, don't be joined together with non-believers.'

'Do not be mismated with unbelievers. For what partnership have righteousness and iniquity? Or what fellowship has light with darkness?'

2 Corinthians chapter 6 verse 14. R.S.V.

I felt her words though true, were a bit near to the bone. In the past I had envied my close friends, who had all married Christians. How easy and relatively straightforward life must be for them. Three of my friends had even settled down with members of the same church. It had not worked out like that for me. I had married someone who did not share my Christian beliefs. In spite of John's lack of faith: he was a truly caring person, such a very loving husband and father. I knew that I could not have found anyone better. Yet Angela's words did rankle. Had I deliberately gone against God's wishes? If so, was I now paying the price?

I could talk about my faith quite openly with friends who were on my spiritual wave-length but I had never been able to talk about it to non-believers. I had never witnessed as Christians are called to do. Early on in my Christian life, I had tried to talk to Mum and Dad but it was in a bulldozer sort of way. John always had an answer to shoot down my inadequate way of talking about my beliefs. Therefore, things remained unsaid. John had turned away from God at the age of thirteen, in October 1966, when the Aberfan disaster occurred. A slag heap totally engulfed the village school killing 116 children and 28 adults. He could not reconcile this horror within the context of a loving God.

Joan, the lady in charge of the junior Sunday School team, was very helpful to me; especially during some very low periods, when John lived away in Grantham. Busily chatting to her after a Christmas activity in December 1985, I had been discussing John's lack of faith. She amazed me by saying, 'I felt like you, despairing because my husband did not come to church. Don't give up hope. He may change. My husband suddenly surprised me, by coming along two years ago. He made his commitment and his faith now means everything to him.' Hearing that absolutely stunned me. Her husband looked and acted as if he had been involved in the church for years. Though obviously very heartened by her words: I immediately dismissed them as of no consequence. It was the most unlikely happening in John's case. Conversely, the thought did occasionally strike me: as to how much John would have to offer God. I was thinking particularly of his musical ability.

One advantage to John having lived and worked away at Grantham; was that I had used the extra time on my own to re-establish my daily time of prayer and Bible reading. This 'quiet time', once so vital to my daily routine, had been sadly neglected once I had begun teaching. I began to feel that at long last, I was regaining that closeness with God; that had once been paramount to my daily welfare. It was as if God was very slowly and very gently being welcomed back into a greater part of my life.

In September of 1986, the friend of an ex-teaching colleague asked me if I would be interested in some private French teaching, for her eight-year-old son. This request shocked me but I decided that it would be worth pursuing. James came weekly. I thoroughly enjoyed teaching French again and thought that this was certainly something that I should develop further. Plus, it was marvellous spending this personal money. My own very welcome bit of independence.

By now John was becoming more and more desperate to leave Ops. Room. He was bored out of his mind. He had paid a high price for maintaining our status quo. In late November 1986, he was informed that before further promotion to Inspector, he needed far greater experience of being a Patrol Sergeant. Then, came the awful shock. From 12th January 1987, John was being transferred to Boston...!

My world fell apart. I had just benefited from a year of feeling that at last I belonged to a community... and now it was to end. Was I mad! I cursed the Police. I even cursed God, as I vented out my fury and bitterness. I considered that we had been through enough trauma, the last time when we tried to move. Besides, Thomas was due to start school after Easter. I really could not accept it. I had always stated categorically, that Boston was the last place that I wanted to live. I could not return to my home town. I could not go backwards. I had even said years before, when John had enquired as to what my reaction would be if he were moved to Boston, 'Over my dead body!' I had bristled with hostility at the thought, all those years before. I made no secret of these negative thoughts. At least two of my friends, in their Christmas letters to me, had something very positive to say about our impending move. My old college friend Sandra O'Toole (née Morris) even quoted the verse from Romans 8 verse 28 Authorised K.J.V. which had spoken to me so vividly at our wedding:

'And we know that all things work together for good to them that love God, to them who are the called according to his purpose.'

Nevertheless my anger still raged. I could not understand why God had to play such a mean trick as this. Oh yes - I had had to learn many painful lessons in my life before. Nothing ever happened easily for me. I thought, *God, this really does take some beating. Why do you have to do this to us? Why Boston?*

John, almost did not commence work on 12th January 1987. His starting date at Boston coincided with the first snowfall of the winter. He managed to reach Boston, before it was virtually cut off from the outside world. School was closed for the entire week. The children and I spent a wonderful week: tobogganing down a steep slope in the woods.

Fortunately, there were some pluses to John working in Boston. My Mum still lived there and had in the past taken in police lodgers. John was able to stay with her. John's parents, his brother and two sisters, all lived locally; so he had a few people to visit. Gradually, I began to realise that it might well be a good move for us after all. Mum then aged nearly seventy, was not getting any younger. She would not always be mobile and able to visit us. My brother Alan and his family, lived miles away in Honiton, Devon. Sadly, Mum did not see much of them. I could understand how much better for her it would be, if one part of her family were conveniently near. We also thought that at last we would see more of John's parents. Unfortunately, Charlotte and Thomas had seen little of John's side of the family. Since he came from a much bigger family than mine, it seemed such a pity. Moreover, the fact that my children had not got my father around, made it more crucial for them to spend more time with the one grandfather that they did have.

Sudbrooke woods were breathtakingly beautiful in the snow. Yet, with our house once again up for sale: I began to realise the difficulties of living there. Charlotte and Thomas would not want to walk in the woods with me for ever! Apart from the church and a hairdresser, there were no other amenities. The nearest shop was one and a half miles away. As they grew older, they would want more than what was on offer here. Ever since Charlotte had started school, I had my own car to do the school run. I hated having to rely on a car to get anywhere. I found driving quite a strain. At least if we moved to Boston: we could rid ourselves of that unnecessary expense, by choosing somewhere more conveniently situated.

Once spring arrived, there were a few enquiries, from prospective buyers. It seemed that this time we would be successful. We started to house-hunt round Boston. I favoured a location in town, so that I could manage when John had the car. We intended to sell the orange Ford Escort (the juice car!) as soon as possible. I fully expected us to settle somewhere in the Tower Road area. My old primary school had always maintained a high reputation and I wanted Charlotte and Thomas to go there. As likely as not, I was destined to return to Holy Trinity. Why else would God want me back in Boston, if it were not to go back to my roots?

One Sunday, I attended Holy Trinity with Maureen Edenbrow (née Parker). Charlotte and Thomas went along to try out their Sunday School. I was beginning to feel far more positive about our intended move. It would be wonderful to be worshipping at Trinity again. Things did seem to be working out after all...

Three weeks before his fifth birthday, Thomas started school. As the time approached, I became increasingly sad about the final ending of that phase of my life: being at home with pre-school children. For the main part, I had enjoyed the time immensely. I dreaded my younger child taking those first few steps of independence: that inevitable growing away from his mother that starting school put in motion. However, it turned out to be far less traumatic for me than I had anticipated. Thomas settled well. Surprisingly, I really took to having time to myself.

During her early years at school, Charlotte's development educationally, was quite mediocre. At first we (including her teachers) had attributed this to poor concentration and a general lack of interest. It was only after a series of ear infections and a subsequent hearing test; that we discovered a substantial hearing loss of forty per cent. This was only detected early in 1987. By then, she had been at school and sadly under-achieving for almost three years. She was diagnosed as having 'glue ear'. This condition being common in young children; occurring when the eustachian tube is blocked by mucus. Grommets are inserted into a hole made in the eardrum, to allow for drainage of excess fluid and ventilation of the eardrum.

On 4th May (John's birthday) Charlotte aged seven, was admitted into the Bromhead Hospital for this small operation. The Consultant E.N.T. Surgeon at Lincoln, inserted stainless steel grommets instead of plastic ones, because Charlotte liked to swim. At the same time, he removed her adenoids. I had no qualms whatsoever about Charlotte having surgery. John stayed with her right up to the operation (she was by then very much a Daddy's girl), whilst I went swimming with Thomas.

Fortunately, John had been in a private health scheme at work for a few years. Therefore, we took the opportunity to have Charlotte's hearing problem speedily resolved. John also took advantage of the scheme, to have his left knee investigated (a result of being knocked off his bike while on duty). Ironically, when we really needed swift medical attention, (my eye problem) we were not in a medical scheme and there was no way that we could have afforded private health care.

That summer, Charlotte's long cherished dream came true. She was a bridesmaid for friends who played in the Ruston Bucyrus Band. At the age of eight, with her fair shoulder length hair, she looked lovely. We were thrilled that her wish had come true, especially as we knew that apart from this particular couple; there was no one in our circle of family and friends, likely to be getting married.

Chapter 13

Boston Again!

Towards the end of the summer, I showed a couple with a young boy around. They immediately liked the house and talked of buying it. Much to our consternation, they made an offer to our building society, but at a much lower price than we were asking. Our hopes were dashed. However, after a lengthy telephone call, John persuaded the purchaser to accept our price. So the wheels of the complicated business of house conveyancing, were finally put in motion. We had begun to think that it would never happen. It was hard to grasp the fact, that at long last we would be moving. Family life apart was very difficult and we desperately wanted to be settled.

House-hunting now began in earnest. There was absolutely nothing that appealed to us in the Tower Road area. After living in such a tranquil location, I hated the prospect of being on a large estate. We looked everywhere; even in the outlying villages. At that time there was very little property for sale.

The chap buying our house lived in Skegness and was hoping to get a job in Lincoln. John, had cautiously checked with him, whether he still intended to move to Sudbrooke, even if his job application was unsuccessful. He assured us that he would. So we doubled our efforts because he wanted to be in as soon as possible.

After a great deal of fruitless house-searching, we were getting despondent. I just did not know what I really wanted. John had no preference. At the back of my mind, nothing could ever compare with our lovely home in its beautiful setting. Finally, we settled on a modern detached house in Woodville Gardens, off Woodville Road. It was in a cul-de-sac. The houses were very close together and all the kitchens overlooked the front. I felt that it was not really my type of place. There was not much privacy and I did not like the idea of the children playing out in the front. Yet, I kept quiet. The house itself was spacious. The children were very impressed by the three toilets and the huge walk-in wardrobe in the master bedroom. We knew that the location would be ideal for the police station but it would be a good walk to the nearest school. Moreover, getting out of Woodville Road onto Sleaford Road, would prove very difficult, especially at peak times. We did not look deeply into these disadvantages; by then we were quite desperate to find somewhere. Our offer was accepted. We made arrangements to have the house surveyed and to visit the local school. Contracts were drawn up and the 23rd November was fixed as a moving date.

Feeling more settled and now in the waiting period, we had a weekend away in Wimbledon. We stayed with my oldest friend Angela, husband Alastair and their two girls. Since our marriage, they had become very good friends with John and they were Thomas' godparents. Both were deeply committed Christians and very involved with church life. As always on our visits, the children and I went to church, leaving John to his own devices. Al in particular, always had long theological talks with John. I had never been able to talk to John properly about my faith; so I was pleased that Angela and Al always seemed to manage it. These talks would go on well into the night. I usually retired to bed.

On the Sunday afternoon, as we said our goodbyes, Al handed John a paperback saying that he might find it interesting. It was 'A Fresh Start' by John Chapman. John took it graciously. I immediately thought, *he'll explode and say something very rude about it. He'll not want anything to do with it.* Strangely enough, John made no reference to his gift, so neither did I. I fully expected him to give me the book, for I knew that it was not his choice of reading. After a few days, I could not find the book anywhere. I searched, wondering what on earth John had done with it. I then discovered it in his work-bag, with a bookmark in it. I felt quite shaken and very humbled but had the sense not to say anything.

Every morning, once the children were at school and I had the house to myself, I would settle down for my 'quiet time'. One day in early October, I was reading about the setbacks that God often allows to happen. Just when things are going really well for us... wham! Something happens to knock us for six! We go backwards for a time but then in the end, having worked the disappointment through: something far better happens and we come out very much the stronger. I was extremely perplexed by what I had read as uneasily I questioned, *what can this possibly mean for us?*

One Friday afternoon in mid-October, the building society rang to say that the offer on our house had been withdrawn. The intended purchaser had failed to get the job and had no intention of moving to Lincoln. Initially I felt gutted with the awful feeling of being let-down. The Bible reading commentary, which had puzzled me a few days earlier, now made sickening sense. John took the news very badly. He seemed almost broken by it. I had never seen him so dispirited. Paradoxically, I now began to feel strangely relieved: may be we would not have to buy that modern house and something much better would turn up. I was convinced that God was with us in this. After all, He had pre-warned me. I could not share John's hopelessness at all. I tried to explain something of this to John, but as usual I found that I was unable to talk about my deep personal faith without feeling awkward and very ineffective. Apparently, I did get something across though: because much later on, John admitted to me, that he could see that my faith was helping me through a difficult situation.

John immediately contacted the owner of the house that we were hoping to buy. She told us that if we managed to get another buyer straight away, her house could still be ours. That weekend we were inundated with potential house buyers. At church on Sunday morning, I told Joan our bad news, but I also told her that I felt certain that we were going to get another buyer very soon. Sure enough, the following day, the retired couple who had looked round on the Saturday, made an offer. We were ecstatic. When John contacted the lady in Woodville Gardens, she informed him that she had accepted another offer. John and the children were very disappointed. Secretly, I was most relieved. The location would not have suited me at all, I liked my space and privacy.

The following weekend we went house-hunting again! During the week, John had viewed a house in Kirton. He thought it the most suitable of the few that he had seen. I had never seriously contemplated being out of Boston. This was all so different from what we had originally envisaged. We all viewed the house on the Friday evening and were favourably impressed. It had been built as a three bedroomed house but had since undergone an extension above the garage. There was a large open-plan extra room which could be multi-purpose. (Ironically enough, on the previous Sunday afternoon, before making up our minds to make an offer for the other house; we had actually stopped outside this house in Kirton. No one had been in, so we drove on to Woodville Gardens). The next day we returned to view it in daylight. The only disadvantage, was the small rear garden. There was less garden area than at Sudbrooke but there was far more space inside.

On Monday 23rd November 1987, Charlotte and Thomas were taken by my mother, to start at Kirton Primary School. I drove from Sudbrooke, in the orange Escort, whilst John travelled later in our red Nissan, followed by the removal van. What a wrench it was to leave my beloved woods. They had come to mean so much to me, in our six years at Sudbrooke. I felt extremely sad to have to say goodbye to some of the friends that I had made at Nettleham Methodist Church. The warmth and friendship that I had received there: had really helped me throughout the traumatic days of trying to move and of those long periods, of being on my own with the children. It had played a significant part in rekindling my Christian faith: to the extent that it had once again resumed its high priority position in my life, just as it had done in my late teens and early twenties, before my marriage.

After a few days of inevitable muddle and chaos, surprisingly we soon felt very much at home. Fortunately, Charlotte aged eight and Thomas aged five, appeared to settle quickly. From the old village school of Scothern (with 120 pupils): they were pitched into one of the largest primary schools in the area (approximately 400 pupils). This school with its modern buildings and ample facilities was a considerable change for them both. They had the advantage of joining their new classes, prior to the start of Christmas activities, when serious work was being somewhat relaxed.

Much to my amazement, I did not pine for Sudbrooke. I was too busy settling in, organising the chaos and preparing for Christmas. The advantages of living in Kirton, had soon won me over. It was great not having to rely on a car. I could get whatever I wanted locally: there being a wide range of shops and services available in

Kirton. Moreover, Sentance Crescent was only a ten minute stroll away from the village centre (less if you walk as if on a route march, like I usually do)! I have always enjoyed walking: finding it very calming, giving valuable time to think and pray. The daily walk to and from school, twice a day, was much more preferable to me, than having to drive two miles each way. As we had been very happy at the large active Methodist Church in Nettleham, I automatically assumed that we would attend Kirton Methodist Church. After considerable disappointment, I had accepted that Holy Trinity was no longer viable.

On our first Saturday in Kirton, the children and I attended an Autumn Fayre at the Methodist Church. It came as a tremendous shock to realise that there were very few young people there. On our way out, we met Sheila Lymer, who welcomed us very warmly. She invited Charlotte and Thomas to come along to their Sunday School. I explained about John working shifts and that he did not have a faith or an interest in church. Returning home, a sudden feeling of gloom swept over me. In spite of meeting Sheila, the place had not felt as I had expected it to. In contrast to the lively place that we had grown accustomed to; it had seemed quite lifeless.

We returned a week later. The service was not well attended and there were only six children in the Sunday School. They were busy preparing for the Christmas Nativity. With so few children to choose from, Thomas got the part of Joseph! Charlotte was to be the innkeeper's wife. Thomas was a handful at rehearsals. I dreaded how he would behave on the day. Sunday School also had a Wednesday Club. The children attended its Christmas party. By then, they already knew quite a few children from school. It seemed as if my feelings had been wrong.

One Sunday afternoon, about two weeks after our move, Charlotte, Thomas and I, went for our first bike-ride. We cycled along to Frampton, for I was curious to see where the church was. By now, the sun's brightness had gone, everything seemed damp and gloomy on that cold, raw December afternoon. As we stood by the church wall, I thought how isolated and uninviting the church appeared: standing on its own surrounded by fields (I had become so used to a church being adjacent to other buildings, not a dramatic landmark such as this). I thought most definitely, *this isn't the place for us.*

As December progressed, I was beginning to wonder even more about John. He had made a few out of character comments. The day before the Christmas Nativity was due to take place: he had commented that he might perhaps come along to see the children. Since I had known him, he only ever attended church for baptisms, weddings and funerals. I knew that he would not go along merely as a spectator. He had never felt right about doing this before. At Nettleham, Charlotte and Thomas had been in a few Christmas events but John had never gone along.

Sunday, 20th December, I was frantically preparing for the 10.15am service; quite nervous for the children, particularly anxious about how one awkward five-year-old son would perform! John was still in bed. I went to speak to him and was surprised to find him sat up with a book open. It seemed as if I had disturbed him. He said simply, 'I'm coming with you.' Quite stunned, I just burst into tears. The children could not understand why I was crying... but they were tears of joy. I think John was very much taken aback by my reaction. I had indeed interrupted him. He had been praying. The reaction of bursting into tears, was exactly the same response, that I had made many years earlier on being told of my brother Alan's commitment. After months of intense prayer for him; the news that he had become a Christian, was simply too much. Tears of course, being a tremendous release of deep feelings: whether they be of sorrow or of joy, as they were in both these two instances.

It seemed so strange going into church with John. He had not attended an ordinary service for years and he felt like a fish out of water. Just as well that it was not a complicated Church of England service. As expected, Thomas squirmed his way through the Nativity play. He was a Joseph with a difference, even crawling under a table at one point. Instead of a sermon, a young lady called Helen Brackenbury, read the story of 'Papa Panov' (an adaptation by Leo Tolstoy of a delightful children's story by Ruben Saillens). It was the moving account of a shoemaker, who gave hospitality to needy people on Christmas Day. In a dream, he had been convinced that Christ would visit him that day. How disappointed he was, when at the close of the day, he had waited in vain. Then, came the wonderful realisation: that in meeting the needs of the poor, he had in fact welcomed Christ into his own home. John found this story very inspiring but he had not been at all comfortable during the service. Furthermore, out of the small congregation, not many people had spoken to him. Though we discussed the service, the reasons for John deciding to come to church, were left unsaid. I suspected that John had made an important decision but I did not feel right in asking.

For years, Mum had spent Christmas with us. This year was no exception. As John was off that Christmas Eve, we went for a drink to his parents. They only lived two miles away at Wyberton. He had muttered something earlier in the week, about wanting to go to Midnight Mass. Rather strangely, I had chosen to ignore his remark. Over drinks, John's Mum was busy telling me all about the popular vicar, the Revd. Neil Russell, who was at St. Mary's Frampton. He had joined Norprint, a short time before John had left to join the Police on 30th November 1970. John could vaguely recall him.

We left his parents after 11.30pm, so I knew that we had missed the service. I had not attended Midnight Mass for years. It was something I loved to attend at Holy Trinity. In thirteen years of marriage, I had only been along twice, when John had accompanied me. Again John said, 'Let's go to Midnight Mass.' I was not keen at all. Fear of the unknown made me so reluctant. It was 11.45pm as we drove past St. Mary's. It looked beautiful with the floodlighting: there were cars everywhere. John's Mum had told us that the church attracted a large congregation. I did not like the idea of going into an unfamiliar crowded church, after the service had started and so we drove home.

After Christmas we finally talked. Unknown to me, John had been considering Christianity for some time. Al's book had helped point him in the right direction. Having made a Christian commitment a few days before the Nativity play, he had felt very strongly that he wanted to attend church. He had not felt right at Kirton and in all honesty, neither had I. It was obvious that we needed somewhere with people more our own age and with young children. I still toyed with the idea of Holy Trinity, whilst John seemed keen to see what St. Mary's was like.

To me, it was a miracle. It is impossible to convey the intense joy and overwhelming emotion that I experienced at John's conversion: especially as I had never believed it possible for John to change. John seemed such a strong, self-sufficient character and to my way of thinking, people like that, never acknowledge their need of God. Though inwardly, I had perceived that life would be so much better for him and for me, if he were to share my Christian conviction. My lack of faith had really been shown up!

Oh yes, I could thank God for his goodness in the past but this was in a totally different league. I felt like a child being given the most wonderful gift imaginable, something he or she knows that they do not deserve. This was the most incredible blessing. God had far surpassed my very human and very limited expectations. In my case, the impossible had happened. God had proved that He is the God of the impossible. I was shocked by this tangible proof of God's love for me. I had been given a second chance. I could have the sort of family life that I had always dreamed of. John and I, could now bring up our children together in a Christian environment.

There really had been a purpose for us to move back to Boston! God had blessed our return by granting the one thing, that through my lack of faith; I could not openly ask for. The verse in Romans that Sandra had quoted to me before our move, was now making sense.

Chapter 14
St. Mary's

On Sunday 3rd January 1988, the four of us set out for church. Even as we drove out of our estate, John and I were unsure whether we should attend Holy Trinity in Boston or St. Mary's in Frampton. John thought that we should give the local church a try first. That did seem to make sense.

Apprehensively walking along the long church path: I had just reached the porch, when I recognised a loud male voice behind me. Turning, to my utter amazement I saw Mr. James Lewis, my A-level English teacher, from Boston High School. He remembered me and I introduced John and the children. It was a lovely surprise.

Before the service had even commenced, the vicar came to speak to us; mentioning there was Sunday School, if the children were interested. They preferred to stay with us. John of course, had to contend with the complicated order of service. The vicar announced the page numbers which helped somewhat.

After the service, a lady sitting behind us; tapped John on the shoulder and asked, 'What are you doing here?' John was astonished to see Miss Joan Mills, who had been Deputy Head at Kirton Secondary Modern School, when John was a pupil there in the sixties. He had in fact seen her a few years earlier, when she and her elderly mother had been visiting Lincoln. I recalled him telling me about this chance meeting and her pleasure at seeing him.

Many of the congregation greeted us warmly. The Revd. Neil Russell seemed very pleasant. He too, had a vague recollection of working with John, at Norprint in 1970. I informed him that John had only just started coming to church, since recently becoming a Christian. He arranged to visit John. A suitable date was fixed for three weeks ahead, when John would be off duty. We were highly delighted at the way things had gone that morning. What a wonderful reception we had been given. Without a doubt, we had been made to feel at home.

We never did return to the Methodist Church. I suffered pangs of guilt about that; especially since Sheila Lymer had given us such a friendly welcome. A few weeks after we had been attending St. Mary's regularly, I met Sheila at school. Rather sheepishly, I explained why we had chosen to worship at St. Mary's. Sheila was overjoyed to hear about John. Our circumstances had changed dramatically. John's developing faith was the prime consideration now.

A week later, I was busy preparing the evening meal when the doorbell rang. It came as quite a shock to see the Frampton vicar standing there. John was at work but we had a good talk. When I mentioned that I had done some Sunday School teaching; he was most interested. Neil thought that I could possibly help with that. I was quite pleased to think that there was a need that I could fill. Although he was at pains to say: that he did not want us to feel compelled to attend St. Mary's, especially if we still wanted 'to shop around'.

I was in no doubt and neither was John. It all made sense. The fact that the vicar and John had vaguely known each other years earlier, had played a part in bringing us to St. Mary's. After the welcome that we had been shown, how could we wish to go elsewhere!

Incredibly, throughout those early weeks of 1988, it seemed as if we had lived here for ages. Life in Sudbrooke became a distant memory. The woods were the only thing that I missed. We had so much more now. Our family life had been blessed in the most marvellous way.

We really felt at home in the community and especially at St. Mary's. Now John was a Christian, it was not sufficient for him merely to attend church on Sundays. Besides, with shift work, he could only manage two out of four Sunday mornings. That spring, John joined the Lent study group. He got to know some other Christians in the church fellowship, on a much deeper level than before I did. I was more than happy for him to attend, whilst I remained with the children. He needed the contact with his 'new family', far more than I did.

I shall never forget his Dad's reaction on turning up on our doorstep one Sunday morning. 'We're just about to go to church!' announced John. 'What! You as well?' his father asked absolutely dumbfounded. His family did not understand the change in John. He had to endure a considerable amount of criticism and negative comments, concerning something that had become so important to him. I was convinced that they blamed me for it all.

We had not been worshipping at St. Mary's for very long, when I was asked if I would like to join the group of volunteer ladies, who fortnightly cleaned the church. I regarded this as something practical which I could do and agreed. John and my mother saw the funny side of this. Housework has always been the most unwelcome of chores!

The first talk that John had with the Revd. Neil Russell, lasted for over three hours. It was obvious why Neil was such a popular vicar. He had such a lovely and very gentle, caring manner. John and I both felt at ease talking to him. Soon we began to regard him, not simply as a very pleasant and approachable priest but as a friend whom we could trust. I was thrilled how things had worked out and that here was someone keen to encourage John in his Christian development.

At Easter, our dear friends Alastair and Angela Steven, came to stay. We were really looking forward to seeing them, to share our wonderful news. I had given a slight hint to them on a card, on which I had written *we are all going to St. Mary's.* They were really thrilled about John's conversion. They had been praying regularly for him, at their housegroup.

After Easter, I started to help with the older Sunday School, for seven to elevens. There were two other teachers and we worked a rota. The first time that I took the group there were ten children. It was wonderful, just like having my own small class again. I thoroughly enjoyed it. The numbers fluctuated slightly but there were usually at least six children. Sunday School teaching appealed, particularly because Charlotte was in the group. I had a vested interest, in making the children feel involved and part of the church family. The role of Sunday School, was not merely to keep children occupied away from the main service. I was very keen to make it meaningful to the children.

Charlotte and Thomas were delighted that their Daddy now attended church with them. John would also say prayers at bedtime with them. Family life had never been so good. John with his love of music, joined the singing group and was also on the rota for reading the lessons. The first time that he read in church, I had to almost pinch myself, to realise that it was really happening. I was so proud of him. His faith really shone out from him. He communicated it with such warmth and conviction. He was certainly growing in his Christian faith.

Mum started to worship at St. Mary's with us. One morning, she was busy chatting to a lady whom she had known from her W.I. and Art and Craft days. Mum introduced me to Ann Langley: (née Miss Ghest, my orthoptist from childhood). What an unexpected surprise that was: to meet up with someone from my past, who was a regular member of St. Mary's congregation.

During the spring, I had a long and very honest talk with Neil. Until then, John's spiritual progress had always been our main topic of conversation. Now I knew that I needed to open up about my own deep-rooted problems. My acute shyness had been a heavy burden to me throughout my life. I tended to put up barriers and then wondered why people did not respond warmly towards me, or why I found it difficult to make new friends. I had always had an inferiority complex; finding it hard to believe that people (other than a few close friends) could be at all interested in me. The despair and frustration at the sort of person I was, (and seemed destined to remain) often manifested itself in a very nasty temper, especially towards Charlotte. At the age of nine, she was no longer my sweet, obedient, young daughter. We clashed. I always deeply regretted my outbursts and suffered pangs of conscience for ages afterwards. Nevertheless, they still occasionally happened. Although Neil could not offer instant solutions, it was helpful to unburden myself. I sensed that at last there was support for us all.

We also discussed John. Neil admitted to me, that he was sure that God had sent John to help him. Moreover, he recognised that John had many leadership qualities which needed nurturing. Neil stated that he would have to develop this with him later on. His words both shook and delighted me. I told Neil that many years earlier I had thought, *what a lot John had to offer God, if he were to become a Christian, with regard to his love of music and singing.* Now the fact that he was such an extrovert and seemed able to communicate on a deeper level, so effortlessly as it appeared to me, was an entirely different sort of gift.

Once I had started to enjoy Sunday School teaching, I began to consider giving supply teaching a try. I had never wanted to return to full-time teaching but thought that it might suit me to teach occasionally. I discussed the possibilities with the headmaster of Kirton Primary School. This was the only school which I was interested in: it being within walking distance from home and where Charlotte and Thomas attended. He informed me that supply teachers were in great demand and that if I were to offer French, I would probably get a great deal of work in secondary schools. This did not appeal. I had no experience whatsoever of working with secondary pupils. He assured me that the problem with John's shifts could be avoided: I could merely cover for pre-arranged days; as opposed to an early morning call to fill in at short notice. I have always liked to organise things properly and knew that I could not cope well with last minute decisions.

There had been no pressure for me to return to work. Fortunately, we were able to manage comfortably on John's salary. Once I had decided that I wanted a family and with the subsequent arrival of my first child: motherhood had seemed to take over and family life became the most important thing to me. My teaching career was in the past and I was quite content to leave it there. My nine years of teaching had been quite rewarding, although extremely draining. I knew that my family would not come first, if I went back to full-time work. However, the occasional day of supply teaching would be a welcome outside interest. Being at home and having a few church based activities did satisfy me ordinarily: yet there seemed to be an underlying desire to have something further. When it occasionally surfaced, it was accompanied by the fervent belief that God had another role in mind for me: besides that of wife and mother. On a merely practical level, it would be great to earn my own money.

I still toyed with the idea of using my French. Quite a few of the Frampton congregation spent their holidays in France. Neil was particularly interested in keeping up his spoken French and suggested that I start a class. I dismissed this idea initially. The idea of doing French with a group of adults seemed rather daunting.

Besides, I was already doing German. In January 1988, I had joined a German evening class at Boston College. I thoroughly enjoyed the class and soon felt at ease with the established group. I was highly motivated because the family and I were looking forward to the Ruston Bucyrus Band's third trip to Neustadt in June.

Charlotte aged eight and Thomas aged six, had time off school for this, their first foreign visit. It was a marvellous holiday, especially because we were staying with a German family. The highlight for me, always being the opportunity to speak German. It gave me a terrific buzz to be able to communicate in another language. My French came in very useful as well. On our journey, we stopped for lunch in the city of Luxembourg. We found a small family-run restaurant, away from the main tourist area. The children were desperate for the toilet, so I was able to switch over to French and explain. We enjoyed a pleasant lunch, with the most attentive of staff. In comparison, the rest of our group were charged exorbitant prices in the city centre.

Throughout the summer, we made regular visits to Spalding Swimming Pool. It had the advantage of a small learner pool, which was ideal for Thomas who had not yet learnt to swim. My godmother Mary Marriott, now in her eighties, lived in Spalding. After years of excellent health, she had become quite poorly. Mum was very concerned about Mary's sudden deterioration. During a visit, Thomas and I were talking to her husband Bill, while Mum and Mary were in another room. Mary informed Mum that she had cancer in her lungs. Poor Mum had expected something like this but it came as a huge shock to me.

In late November, Mary was admitted to Pilgrim Hospital. In there, she came to know Edie Desforges, a lovely lady from our church, who was also suffering from cancer. I had intended to visit Mary in hospital but unexpectedly she was transferred back to Spalding. I never did see her again. Her funeral was the same afternoon as Edie's. I found it comforting to believe that they were still together.

After our successful holiday in West Germany, I was determined to form my own local French group. At one point there were half a dozen people eager to join. I had even fixed up dates and a fee.

However by the end of the summer holidays, all interest had waned. I was so downcast and in my usual manner, when feeling let-down, took it out on John and the children.

The weekend before my class would have started, we stayed in Wimbledon with Angela and Alastair Steven. For the first time, John attended church with us. In striking contrast to St. Mary's: theirs was a large town church, overflowing with families, with a variety of activities to cater for the whole age range. It reminded me somewhat of Nettleham Methodist Church, with its very lively and bustling atmosphere. We were amazed by the number of house fellowship groups on offer. This was something we thought that we should like to attend but there was nothing like that at St. Mary's.

The following Monday morning, while shopping in Kirton, I met Neil. He fully intended to come to my first French class that evening and was surprised to hear that it had become a non-event. By then the French class no longer mattered: I was keen to tell him all about the church in Wimbledon and about the need for a house-group here in Frampton. Perhaps my enthusiasm was a bit much for him early on a Monday morning! He stated that it was time to have a long talk with John.

That Tuesday morning, Neil and John discussed the idea of a house-group. Neil suggested that John and I host it. It seemed as if God had used the idea of having a French group in my home, to prepare me for being involved in something else. It appealed to us both. However, Neil had something far more startling to suggest. Neil asked John what he intended to do after his confirmation in October 1988. Neil broached the subject of John training for a ministry within the Anglican Church. The choices were narrowed down to either ordination as a non-stipendiary priest, or lay ministry as a Reader. The matter needed a great deal of prayerful consideration.

On 16th October 1988, John was confirmed by the Bishop of Grantham, The Right Revd. Bill Ind. What a wonderfully moving service that was for me. It was hard to believe that roughly a year earlier: John had been utterly demoralised over the prospective house-buyer's deceit. It had been a very low period in his life. Now a year later, he had gained such a deep meaningful faith, that he could not keep quiet about it. Jesus Christ had transformed his life. His confirmation was a really joyful occasion for me. Again, tears of joy being shed.

That October, Kathleen Cockerill and I helped Maureen Edenbrow organise a reunion for the 1960 year group of Boston High School (now all aged about forty). It was years since the three of us had all met up together. We had a lovely time planning for the event, as well as re-living many happy shared memories of church, Covenanter and school days.

The evening was a huge success, with approximately two-thirds of our year attending. It was fascinating to speak to people whom we had not seen since O and A-levels. There were considerable surprises in seeing how some pupils had turned out. It struck me forcefully, that out of all my ex-French teacher's more favoured pupils (of whom she had very high career expectations): the only pupil who had actually gone on to teach French, had been me. I felt rightly proud of that. Life is full of twists and little ironies.

Our former headmistress, Miss Esmé Thomas and the deputy Miss Joan Carter, had been unable to attend the reunion. As they both lived in the Stamford area, Kathleen who lives near Bourne, invited them to join us for lunch. Even in retirement, they had maintained contact with many ex-pupils. How they enthused about the high-powered life-style of many of our peers: who had achieved considerable status in their chosen careers. Whereas the three of us, had devoted our time and energies to our families and our various church activities. It left me feeling very inadequate and quite worthless: that I had not combined a successful career, with family life.

That October half-term, we experienced our first package holiday abroad. We had a fantastic ten days in Santo Tomas, Menorca. It was the best family holiday that we had enjoyed up to that point. The weather as expected, being very warm and it was so relaxing to spend hours of carefree fun in the Mediterranean. For me, the main attraction of any holiday, was being able to have regular dips in the sea.

The day after our return, we held a coffee evening to discuss the proposed house-group. It was decided to have a morning session one week and an evening session the following week, to accommodate those who worked during the daytime and John's shift pattern.

As I was one of the Sunday School teachers, I assisted with the Christmas Nativity. Both groups had large numbers of children, so there were at least twenty to organise. Charlotte at nine, was one of the oldest girls who regularly attended. She was eligible for the star role of Mary. Thomas and two other six-year-olds were shepherds. On our last rehearsal, Neil asked me to do one of the readings for the service. I had not read in a service since college days, when I used to be a chapel helper. Although, extremely nervous about the prospect of reading before so many people, I felt delighted to be actively involved. The number of people who made a point of commenting on how well I had read, specifically remarking on the clarity and the significant way that I put it over, astounded me. I began to think that may be here, was a gift that I should cultivate. When I mentioned this to Neil, he invited me to join the rota for reading the lessons. This I gladly did. To me personally, it was a most fitting way to conclude our first year in Kirton. It marked the end of a most eventful and happy year for us all.

Chapter 15

Mission and Ministry

By January 1989, our house-group had settled into a pattern of meeting every Thursday morning. If John was absent, Neil or I would lead it. I had never done anything like this before. I had always found it virtually impossible to say anything, when in a group situation. I froze in shyness and felt totally ill at ease .All the same, I could manage to say a short prayer at prayer meetings. That was different somehow, no one was looking! My acute self-consciousness continued to be a real burden to me.

The study notes which we followed were very comprehensive and I seemed to manage. However I was uncomfortable in this leading role for I could hardly put my own thoughts forward, let alone draw those out from other people. Although at college, I had contributed to Christian Union activities, yet that was in another life!

At the beginning of the year John commenced his formal Reader training. Before being accepted by the Lincoln Diocese: John required the support of Neil Russell our vicar and the P.C.C. He was formerly interviewed by Reader Alan Kemp and Canon Peter Fluck of St. Botolph's Church in Boston. The Revd. John Duckett, vicar of Sutterton, became John's tutor. John soon knuckled down to an intensive study of parts of the New Testament. On the whole, I was very supportive of this involvement. Occasionally there was slight friction: time when I wanted John to be with us as a family, instead of having his head in a theological book. He usually studied on his rest days, while the children were at school. Tasks such as decorating were put to one side. I believed that there was far more to our lives than filling it with a constant round of home improvements. Developing our work for God, was most important.

By July 1988, in spite of receiving the necessary contract from Lincolnshire County Council; I still had not done any supply teaching. I mentioned this once to the Kirton Head: only to be told that there would not be much work, for someone who imposed restrictions on their availability. I had thus begun to think that I would never get any work: when a late Thursday afternoon call from the school secretary, threw me into a right panic. Charlotte's teacher, had gone home sick and they needed someone to cover for the following day (Friday 3rd February 1989). It would mean having a small group of sixteen in the morning and then the whole third year class for the afternoon.

I was in such a state of nerves! I had not taught in a school for almost ten years. I slept very little that night. I seemed to be 'clock-watching' for ages before it was time to get ready for work. I muddled through the morning, with the small group that Charlotte was in. I enjoyed part of the afternoon more: when with the full class I tackled the subject of fear and we discussed individual fears. I went home absolutely shattered, very relieved that my initiation day was well and truly over.

How I enjoyed domestic chores on Monday morning, after my day of teaching. However, staff at school were being hit with a flu-bug. In the ensuing weeks, I had the opportunity to work with a variety of classes. Slowly, my confidence grew, as I became better acquainted with the staff and school routine. I was much happier not being in Charlotte's year. On the whole, I enjoyed the challenge of doing something different out of the home. I planned as much as possible, though with teachers going down like flies: it was a case of muddle through with very last minute decisions (not my style at all) as to what on earth to do, with the class sat expectantly waiting.

In February 1989, the Christian Police Association, which John had joined, took a service at Nettleham Methodist Church. The children and I had never been back there; although I had contacted Joan the previous year, to inform her about John's conversion. I knew how thrilled she would be. Joan had been the only person to urge me, to never give up on John's lack of faith.

I was really excited at the prospect of returning: this time with a deeply committed Christian husband. I felt that it was a heaven sent opportunity to give thanks to God, in a place where the children and I had received so much loving support; during difficult days, when John worked and lived at Grantham and Boston. In all the time that we had worshipped at Nettleham, John had never been to a service with us. Now, he was to take a leading part in it. He gave a moving testimony of becoming a Christian. It was such a joyful return. Quite an emotional reunion, with a few people who had been very supportive in the past.

Before Easter, Neil invited me to help with the Good Friday Workshop. I was delighted to be involved. At our planning meeting, I mentioned the simple Easter service that I had once done, with my favourite class at Woad Farm. Consequently, Neil delegated me to lead the service! John was busy working, so he could not be involved.

At 10.30am about thirty-five children, aged between four and thirteen, descended on the vicarage. The programme consisting of a morning of various craft activities, followed by a picnic lunch and concluding with a short act of worship. My craft group made a huge, torn-paper collage, depicting three crosses on a dark hillside. It was effectively stark, in its extreme simplicity and formed a dramatic backdrop to the service. Charlotte read a poem *'The Flowers Sleep.'* Unfortunately, her usually audible voice was marred because our background music of *'Morning'* from the Peer Gynt Suite, was too dominant. I thoroughly enjoyed leading the short service. I felt quite elated that I had been able to do something so public. In fact, I was really very smug, that I had led a service in St. Mary's, before John ever did! For part of his Reader training, was to be involved with the practical issues of leading worship.

My brother Alan had come to stay for Easter, with his two sons, who were of similar age to our two children. It was the second time that he had visited without his wife. On Easter Saturday, Mum, Alan and boys, joined us for a day out. Before we set off, Mum spoke to me privately. Alan and his wife were getting divorced. What a difficult weekend it was. Alan, as usual, kept his feelings very much to himself. The boys seemed no different. Our two had no inkling of the change in circumstances until Alan returned home to Devon. At one point on that Saturday, Alan and I happened to be walking together; everyone else was a long way off. He never brought the subject up; it was left to big sister to try and convey my feelings of concern for him and the children. Alan, maintained a calm exterior: as I floundered, very upset; feeling totally inadequate in a situation that I had never had experience of. Mum, had taken the news very badly. It seemed much worse because we lived so far away from Alan.

On Easter Sunday, Alan, Mum and boys joined us all at St. Mary's. John was involved in the service, by leading the prayers and giving his testimony. The children and I, were obviously mentioned. My faith over the years, especially the way that I had handled the trauma of our house sale let-down, were all included (I tried not to squirm too much with embarrassment). John introduced a song that he had composed, to be sung with keyboard accompaniment, entitled 'Jesus Is My Saviour.' This he demonstrated with the children leading the singing. I was so proud of them all.

On the first Sunday after Easter, I took part in a M.U. Deanery Evensong, which was hosted by St. Mary's. Neil had kindly volunteered me to do the prayers! Many hours of preparation later, clutching two A4 sheets of hand-written prayers, on the theme of Mary... and was I nervous! The church was packed. I had never seen so many clergy before. I really was shaking. My heart was pounding away furiously and I felt so churned up, as the time came for me to approach the lectern.

Once I stood there, a tremendous feeling of calm descended upon me. It was as if God took over from me. Remarkably, this has often been my experience when taking part in a service. Many people congratulated me on my meaningful, clearly delivered prayers. It was a shock to receive so much praise. Naturally, it boosted my ego considerably and I felt really pleased that I had been blessed with the gift of clear speech, to enable me not only to read lessons but also to lead prayers.

As a member of the Police Federation, John attended their annual conference each May. To my great annoyance, my fortieth birthday was to occur during conference week. Hating the thought of being another decade older: I had turned down John's offer of a party (being very shy, I always disliked big dos). Accordingly, it was almost a non-event. In all honesty, I was quite upset by the lack of fuss from the family. Though Charlotte and Thomas did hang a sign outside the front door and Mum made me a cake. Nevertheless, thanks to Neil and my friends in the M.U. it turned out to be a day to remember. May 18th coincided with their outing to Gibraltar Point.

Our picnic lunch was livened up by the German wine that I had taken along and by the lovely surprise birthday cake that Judy Williams had made for me. They really made the day special for me.

After those hectic days of supply teaching in the spring, there was a lull until the beginning of July: when I taught the middle infant class of five to six-year-olds for seven consecutive school days. I became really fond of them and for that short time, regarded them as my own class. I enjoyed the continuity; it was far better than having many different classes. Consequently, by the end of the summer term, I had earned a considerable amount. It seemed right to spend that on an extra holiday. We had already booked a return holiday to Menorca in October. Now, we felt strongly that we should go to Devon and see my brother Alan. Mum travelled with us. We booked a caravan on Beer Head in East Devon. It was a beautiful location and we all enjoyed a lovely holiday.

That September, nine of us from Frampton embarked on the two year Bishop's Course, *'Exploring our Faith.'* This course had replaced the former Bishop's Certificate, with its emphasis on formal study. The purpose for doing the course was to prepare us for greater involvement in church life. We met fortnightly. It proved to be very challenging, although at times quite disconcerting: to rethink matters of faith, which had once appeared to be so black and white.

Our meetings became great times of learning, interspersed with much hilarity, especially when we tackled role-play. In one scenario, I portrayed a most convincing tree, being watered and then dying very dramatically. Everyone was in stitches at my performance. Was that another hidden talent...? Another hilarious evening was when I as a BBC interviewer, had to question Zacchaeus who had climbed up a tree, to gain a vantage point in which to see Jesus. Those were memorable moments of laughter, but we actually shared all sorts of emotion. Very soon, we became a close-knit group. Our tutor was the Revd. John Duckett who was John's Reader tutor. John was excellent. He made our sessions so lively and purposeful.

I firmly believed that Sunday School was still my main role. For that reason, as the number of children declined, I grew most disenchanted. In addition, Charlotte and Thomas began to moan about having to attend church. I knew that if there were more children: Sunday School would be much more appealing for them. Fortunately, they were still keen to say prayers at bedtime. Charlotte was now in the choir and helped serve at Holy Communion; a sight which made me so proud.

I seemed to have a continual bee in my bonnet about making faith and church relevant to youngsters. Once, I even spoke to our M.U. on the importance of Sunday School. For me personally, circumstances may have been so different, if I had not been invited along by the Cole family. As a child I owed much to my introduction to Sunday School and church. It was the first talk that I had done and there were very favourable comments on its thoroughness and preparation.

In Sunday School, I always encouraged the children to say their own prayers. I tried to show them that God was interested in all their concerns (however small and unimportant that they might seem to adults). Occasionally, the children would participate in the service.

Not long after the Tiananmen Square massacre in China (4th June 1989); Charlotte had written a one sentence prayer, simply asking God to help the people of China. The following Sunday I asked Neil if Charlotte's prayer could be included in the service. In its simplicity, it echoed what we all felt. Our prayers do not have to be long-winded.

My interest in prayer continued. Frequently on a Tuesday morning, I would join Neil and Val Marriott for a short said service of Morning Prayer, at St. Michael's, Frampton West. I valued enormously these times for prayer and fellowship. At St. Mary's, I set up a prayer board: a note-pad nearby, to encourage prayer requests. Our Sunday School children used it considerably, as did John and I; but to my disappointment most of the regular congregation, seemed to ignore its function. I found this very disheartening and would moan at poor John, about the lack of spirituality and prayer awareness at Frampton. To my perception, prayer was paramount to Christian survival and growth.

Charlotte had a lovely clear speaking voice and read in services occasionally. She was always beautifully articulate and so expressive. We were both tremendously proud of her. Her first public speaking part (aged eight years and nine months) was in April 1988, when she was asked to say the Brownie promise at the St. George's Day Service at Boston Stump. The following day, Ann Pilbeam her teacher was commenting to her class, that she had never heard such a well-spoken Brownie promise. She was quite amazed on being told that the Brownie in question was Charlotte. John and Charlotte were extroverts. She would talk easily to anyone, whereas, Thomas and I were the introvert members of the household.

Quite naturally at this stage, Charlotte was a 'Daddy's girl'. Moreover, she seemed to be following in his footsteps, by her aptitude for music. When she was nine, John taught her to play the tenor horn. She then joined the Kirton Band as a junior player in 1989. She was very keen and enjoyed the weekly practices and the numerous fêtes and concerts that they performed at. Obviously, it filled me with such pride to watch her. I had no musical ability at all but I recognised how marvellous it must be, to have that gift.

During those years when Charlotte and Thomas were both at primary school, they were largely content to be in each other's company. Very rarely did they have friends round or go elsewhere. As a family we spent a great deal of time together, doing a variety of activities. Those were happy days.

Chapter 16
Romania

In December 1989, after forty years of dictatorship, under the Communist tyrant Nicolae Ceausescu: Romania was now open to the West. Dreadful conditions had come to light. Early in January 1990, Duncan Howells a social worker, contacted Lincolnshire Police to request assistance in collecting basic dried food items for Romania. Within a couple of days, John had informed all our local churches. Consequently, several hundred pounds worth of goods were donated or bought with cash from a local supermarket. Furthermore the proprietor added a substantial contribution.

In early March, Duncan Howells spoke during a morning service at St. Mary's. He gave the most moving account of the unbelievable deprivation that he had discovered, while visiting Romanian orphanages; powerfully illustrated by the use of disturbing photographs. By the end of his presentation, he had captured everyone's support and we felt compelled to continue helping. His second trip, at the end of March, was to concentrate on: medical items, baby food, bedding and clothing. John was allowed to use a police van to take a load of donated goods to a depot in Lincoln. Four of his police colleagues were joining Duncan for the second trip to Romania. John told me how he wished that he was going. How relieved I was, that he was not!

From then on, John became more and more involved with fund-raising for Romania. He related extremely well to Duncan. Indeed we both did. Duncan was a super person, with a tremendous driving force, necessary to motivate and involve others in something that was so dear to his heart.

In February, Charlotte and I took part in the Candlemas pantomime. The thirty minutes of after-supper entertainment was a yearly ritual at Frampton. That year's story was loosely based on Snow White. Charlotte aged 10, almost the youngest in the cast, played a dwarf. Mine was a very minor two or three line part but I was glad of the opportunity to take part. It was very nerve-racking being on stage, but great fun.

Prior to the second Romanian trip, I handed out notices around the village about the items needed. I visited Kirton Primary School. The headmaster did not seem his usual friendly self when I spoke to him. He sat there looking ghastly white, as he took my notice. Without further words, I left. Shortly afterwards, he was in hospital, very ill with cancer. I felt dreadful that I had bothered him, when unbeknown to me, he was so ill.

At the end of March, we visited a family whom we had met in Menorca the previous October. We collected the children after lunch on the Friday and travelled to Coventry. On the Sunday morning, we visited Coventry Cathedral, where we lit a candle for our Kirton headmaster.

That evening on our return home, a double shock awaited us. Before our weekend away, we had been aware that a very dear member of our church community and a staunch M.U. member, Joyce Newton, had been admitted into hospital, following a minor stroke. Sadly, Joyce suffered a massive stroke during the weekend and died. Moreover, the head of Kirton Primary School had died on the Friday that we travelled to Coventry. The entire community were deeply upset by his death. He had been such a well-loved headmaster. Cancer had reared its ugly head again.

On the Saturday before the start of the Easter holidays, I was helping to sell refreshments, at a netball tournament at Kirton Primary School. The deputy head Mr. John Thomas, who had been acting head since the headmaster's death, wished to speak to me. Rather puzzled, I followed him to the staff room, only to be absolutely bowled over by what he had to say.

Mr. Thomas asked me to consider taking over his teaching duties for the summer term. The fourth year had very large numbers; so those children requiring more help in the basic subjects, were in a small group and returned to their respective main classes every afternoon. It would mean having a group of sixteen pupils (6Z) every morning and then the whole class (6X or 6Y) for the afternoon. Fortunately his afternoon timetable meant that he took a variety of other classes and so I would not have to teach an entire fourth year class every afternoon.

I sauntered home in a daze, feeling quite flattered to be asked and most tempted by the prospect of earning a full-time teacher's salary, holiday pay included, instead of the daily supply rate that I usually earned. What a quandary to be in. I had never wanted to return to full-time teaching. I had always vowed that I never would. My children came first. Charlotte was then nearly eleven and Thomas almost eight. Occasional supply work was one thing but full-time teaching even for one term, was another matter.

Ever since our move to Kirton and John's conversion: with our subsequent church involvement and my new lease of spiritual life; I had become all the more determined to put God first in my life. With regard to any personal ambition; I was content to play a supportive role for my children and especially for John, in the exciting way that opportunities were now opening up to us because of his changed outlook. A verse that I often considered:

'But seek ye first the kingdom of God, and his righteousness; and all these things will be added unto you.'

Matthew chapter 6 verse 33 Authorised K.J. V.

Nevertheless, after considerable discussion, I decided to take up the temporary teaching appointment. Another advantage in my favour, was that for the entire summer term; John was to work Monday to Friday at Police Headquarters at Nettleham, near Lincoln. There would be no awkward shifts to work round. John thought that we could surely survive for one term. It would be good experience for me: a useful exercise in determining whether eventually, I should return to full-time teaching. The only problem being our weekly house-group, which we hosted on Thursday mornings. Fortunately the group were keen to continue without us.

At Easter, Alan came to stay with Mum, bringing Lynne and his boys. Lynne and he had met late last summer. Their friendship had quickly blossomed. We were eager to meet her and liked her immediately. They were very happy together and appeared well suited. Our initial meeting was at our Good Friday Workshop, when I was very occupied and rather fraught! On Easter Sunday, they all came to us for lunch. Later that afternoon, Lynne seemed keen to look round our home. During our tour of inspection, Lynne and I really opened up to one another. She admitted how anxious she had been about meeting me and whether I would approve of her or not (Alan must have told her she would get the 'third degree' from his big sister)! I felt totally at ease with her. Lynne and I seemed on a similar wavelength. Before rejoining the others, we had given each other a warm hug.

Mum and I were so relieved, knowing that Alan had again someone to share his life with. My prayers thankfully had been answered. It seemed as if things had indeed worked out for the best. Alan and Lynne became engaged in December 1990.

That Easter, I was extremely busy, trying to prepare for the summer term of work. After Alan's visit, Angela, Alastair and their two girls stayed for a couple of days. As usual there was much to catch up on. On the Thursday that they were due to return to Wimbledon; John attended the National Assembly of the Christian Police Association: held in County Armagh, Northern Ireland. That caused us all some anxious moments. We were all greatly relieved when he returned in one piece! John enthused about the wonderful hospitality that he had received and how spiritually uplifting the fellowship had been.

On Monday 23rd April, there was a training day at school. What a novelty, to leave John and the children at home, whilst I went into work. However, after the first week of only four days' teaching: I was panicking - *eleven weeks to go, I'll never survive*! Indeed that first weekend, I really regretted my decision.

I was timetabled to teach 6Z every morning, unless another member of staff was absent, when I would be asked to cover for them. This was dreadfully unsatisfactory, because the sixteen children in 6Z were then denied the extra help that they needed: being simply re-absorbed into their already overcrowded base classes, for the entire school day.

There were a few difficult boys in 6Z, but fairly soon I began to enjoy my little class. The afternoons were far more taxing. In a normal week, I taught seven different classes. I hated taking the two fourth year classes. By then, they knew which secondary school they were transferring to and being at the top of the school, they thought nothing of making life difficult for a new teacher. It was far worse teaching Charlotte's class; I loathed it. I have never tolerated rude, ill-disciplined children. I probably over-reacted, making the situation worse. Charlotte had a hard time too, having to listen to nasty comments about her mother.

On the plus side, I enjoyed the social contact in the classroom. I found the staff very friendly and most supportive. The National Curriculum was causing a considerable amount of extra work on already over-pressurised teachers. Schemes were being constantly drawn up and I had to attend weekly planning sessions, both at lunchtime and after school. It was all meaningless jargon to me and I felt greatly relieved to be only there for the term.

I was into my second week of teaching, when Duncan Howells invited John to join the third trip to Romania, planned for that June. John by now, was well and truly hooked on supporting the project. I knew that there was no point in trying to dissuade him. Besides, I was as keen as he was to do something; but unlike John, my concern was less direct. I could not cope with the reality of seeing such distress at first-hand. T.V. reports of harrowing events have always haunted me for days afterwards, as I have seethed angrily and helplessly, at man's inhumanity to man.

It was necessary to hold many fund-raising events to finance the convoy. Another good reason for my working in school that term, was because it gave the opportunity to engender interest and support for the project. With abundant media coverage on Romania, the children were being made aware of the terrible plight of the Romanian orphanages.

My next-door neighbour Margaret Harmston, suggested a few fund-raising ideas. For 6Z, we came up with the idea of having a large map of Romania, divided into a grid of $2cm^2$, a thousand plus in total. The map would be divided into the three horizontal bands of the new post-revolutionary flag of red, blue and yellow. We would charge ten pence to buy a coloured sticker, to place on the appropriate square of the flag.

My class were involved with preparing the map for display, making and selling the stickers. It became our mini-project. It was lovely to involve some of the less academic children, in something so worthwhile. We worked a rota for selling stickers during break-times and for totalling the daily cash and plotting it on a graph. It really gripped their imagination.

Before we began in earnest, I had to introduce the fund-raising project to the whole school. Quite incredibly, this was not the ordeal that I had anticipated: having never before, spoken to a hall full of approximately 400 staff and children. In all my years of doing class assemblies; I had always made sure that the children did all the speaking!

The fund-raising went very well. In less than two weeks, 6Z had raised £110. A photograph of our efforts, with the children holding the flag, appeared in the local newspaper. By then, another £15 had been collected. My class were thrilled. We had well exceeded our original target of £100.

John's parents disapproved strongly of John's intended venture. They thought it highly irresponsible of a family man to take such risks. I did not share their qualms at all. I knew that it was right for him to be so involved. I certainly believed without doubt, that God would take care of him.

On Friday 22nd June 1990, six police officers accompanied Duncan. There were two lorries, a van and trailer, laden with medical equipment, drugs, beds, clothing, food, toys, books, typewriters and calculators. Many tablets of soap had been donated by schoolchildren. They were given out individually, as a gift to the many elderly people, to whom such an item was a real luxury.

It took John a long time to readjust when he came home. Some of the distressing scenes, really haunted him. He became even more determined to continue to support the relief project. By then it was affiliated to Romania Project U.K. a registered charity.

Shortly after his return, John spoke to the entire school of five to eleven-year olds. He captured everyone's attention for a full forty-five minutes. His talk was a tremendous success. Indeed, this was to be the first of many talks that he was to give in the next couple of years.

I encouraged my year six classes to write letters, to schoolchildren in Romania. There was an excellent response. It was quite mind-blowing for them to be told, that children in Romania did not have such basics as soap, sweets and chocolate. For many it was a very sobering lesson, to learn that the horror of Romania was real and being experienced by children their own age.

As the summer holidays approached, I began to feel that the end was at last in sight. By now I was utterly exhausted. Furthermore, the last few weeks were made worse by the extremely hot weather that we were experiencing. Frequent timetable changes due to sudden staff absences; made me realise just how vital supply teachers were for the system to continue with the minimum disruption. I therefore agreed to be added to the list for the early morning call-out. I knew without a doubt that I would not want to tackle full-time teaching again. I had enjoyed certain aspects of the experience but knew deep down that it was not for me. Similarly, when I had taught before, the demands of school had simply taken over.

Consequently, that term I had had very little time or inclination to be with my own two children, let alone John! I had had to forego various church activities during the week and had even skipped Sunday services. As for my quiet times for prayer and Bible reading! Impossible! This had all happened a long time earlier: at great cost, when I had for a few years forgotten all about God and gone my own way. I knew that it was not right for the most important aspect of my life, to be squeezed out for full-time teaching.

That summer we enjoyed a superb holiday on the Istrian peninsula of Yugoslavia. The scenery was breathtaking. The rocky coastline was such a contrast to the large open sandy beaches of Menorca. We had to wear plastic shoes to avoid the prickly sea-urchins and the stony shore. In fact, most of our swimming was in deep water. The children loved jumping off the rocky headlands into really deep sea. Fortunately, they were both good swimmers. I was much happier when I knew that I could touch the bottom!

We stayed in a post world war two hotel on the small secluded island of Katarina, overlooking the old fishing port of Rovinj. By western standards the hotel was rather run down, but yet there was a certain charm and character about it. The hotel and indeed the entire island were scheduled for redevelopment in the near future. We had already visited a smaller island, where the accommodation looked more lavish. I hated its gleaming facade: it could have been anywhere. I recall thinking how sad it would be if Katarina were to be redeveloped. To my mind, its beauty would be spoilt.

During our holiday we visited Venice, a five hour coach journey away. The gondola trip was absolutely magic. Unfortunately, the heat and the crowds were too intense for comfortably enjoying the remainder of the itinerary. All the same, John and I were very impressed. My most treasured memory was the sight of Thomas (then aged eight) kneeling in prayer in St. Mark's Basilica. On that beautiful August day in 1990, during the return journey from Venice: we listened incredulously as our guide spoke gravely of the possibilities of civil war erupting in Yugoslavia.

Our final and most vivid memory of that special holiday, was of a huge firework display. It was the most elaborate that we had ever witnessed. It took place across the harbour at Rovinj. Thomas, who hated fireworks, slept solidly through it all. Quite amazing: considering that the deafening noise-level brought to my mind the terrible sounds of warfare. Tragically, as our guide had predicted, Yugoslavia was to become a savage and very bloody battlefield, within less than a year.

Chapter 17
Difficult Years

In the autumn of 1990, I delighted in once more having time to myself. Charlotte settled quickly into life at The Middlecott School, Kirton. From being taken absolutely everywhere by me: she was suddenly plunged into the deep end of secondary school life. Having an August birthday, she had always been one of the youngest in her year and so had only just turned eleven. Whereas, most of her peers were quite a few months older and unlike Charlotte, they all had older siblings.

During that first term, she rose early, being usually out of the house by 8.15am. She made friends with a wide age-range of pupils and seemed quite happy. As Charlotte already played in Kirton Brass Band, she automatically joined the school band and was eligible for peripatetic music teaching with her tenor horn. To my way of thinking, it made her an integrated member of the school from early on. I recognised this as a definite plus. Always the over anxious parent-teacher, I was extremely zealous in checking her homework. Initially, Charlotte was keen to take up my offer to help with her French. We used to practise conversation and she willingly spent time on vocabulary testing. I enjoyed helping her. Obviously, I hoped that she too would develop an avid interest in French.

In the following summer, Charlotte started confirmation classes. In a sense I knew that she was too young but as she already served at Communion, it seemed a natural progression. Our vicar Neil Russell, was of the opinion that even if youngsters stopped attending church as countless teenagers do: having already been confirmed, it makes it far easier to return in later life.

Neil had also broached the subject of confirmation to my mother and she joined the adult confirmation class. Mum always kept her inner beliefs to herself, so we had never talked easily about our personal faith. Since our move to Kirton, Mum had been able to spend more time with us. She had been extremely supportive of John in his new role. Mum had become part of the regular congregation at

Frampton. She was very gifted at sewing and had joined the kneeler group. They were gradually replacing all the church kneelers, with new ones embroidered with flowers mentioned in the Bible.

It was a most moving occasion: to witness my mother and my daughter being confirmed by the Bishop of Lincoln, The Right Revd. Robert Hardy. It meant so much and I shed tears of joy, watching my mother kneel before the Bishop. Prayers of many years were answered for me on that Sunday.

Supply-work continued at a fairly gentle pace. The early morning calls were unwelcome though. Very often I would awaken early 'on edge' praying that I would not be called in. I usually rallied round at short notice but occasionally I declined. I still covered for pre-arranged absences and was much happier liaising with the teacher and organising a proper programme of work. The National Curriculum now meant that time was at a premium and the normal timetable had to be followed. This was much better for the children and I found it more worthwhile. I always enjoyed the contact with the staff and the one-to-one relationship with pupils. I did like some aspects of being in the classroom. I know that if I had been teaching French, I would have been far more enthusiastic. On the other hand, when I was being swamped by umpteen young children, all demanding spellings for story writing: then it all became far too tedious and I would long to be back home cleaning up, albeit that I loathe housework!

Irrespective of whether I had enjoyed a good teaching day or not: I hated having to go home to start preparing a meal. Due to the effect on my temper, John would say, 'It's not worth it, you might as well stop. We don't need the money.' I ignored his advice, because I did enjoy having my own pay cheque. It all went very nicely towards our foreign holidays. Most importantly, it was fulfilling my need to have some measure of independence: something to take my mind off family and domesticity.

Since John's Romanian trip, he had gained much local publicity and had become somewhat of a hero. As well as his Reader training with its regular study days and time spent on practical work in our church services: John also gave talks and slide presentations on

Romania. He was inundated by requests from churches, schools, youth groups, W.I., Rotary, Lions, etc.

His charity involvement was to be recognised in the spring of 1991. On 22nd March, Lincolnshire Police awarded John the Harold Chappell Rose Bowl, in recognition of his outstanding work for the community. His parents and I, attended the award ceremony at Police Headquarters, Nettleham. It was such a proud occasion. I was thrilled. At long last the work that John found most rewarding (his voluntary unpaid work) was being publicly recognised.

John and I, had of course heard a great deal about children becoming rebellious, once they reached secondary school. Rather naïvely, I certainly never expected to experience it. Once Charlotte's first term at Middlecott was over, the problems began. The first sign of her rebellion was the change in her attitude towards church. No longer wishing to attend, she became most concerned as to what her friends would say about her involvement. Comments such as: 'church is crap,' 'you and Dad are Bible-bashers,' 'you've changed Dad,' 'it's all your fault;' became part of her daily conversation. I found it very hard to bear; my own daughter saying such hurtful things about us and our Christian faith.

Setting off for church with Charlotte became a ridiculous farce. Very often the three of us would be sat ready in the car waiting for her. It often resulted in John putting her in the car! Hardly the right mood to go to church in! By summer, we realised that forcing her, was definitely wrong; but the alternative of none of us going, would also be wrong. Reluctantly, we agreed to her staying on her own. Indeed it was the first time that she had ever been left alone by us. It was upsetting the first time that we did this and of course everyone missed her. Yet, I soon adjusted to going out without the unpleasant hassle and put it down to something she had to go through.

I could well recall my own decision to stop going to Bible Class not long after I had started secondary school (though, I only stayed away for a couple of months). More significantly, there had been the time in my twenties; when for years God was pushed right out of my life. Therefore I knew, that it was not necessarily the end of her involvement.

At Christmas 1990, we had bought Charlotte a hairdryer with a diffuser attachment. Until then, she had shown only a moderate interest in styling hair. From then on, her hair became a time consuming obsession. I had never bothered about doing my own hair, merely having it permed, so that very lazily, I could wash it and go! To me, messing about with hair was a real bore. I simply could not see the appeal. Another bone of contention between us was beginning to surface. Whereas, Charlotte's hair had to be laboriously styled before she would leave the house. Very soon, she would be rising at 6.30am, to start the elaborate ritual before going to school at 8.30am.

In July 1991, John and I attended the end of term parents' evening. What a shock, to discover that her overall report was very poor. Most of the teachers said of Charlotte, 'Lots of ability but wastes her time!' She was frequently messing about in certain lessons and not giving her best. It was pointed out to us that her choice of friends was also rather dubious. We were both furious. It was a real kick in the teeth. I just could not believe that my own daughter was turning into the sort of pupil that I could not have tolerated. We hoped and prayed that Charlotte would settle down after the summer.

By the autumn of 1991, we were well established into our second year of the Bishop's Course. Although I always intended to tackle the recommended reading list, somehow I never did. I hardly found time to read, apart from an occasional Christian paperback, or a children's book.

John was frequently buying theology books for his studies. On one of his book buying sessions, John brought home, Lyn Ellis's book 'I Didn't have Cancer For Nothing.' Since moving to Boston, I had been vaguely aware of her fund-raising activities for DOCATEF (Detection Of Cancer And Treatment Equipment Fund) and had seen her picture in the newspaper on numerous occasions. John read it and recommended that I should also. I put it on the bookshelf. There was no way that I wanted to read about someone's experiences of cancer. I could successfully blot out my own painful memories of losing Dad, most of the time. Yet when they were allowed breathing space, it was too distressing. I did not want reminding of Dad's suffering, of his untimely death and of all the regrets... Somehow, curiosity overcame my reluctance. Once I began her book, I found it to be such compelling reading. Instead of being upset, I was simply filled with admiration for the way that Lyn Ellis had battled against cancer for so long. Sadly, by the time that I read her book, Lyn had died.

At a similar time: I happened to read an article in our local newspaper, entitled, 'Cancer Of The Mouth And Throat.' It mentioned that heavy drinking, (especially of strong spirits) and smoking were the most common causes of this type of cancer. Apart from an occasional glass of wine, I did not drink or smoke. I read on totally unperturbed. As well as listing the obvious things to avoid, the article developed the idea that any weakness in the tissues of the mouth, could lead to cell irregularities and subsequently to the development of cancerous cells. I literally, went icy cold with fear. Instantly, alarm bells had begun to ring.

My obstinacy as a child, in refusing to abandon my thumb-sucking habit: had resulted in prominent upper teeth, which had made deep indentations in my lower lip. I had always been acutely self-conscious of this blemish. Could this be a weakness? The article terrified me. For a few weeks it really preyed on my mind, though I never mentioned it to anyone. Then, it just seemed to fade completely from memory and I never thought of it again.

During the spring of 1991, everything seemed to focus on preparations for the next trip to Romania. This was to take place at Easter, for two weeks. Virtually, all John's spare time was spent in giving talks, fund-raising and nearer the time, in collecting goods. John contacted Chris Cook, (my ex-pupil from Woad Farm School) who played for Boston United. Chris very kindly donated a full football strip and some footballs. It was lovely to see my ex-pupil again. The children even collected his autograph.

John launched an appeal with local schools, for small chocolate cream eggs. He thought it would be appropriate to take them as small Easter gifts. Our hall, one of the coolest places in our home, became full of boxes of chocolate eggs (Approximately 2,400)!

I have already explained how I fully supported John in this work. However by the last week, the children and I were beginning to feel the strain and to resent the intrusion. John's involvement with

Romania had taken over our lives. Meal-times were constantly interrupted. Answering the telephone gave my non-existent secretarial skills ample time to improve!

Instead of resting up in preparation for the gruelling long journey (a 4000 mile round trip): John was flying round sorting out numerous crises and unavoidable last minute details. Consequently, he was shattered before the journey had even begun!

With the visit being in the Easter holidays, I experienced the strain of John being away, far more than previously. This time, the children were at home: whereas before, we had all been at school and I was far too busy with teaching to do much thinking. In addition, Charlotte was now in her difficult phase.

My dear friend Maureen Edenbrow, had an insight into what I was going through. On Easter Saturday, she rang up to say that she and her Mum felt that the children and I were in need of prayer support; for we were the ones left at home. In comparison, John had been swamped with so much attention and publicity: everything had focused on him and his visit. I was very touched by Maureen's deep concern.

It was only after John's return that my true feelings surfaced. I sank to an extremely low, quite depressed state of mind. Apart from a few friends praying for us and of course Mum's unceasing support, I had felt terribly alone and very vulnerable. With it being holiday time, everyone was involved with their families. It had been a most difficult time for me. In spite of telling John how I had felt: he could not fully comprehend what I had gone through, or what I continued to feel.

One Friday, shortly after John's return, we held our Bishop's Course meeting at John Duckett's. Against a background of soothing classical music; we were spending time in quiet, contemplative prayer. In spite of being amongst some dear friends, I was in a very subdued mood. Charlotte and I had rowed at dinner. Suddenly, sat in that peaceful candlelit room, I was overcome by floods of tears and had to leave the room. Jayne Featherstone came to find me and I poured it all out. I felt so much better for offloading to her: Jayne was a great comfort. By the time the rest of the group were drinking coffee, I was able to rejoin them without feeling embarrassed.

Sensing that they were truly concerned; I realised how wrong that I had been to even think that I had been on my own and that people did not care. I felt ashamed of myself.

After their fourth visit, 'Romania Project UK' realised that long-term aid, ought to be the next step, rather than continuous convoys. Valuable contacts had already been made with both Pilgrim and Lincoln County Hospitals. They had supplied a considerable amount of redundant medical equipment. In June 1991, the authorities at Pilgrim Hospital, agreed to provide training and accommodation for a Romanian doctor, for a period of three months.

During May half-term, John and I escaped to France, for a five day stay at Di and Ian's cottage, in the tiny hamlet of Désertines, Normandy. Their offer of free accommodation had been ours for some time. We had never taken our car abroad before, so I was most apprehensive. It was a fantastic holiday, a second honeymoon! Désertines, was in such a quiet but very pretty rural area. It was great to escape the hustle and bustle of ordinary life. The weather was glorious, enabling us to spend hours cycling round the country lanes. It was really idyllic.

The highlight for me, was returning to France after thirteen years' absence. For once, I could not take my usual easy way out and allow John to do all the talking. John had only a limited command of spoken French. Therefore, I was the one to do most of the conversing, whilst he became the listener! We found the locals extremely friendly. The proprietor of the village bar, spoke very little English, so I acted as interpreter. The experience boosted my ego, especially after being so dispirited, a few weeks earlier. John and I even managed to communicate with the elderly neighbour, whom Di and Ian had not really met. We were invited to drink coffee and cognac with her. She was an incredibly ancient lady, toothless and with a strong regional accent; which caused me some problems in understanding. Nevertheless, I managed to converse with her. We were thrilled to have been welcomed into her cottage. We returned from France, quite determined to return the following year.

In August, we made a wonderful return to Santo Tomas in Menorca. After two excellent holidays in October of 1988 and 1989; we obviously found it much hotter and busier, to be there in peak season. All the same, it was a lovely holiday. Halfway through our stay, Charlotte developed an awful prickly heat rash. Two days before our return, she had sickness and diarrhoea. She was very poorly and we had to call in the local doctor. I treasured the time that I spent at Charlotte's bedside. It was a welcome return to our former closeness. Of course, once she was better, we were back to the tension and conflict that had almost become a daily occurrence.

A few days after our arrival home, a Romanian student, Monica Cotoranu, came to stay. John had met Monica and her family on his last visit there. Her parents were both doctors and she was also hoping to follow this profession. Dan, Monica's father, had agreed to find a suitable Romanian doctor, to take up the attachment at Pilgrim Hospital.

That autumn, the nine of us who had just completed our two year Bishop's Course; met up in the hope of working out some sort of follow-up. We had learned so much together but most valuable of all, was the bond that had been formed. We did not want this to end. By then, John Duckett and Dr. Joan Butterfield, had become very good friends. It seemed as if our group had brought them together. Joan had been involved in the production of the course material and we had been the guinea-pigs. We never continued our studies but the friendships continued. That harvest, John Duckett was due to take an evening service at St. Mary's. We all took part and thoroughly enjoyed working together as a team. There was a tremendous feeling of oneness.

Later on that term, we shared a quiet day at Edenham Vicarage, led by Joan Butterfield. By then, John and Joan had announced their engagement. We were all looking forward to their wedding the following spring. Joan asked us to bring before God, all the people who had made an impact on our lives: those from our past that possibly we no longer had contact with; following it through to those we held dear at the present time. I found it a very challenging exercise spiritually. There were so many people that I had to thank God for. Our final activity together as an established group was in November 1991; when the nine of us travelled by minibus to attend a day conference at Lincoln, during which we were presented with our certificates by the Bishop of Lincoln, The Right Revd. Robert Hardy.

By the start of her second year, Charlotte, who had just turned twelve, showed no signs of improvement. From talking to others: it seemed that we were experiencing an extreme case of adolescent rebellion but at a much earlier stage. At home, her behaviour and language became more outrageous and more abusive.

During that autumn term I worried myself silly over her music. Charlotte, no longer wanted to play in the school band and that would mean she would lose her peripatetic teaching. I could not bear the thought of her giving up on something, that she had shown such a talent for. After weeks of anxiety on my part, she dropped the school band. However, she did persevere with Kirton Brass Band, for one more year; before all musical involvement ceased.

No sooner had I calmed down once the music problem had been resolved: when something else occurred. There was a problem with one of her teachers. Initially, we ignored her complaints. With her past record, it was more than likely to be her fault. In discussion with other pupils, I realised that there were grounds for complaint. We did try to resolve the matter by going into school. The situation was closely monitored but it resulted in an even more unpleasant atmosphere at home. Charlotte under considerable stress, vented her anger on us.

It was a nightmare of a year. I literally, lurched from one crisis to another. It was one long battle. I used to breathe a sigh of relief when Charlotte left for school. By mid-afternoon, I would start to dread her return. To say that life between us was hell, was no exaggeration.

I have always been a worrier. Hence, my skinny frame: being able to eat whatsoever I like, without putting on weight. Always the sort of person to foresee problems, before they have even materialised! Fretting about Charlotte became my obsession. John was obviously affected but less intensely. He was the sort of person who could switch off and relax more easily. Besides, he was at work and away from it. I often used to think, that if I had more outside work or interests, it might be healthier. Local friends from church were extremely good listeners and very concerned. Yet, it must have been very wearing for them, to always hear the same thing.

I continued to do the odd day of supply teaching. On at least one occasion, I declined work when contacted early morning. On my next day in school; I explained to the deputy head that home circumstances were stressful. Unexpectedly, she very sympathetically assured me that I was not letting them down. I could simply once again, be on the list for pre-arranged work. That was a huge weight off my shoulders. How relieved I was that I had been honest with school.

Chapter 18
Problems

During the early part of 1992, I was to undergo the blackest period of my life. My obsession with Charlotte, had left me completely drained and utterly demoralised. I could see no way out and that was so frightening. As a mother, I felt a total failure. As a teacher, it grieved me, knowing that Charlotte was not working hard at school. All the pressure that I had foolishly applied, had simply been counter-productive. Even so, I still found it nigh impossible not to interfere and have my say. The extreme dejection that I had endured almost a year earlier; on John's return from Romania, had resurfaced. This time was far worse. I was at rock-bottom; oppressed by many negative emotions: the most painful being those of utter despair and of my worthlessness.

I was generally bored with the monotony of daily life; spending most of it at home, bogged down by loathsome housework. I perceived that there should be more to my life than there was. I accepted that it had been right for me to concentrate on my own family rather than develop my teaching career. Yet somehow, it all seemed to have backfired on me and I did feel resentment. How I wished that I could abandon everything and everyone and just 'be myself'. Sometimes, the pain of failure weighed so heavily that I longed to die. I wanted to be with God.

On one occasion with Neil, I discussed my need for some sort of identity, other than that of wife and mother. Apart from a few hours of very occasional supply teaching: I only seemed to do oddments. It vexed me to think that I was simply regarded as John's wife, rather than as a person in my own right. Neil assured me that although that might have been true once, it was no longer the case. He thought that teaching was not my forte. Instead, he suggested that possibly something such as M.U. might be more appropriate. I could not see that happening. I had not the initiative to do anything other than what I had always done. How could I tackle something new? I was not sufficiently resourceful.

That February, I suffered two unpleasant 'flooding' occurrences during my period. This had never happened before and I was alarmed. An examination revealed that everything was in order. It was a great relief. However, I did begin to wonder if I was alright physically. I seemed to be permanently exhausted. Surely, this was only to be expected, considering my troubled mental state!

In May, still uneasy about my health, I decided to pursue the health checks further. My main concern was to discover if I had an over-active thyroid gland causing an excessive level of anxiety. The test proved negative. I also had tests on my blood, blood pressure and cholesterol level. My weight and height were also checked. As expected, my weight was much lower than it should be for my height. However, there were no health problems to be concerned over. So back to battle-stations!

May, my birth month, has always been my favourite month of the year and with the warmer weather, I began to feel less gloomy. At the end of May, after lengthy negotiations, Dr. Adrian Cozma finally arrived, for his three- month attachment at Pilgrim Hospital. Dr. Cozma, a bachelor in his early thirties, was a good friend of Dan Cotoranu. John collected him from Stansted Airport and he joined us for lunch. Dr. Cozma spoke excellent English. We warmed to him immediately. With a stranger at table, the children, for once behaved impeccably and we enjoyed a most civilised lunch.

During the summer, Adrian became a regular visitor to our home. As a Christian, he was keen to join us at church, especially when John was taking part in the service. John and he got on so well together and I grew extremely fond of him. The children soon relaxed and were their normal selves. Indeed, Adrian became such a close part of our family life, that he soon experienced at first hand, some of our problems. On numerous occasions, he tried to reassure me by saying that it was only a phase and that Charlotte would grow out of it.

Thus, from June onwards, John became a regular visitor to Pilgrim Hospital, as he chauffeured Adrian to and fro. Naturally, he socialised with Adrian in the Social Club and became acquainted with some of the doctors and other members of the hospital staff.

Probably from late May (though on this I cannot be certain): I became aware of a slight soreness in my throat and I sensed that the right edge of my tongue seemed rather strange, even possibly sore! It felt unlike anything that I had previously ever known. Amazingly, it never occurred to me to look in my mouth. I merely thought, *I'll have to get it checked up some time. I can't be bothering about it at the moment. I haven't the time.* Though by now, I could no longer drink pure orange juice or eat fresh grapefruit (which normally I consumed regularly): as they aggravated the feeling of tenderness that I was now far more conscious of. I simply dismissed it and lived with the slight discomfort. After all, I was burdened by far more worrying concerns than my mouth.

I remember thinking, *this is probably how the tip of John's tongue feels like.* The nerve endings in John's tongue were irreparably damaged when his wisdom teeth were extracted in May 1980. Although, he had seen a consultant in London, nothing could be done. Hence, he had lived with the sensation of a permanently sore tongue tip, for years.

By the time that we were holidaying in Portugal in early August; the discomfort in my mouth was much worse and I had to make a conscious effort to eat and drink on the left side. On holiday I was obviously drinking sharper, more refreshing soft drinks and far less tea and coffee, than I normally consume at home. Again, I just thought, *what a bind, suppose I'll have to see the doctor about it sometime.*

Summer holidays, far away from home; provide me with valuable space for reflection: usually done while lazing in warm water. For me, the main ingredient to my annual holiday, is the availability of good swimming facilities. If I cannot swim daily, I suffer withdrawal symptoms! That summer, I had bought a copy of Paris Match. Keeping up my French reading was another holiday ritual. This edition featured the atrocities that had recently been exposed in the Yugoslavian concentration camps. Afterwards, I found it hard to switch off from such disturbing news, probably because two years earlier, we had enjoyed a holiday in Yugoslavia. To see pictures of such unimaginable horror, in a country we had visited, was really shocking.

In contrast, my life, (excluding the continuing daughter problem) seemed to be ticking over quite comfortably. I could look forward to John being licensed as a Reader the following April. I still marvelled at that amazing happening and the way so many blessings had happened to us since our move to Kirton. Personally, I could envisage another year of muddling along, with no specific role: doing a few hours of teaching, Sunday School work, occasionally reading the lesson or leading the prayers in church. I was also responsible for compiling the prayers for our monthly M.U. service. In addition, I was a member of three committees, all of which, I was beginning to tire. In the main I was satisfied to be supporting John in his developing ministry and our family life, by being at home. Yet part of me experienced discontentment at my lack of personal development. May be low esteem, was at the root of the depression that I languished under occasionally.

Returning from Portugal, we learned that parish life was about to change drastically. The Revd. Neil Russell was to move to Stamford, the following January. This was a terrible shock. As well as being a likeable and approachable priest; he had become a very supportive friend. I knew how much John and I would miss him.

At the end of August, Pilgrim Hospital agreed to an extension of Adrian's attachment. He could stay for a further two months. Adrian wanted to take the P.L.A.B. test (Professional and Linguistics Assessment Board), an entrance exam for foreign doctors. If he passed, he could then do practical work, instead of mere observation and study. This could enable him to work in Britain for a further period. We hoped that this would materialise, to be of benefit to Adrian and those in Romania.

Chapter 19
'It's Nothing Sinister'

Two days after Charlotte's thirteenth birthday (when we had spent an exhilarating time ice-skating); John was preparing for an afternoon shift. It was Wednesday 19th August. I happened to mention that my tongue felt sore. Until then, John had absolutely no inkling that there was anything wrong with my mouth: I had kept it completely to myself. John asked me to stick my tongue out so that he could take a look. In some surprise he exclaimed, **'What's that on the side of your tongue? It's a sort of mouth ulcer!'**

In absolute disbelief I gaped at what met my eyes. I saw a nasty ulcerous patch on the right side of my tongue. It was no tiny white pinhead of a single ulcer but an extensive area of white and red inflamed ugliness: extending along the right tongue edge for about two centimetres. There was a development inwards at its widest point of probably two centimetres. In fact the side of the tongue had a horrible 'eaten away appearance' and there was the beginning of an indentation away from the edge inwards. It looked vile.

I had never experienced any mouth ulcers before and could not believe what I was seeing. *How on earth could I have overlooked this...? But then I was unaccustomed to inspecting my tongue!* Just as well that we had examined it today. The soreness of the past few months all fitted into place.

My feelings at that point were of extreme resentment at the sheer inconvenience that this would cause. Now, I would have to see the doctor! I was also extremely disgusted at myself for being so negligent, as to allow something so startling escape my notice. There was no real anxiety. John and the children were the only ones who knew about my tongue. I thought that if I ignored it and or prayed about it, then it would go away. However, the following morning, my tongue still looked hideous. I obviously could not deny the situation. Two days later, I saw my G.P. Dr. Peter Luck. He thought that it was probably caused by teeth erosion because part of the tongue did appear to have been slightly worn away. He prescribed cream to treat the soreness and referred me to my dentist.

During my walk from the doctor to the dentist, on that lovely hot August morning; a brief sensation of cold foreboding gripped me momentarily and I shivered. A couple of minutes later, I was talking to the dental receptionist. By now the unwelcome feeling had been dismissed from my mind as quickly as it had appeared. After all, I had been in tight corners before, when things had looked serious. Yet, God had constantly provided me with a way out. He would not let anything bad happen to me. He would always intervene.

The dentist I preferred to see, had restricted working hours at Kirton and the dental receptionist could only offer me an appointment in five weeks' time. When I explained the situation, she slotted me in, before 9am on Thursday 3rd September.

Two weeks later I saw the dentist. I recall sighing deeply with relief at her words, 'It's nothing sinister.' I suddenly felt as if a weight that I had not even been consciously carrying, had been lifted from me. She asked if I had been under some sort of stress, because in her experience stress often showed itself in the mouth, in the guise of ulcers. I mentioned that things had been very difficult for a long time with my daughter. Along with Dr. Luck, she thought that my back teeth had eroded my tongue. These she smoothed down. She also commented that to her, it looked as if I had bitten my tongue. An appointment was made for two weeks.

In that time it did not improve. My throat and tongue were feeling quite tender, and at times it was painful to eat. I had to stop eating things like toast and biscuits. My throat seemed very dry and I was having to drink more. It felt as if there was something at the back of my throat. It also hurt to talk for long.

On Thursday 17th September, it was not at all surprising that the dentist found no real improvement. Some of the redness had gone, making it look less inflamed but that was all. From this, she thought that referral to Mr. Glendinning, the Consultant Oral Surgeon was necessary. I waited while the hospital was contacted and an appointment made for the following morning.

The letter I took with me was for Mr. Glendinning but instead I saw his deputy, the Associate Specialist. He repeated exactly what the dentist had said, 'It's nothing sinister.' Again, I breathed an even deeper sign of relief and felt doubly reassured. He thought that the severe ulceration of my tongue had probably been caused by tooth erosion, or by being bitten. He also wondered whether grinding of my teeth had contributed to its condition. Trauma which may have been caused years earlier. He prescribed a sort of clear plastic gum shield, called a 'cover splint', to be worn at night and to fit over my bottom teeth to protect my tongue. It would also enable the tongue to heal; though he stressed that any improvement would be very gradual. He advised me to use a mouthwash for greater oral hygiene. Before I left, a plaster cast impression was taken of my bottom teeth.

I returned on Monday 21st September, to collect the awful contraption. This time I saw someone else: dentist Mrs. Tamara Good. As soon as the clear plastic mould had been fitted over my bottom teeth, I just wanted to throw up! It was horrible. A bacteriological swab was also taken from my tongue's surface. Mrs. Good instructed me to return in two weeks, after I had mastered wearing it at night. That date happened to coincide with the start of a week's teaching: for in July, the school secretary had telephoned, to offer me a set of dates for one class. I eagerly accepted, knowing that it would be much more worthwhile to work with one specific class, rather than a variety, as I usually did. John had commented that he did not think that I intended to do further supply work. I assured him that I wanted to do this particular stint.

Having fixed an appointment to return in three weeks; I drove home most unhappily. How on earth was I going to wear the wretched thing for a few minutes, let alone sleep in it? At least I had three weeks' grace.

In my usual dilatory fashion, I let a couple of days pass before I even ventured to try the cover splint. Again, my mouth watered and I began to retch. After a few feeble attempts, I managed to keep it in for a minute. This I built up very gradually over the next few days. After a week, I could tolerate it for roughly an hour. I experimented when alone, while busy doing housework. By the end of the second week, I was wearing it for approximately three hours daily. I never slept with it in, until exactly one week before my next hospital appointment: when I knew that I could procrastinate no longer. Much to my relief, I managed this successfully. Apart from John and the children, no one was aware of any of this. I had not even bothered Mum, which was unusual because I rarely kept anything from her.

The Sunday before my week of teaching commenced; I had a hurried few words with Neil, after the service; before rushing off to organise lunch. I asked him for his prayer support. I would need it to survive a solid week's teaching, especially now that I had this 'sore throat'. Accustomed to teaching at maximum, three days consecutively: I knew that I was in for an exhausting week at school; along with the more stressful demands of family life. John was not at all happy. He knew how bad-tempered I would be. My sore throat had bothered me as to how I could sustain a week of constantly talking; so Dr. Luck had prescribed a throat spray. It was never used.

Unexpectedly, the week's teaching went superbly well. The children were very pleasant and I was glad to be teaching them. Most significantly, it gave me something else to focus on, rather than on the same tedious concerns. How delightful to be back in the staff-room and renew acquaintances, having worked one solid term there, two years previously. Ann Pilbeam, who also worships at St. Mary's, queried how it was going. I blurted out almost in tears, 'I'm really enjoying this week but it's hell at home with Charlotte.' We exchanged words about problems with daughters before dashing off to afternoon school.

On the Friday, as I said goodbye to the class, I was actually looking forward to teaching them again. I had dates fixed for three Wednesdays, in October and November: as well as some days the following spring. One of the girls gave me a 'smiley face' painting, which I pinned on my notice-board at home.

Ahead of us, was the prospect of an enjoyable weekend away. We travelled to Bicester, to stop with my old school friend Di (Diana) Pettifer, dropping the children off en route, with their friends in Lincoln. Thus, benefiting from a lovely child-free weekend, with welcome stimulating conversation. What a tonic for us both.

On Monday 12th October we rose early. John was working an early shift from 7am to 3pm. As Mum was still away in Devon at my brother Alan's, I was using her car. Mum was due home the following day. I intended to visit her bungalow, after my 10.15am hospital appointment, to check on things. I had planned to go early for my appointment, so that I could park easily and was more than happy to kill time by reading.

For the second time that term, Charlotte played up about going to school. The first time had happened a month earlier and had resulted in my taking her and dumping her very angrily, at the school gates. John was sleeping after a night shift, so in an agitated state, I drove to his parents' house at Wyberton. We obviously talked about the problem and it was then that John's Mum made the startling comment, **'What Charlotte wants is a good hard shock!'** For once, John's Dad and I agreed on something. His idea was to send her away to boarding school. Even if we could have afforded to, it certainly was not my idea. Yes, she probably did need a good hard shock...but what?

On this occasion at 8.55am, the time Charlotte should have been at school; she was still fussing about her appearance and even tidying up her bedroom! All tactics designed to wind up her poor old Mum and they certainly worked! I was more uptight than she was about her lateness. Finally, I almost had to physically drag her out of the door and into Mum's orange Mini.

Thus, I was in Pilgrim car park at 9.15am. Much to everyone's amusement, I never go anywhere without my flask of coffee. I drank my coffee and tried to calm down but this second episode had badly flustered me. Once I had regained my composure, I went to main reception and started to read a new book which Neil had recently bought for me: a Christian psychiatrist's report, on parents in pain. I had read no further than the first two pages when I realised that it was not the sort of book to read in a public place. It was too upsetting for me. There I was, nearly in tears again and it would soon be time for my dental appointment.

By the time I saw Mrs. Good, I felt perfectly alright. I was very confident because I had mastered the cover splint. After an examination and her explanation that the swab had revealed nothing unusual: I then asked a few pertinent questions, which John had raised. One of these, being whether the white patches on the tongue edge, could be a fungal infection which had developed after erosion. Mrs. Good then decided that Mr. Glendinning should have a look. On seeing my tongue he exclaimed, 'That's nasty, I'd better have a tissue sample.' As the clinic was very quiet and staff were available, it was suggested that the biopsy be done there and then. It made sense to me.

Preparations seemed to take a considerable time. Mrs. Good administered local anaesthetic. Indeed, I chose to have a double dose, to make sure everything was suitably numbed. Right throughout, Val Thompson one of the dental nurses, chatted to me. She lived locally and I had previously only known her by sight. In fact we had a really good talk. I felt totally at ease and most relieved that Mr. Glendinning, the Consultant Oral Surgeon, had at last become involved. Now something more positive was being done.

I had excellent attention. The three or four people around me were wonderfully reassuring. One of them held my hand while Mr Glendinning took the sample. He seemed to be absolutely ages obtaining it and then had difficulty transferring it into the test-tube. The only time that I experienced a degree of concern, was when Val removed a swab of cotton wool from my mouth and I could see lots of my blood! With a list of instructions, in case the bleeding reoccurred and a request to return at 1.30pm on Wednesday, for the result; I drove straight home. By now I was feeling extremely woozy.

Once at home, the shock of what had just been done, hit me. Although in my naïvety, I did not associate a biopsy, with anything sinister. I was distressed because it had not been a pleasant experience. I knew that I was frightened, in case heavy bleeding started, or I passed out. I wanted someone with me but I did not know whom to contact. John was at work. Mum was away in Devon. I could not bother friends or neighbours. Suddenly I wept, as it struck me that I could not bear the thought of not seeing Thomas, my younger child (then aged ten) grow up. This thought soon passed. After all, I was bound to be disturbed, after such an unpleasant biopsy.

I fixed my attention on the latest problem; that of Charlotte being late for school. However, by John's return from work at 3pm, I was feeling very sorry for myself: the numbness was wearing off and it was so painful.

I was alone in the kitchen when Charlotte returned from school; all bright and breezy, such a contrast to her mood that morning. On seeing my woeful face, she asked what was wrong with me. Somewhat tearfully, I informed her. Immediately, came the question, **'It's not cancer is it, Mum?'** Totally confounded by such directness, I managed to utter automatically, **'Of course not.'** We just hugged. By now, we were both in tears. Mercifully, this went unnoticed by Thomas and John. Charlotte for all her faults, was extremely perceptive. She admitted that this had been on her mind, since the discovery of my ulcerated tongue in August.

Such thoughts were swiftly dismissed from my conscious mind. It was utterly ridiculous. That could not happen to me. I had encountered difficulties in the past. Yet, nothing really terrible had ever occurred. God had always been there and had sustained me. John and I never discussed the possibility of the biopsy result being cancer. It was too dreadful a subject to actually contemplate, let alone broach. Whether on a deeply sub-conscious plane, this unspoken fear existed, I cannot say.

The following day I was very miserable. My tongue was obviously very sore and I had very little appetite. Everything I ate or drank, had to be done on the left side of my mouth. I felt so lethargic. John was busy on the computer when Neil came round. It was on the pretext of returning John's books but he had really come to visit me after John had contacted him.

John was working a late shift, so at tea-time, Thomas and I collected Mum from the railway station. When she enquired how I was, I briefly mentioned my ulcerated tongue and the biopsy. Nothing more was said on the subject.

Later on that evening I visited a friend and neighbour, Margaret Barsley. It was one of the few times that I had really spoken at length to her. **'We all have our cross to bear,'** I glibly remarked to Margaret, after we had spent time discussing the heartache of bringing up a teenage daughter. Little did I realise that **'my cross'** would turn out to be something far more serious: that it would bring me to the lowest point of my life and that all my so-called problems, would be put firmly into perspective.

PART 3

Chapter 20
I.C.U.

John returned to Pilgrim at 6pm. He waited for two very long anxious hours, in the nurses' room on 2B. Michaela Smith, a friendly student nurse, plied him with cups of coffee. At 8pm I was apparently wheeled out of theatre into the Intensive Care Unit. I was covered in a foil blanket to maintain body heat, because after many hours of surgery my body had lost a considerable amount of heat. The surgeons had gone. There was no one to inform John of any results from surgery and he was left feeling extremely distraught. What were the results of the lymph node and thyroid examinations? Had the cancer spread? There were several questions he needed answering, in order to avoid another sleepless night!

At approximately 9pm he was allowed to see me. He was shown to my best side (my left) and observed the awful sight of the ventilator tube down my throat, which was heavily bandaged, in order to secure the tube. It appeared to John, that there were wires and tubes spread all over my body. He insisted on seeing the other side of me and was shocked to see the living tissue of the muscle pedicle, wrapped in what appeared to be a muslin type material and oozing with fresh blood. As he left the ward, the nursing staff apparently asked him if he was alright. He instinctively replied, 'Yes.' Once outside in the corridor, his legs nearly buckled under him, as he steadied himself against the wall, reflecting on what he had just seen.

Although still unconscious from the anaesthetic, once in I.C. my sedation began. This was administered by way of intravenous infusion (drip) and consisted of morphine for pain relief and a sedating agent to keep me unconscious and therefore immobile, while the ventilator was breathing for me.

Early on Thursday 29th October, sedation was stopped. This is usually done between 6am and 8am. I astonished the staff by coming round very quickly. At 9.20am I was taken off the ventilator. Dr. Chalmers the anaesthetist, had to be present, to disconnect it, in case of respiratory distress. My first recollection in my semi-conscious state, was of someone in dark clothing bending over me and a murmur of voices.

Momentarily, a tremendous feeling of utter relief flooded through me as I regained consciousness and realised, *I'm still alive, I've survived!* Then this euphoric feeling dissipated as speedily as it had come. For the grim reality of what I had awoken to, was utterly shocking. I lay there traumatised. I had not been prepared for this at all. I had simply had no real understanding of what it had all been about. In my worst nightmare I could not have envisaged anything so horrendous. Foolishly, I had thought that it would just be like coming round from my eye surgery: then it had seemed as if my head had been hammered unmercifully for hours. That was absolutely nothing in comparison to how I was suffering now.

From where I lay, propped up with five pillows beneath me, everything felt so strange and uncomfortable. I was vaguely aware of unfamiliar contraptions beside the bed. These being the drip stands, pumps, ventilator and an electrocardiograph. I had woken up to a totally bizarre world. Someone else lay where I should be. It felt as if an alien being had taken over my body. It was very unnerving.

Meanwhile, John had spent another dreadfully long, sleepless night. He was up very early and at 7.30am on that Thursday morning, he was having porridge with Neil and Kathy Russell at Frampton Vicarage. At 9am he had actually followed the surgeon into Pilgrim Hospital and had accompanied him up to I.C. John waited outside while the surgeon checked on my condition. He was then introduced to Dr. Chalmers who was responsible for me during my stay in I.C. This fact was something that I discovered at a much later stage. On that Thursday, I recall feeling slightly puzzled as to why Dr. Chalmers had visited me twice, whereas the surgeon had visited me only once.

I had not been conscious long, when the surgeon came to say how well the operation had gone. He informed me that mercifully the cancer had not spread into the right lymph node of my neck or the thyroid, so further surgery had been avoided. This really was no consolation to me at all. I just felt dreadfully shocked and so utterly miserable.

Then John arrived. The first thing that I recall him saying, was that my speech was not bad. Not bad! It was bloody dreadful. It sounded just as Christine had foretold: very slushy, like having a mouth full of gob-stoppers! Although it sounded so awful, I was aware that I could make myself understood. Indeed, I could communicate. Not that it made me feel any better.

John had very thoughtfully brought in my spectacles, so at least I could see more clearly what was going on. My bed was virtually opposite the nurses' station, allowing me to focus on that centre of activity. John informed me that Neil was outside and asked if I wanted to see him. I did not like to refuse but in truth it was all too much of an ordeal, having a friend see me in this state. Neil held my hand and spoke encouragingly, assuring me that he could understand what I was saying. That failed to console me. I was unresponsive. I was living a nightmare.

Later that day, John brought Mum to see me. Mum bless her, had that remarkable quality of appearing to take it all in her stride. She did not display any emotion. At something I mentioned, she asked John what I had said and I recall thinking crossly, *oh mother, that's not very tactful!* John had brought in a few cards and a long letter from Adrian Cozma. He seemed to think that I would be interested in such things. Interested! I could quite easily have slung them at him but I did not wish to hurt his feelings, so merely gave them a cursory glance. I could not feel interested in anything or anyone.

When Paul Elliott, a friend of John's in the Christian Police Association, rang to enquire how I was, the nurse asked me what I wanted her to say. I could not even be bothered to answer her. Pulling a dreadful face, I looked upward at the ceiling despairingly. She chose a tactful reply.

As I lay there in my numbed state of disbelief; I could not accept that my God would put me through something so terrible as this. God seemed far from me that day. I felt that I was in hell! How I hope and pray that I never have to experience anything so dreadful again. I do not think that I was consciously angry with God. I was so hurt and bewildered: almost a sense of being betrayed by having to really suffer in this manner. The physical discomfort was indescribable: not pain as such because I was constantly dosed with morphine. As dreadful as it was for me physically, the torment experienced in my mind and spirit was far worse.

I do not recall even trying to pray. I was too dispirited to even think of verbalising a prayer in my mind. Whether a terse, *God, get me through this, God. You've got to get me through this,* ever went through my conscious mind, I simply cannot recall.

With hindsight, I am certain that much must have been going on at a deeply sub-conscious level. I am sure that God was with me: giving me the necessary strength to endure this ordeal calmly, even though at the time He seemed so distant. After all, I was not freaking out in panic or sobbing hysterically. I was in control of my emotions. Doubtless, the morphine contributed partly to this state.

It was the chaplain's rest day. The Revd. Dennis Clark who was deputising for him, came to see me. I had never met him before but he knew John. It was too traumatic for me. For the first time since surgery, I shed a few tears and became upset at what he said. I could not bear to hear him speak of God loving me: or to hear him say that God would bring me through this ordeal. I could not accept such words of comfort, the way that I was feeling so abandoned. It was too much to stomach; even though I knew that in theory it was true. Here in Intensive Care, I could not believe those reassuring words.

I was attached to a variety of equipment. Drips were in both arms. One drip supplied me with a saline and glucose solution, along with other essential nutrients. The second drip contained morphine for pain relief. As in theatre, an electrocardiogram was still monitoring me. I had an oxygen mask over my mouth and nose, which thankfully did not bother me as much as I would have anticipated. Ever since a ghastly childhood experience at the school dentist, when a huge black mask was put over my face, I have had a phobia of face masks! Fortunately, this mask was lightweight and transparent. It was to assist my breathing until I was able to resume this independently.

It is impossible to convey in words, how awful I felt physically. I remember clearly that my throat was so tight and unbearable. How Thursday dragged! I endured a long miserable day. Unfortunately, I could see the clock. Time seemed to stand still. I had expected to sleep away some of the day but I was far too keyed up and of course propped up with five pillows; far too constrained!

I longed to be safe at home with my family. I thought of how I used to moan at the tedium of all those household chores. Now, I would have given anything to be at home and bodily able to do the cooking, washing up, and the vacuuming... All that seemed absolute bliss to what I was doing now. How I vowed that I would never ever grumble about doing such tasks again!!

The nurse who tended me during the morning and early afternoon was quietly spoken, very gentle and most kind. Checks on my temperature, pulse and blood pressure, were being done half-hourly at first and then gradually spaced out, as my day in I.C. progressed. My heart, urine and the oxygen level in my blood, were constantly being monitored. She obviously had to do for me what I was incapable of doing for myself: washing me, cleaning debris from my mouth and making me comfortable (ha! ha!). During those first few hours I was given a total of three units (1,050 millilitres) of blood. There were small drains near my wounds, where blood collected, which were emptied periodically. I recall my dismay when the nurse came to say goodbye to me. Although the other staff were very kind, I had become quite dependent on her.

When the physiotherapist visited the unit, she literally breezed past me saying, 'You're not talking are you!' Before I could manage some sort of reply, she had called hurriedly, 'Take some deep breaths,' and with that had gone. I was not at all impressed by this, because I had not got a clue what she was talking about.

My long miserable day was surpassed by an even longer and more agonising night, which seemed to last an eternity. I thought that I should go mad, watching the hands of that clock. Obviously I was still propped up with a mountain of pillows, which was hardly conducive to sleep. The reason for my sleeplessness, was that as well as being uncomfortable, I was far too tense about what was happening to me in I.C. Indeed, I was very frightened. My throat was so full of the large build-up of trapped secretions from my lungs, which during five hours of surgery were denied their normal outlet. I was too scared to fall asleep in case I choked! Since coming round from anaesthesia, I had needed to have suction applied to the back of my throat, to clear away this build-up of mucus. The first few times a long tube was put to the back of my throat, was such a dreadful experience. It almost made me vomit. I was also very concerned about my left eye. Under such stressful conditions, could my squint re-occur? I could not bear that. Therefore, I wore my spectacles the entire night.

Staff nurse Sarah McKown tended me during the night. She was so friendly and comforting. I felt more safe and reassured when she was there. That night, I listened to the nurses' gossip. Sarah had offered to move me to a quieter part of the ward; away from the hustle and bustle of the nurses' station but I preferred to stay where I could see and be seen! I had a handbell to ring and this I used frequently during that long night. In the end it gave me something to do! I became very hot and bothered, so they rigged up a fan for me but then it was not long before I felt cold. So the night progressed.

On one occasion during the night Sarah was unavailable to do the throat suction for me. A rather unfriendly relief nurse wanted me to do this for myself. There was no way that I could push a tube into the back of my throat. Rather grudgingly she took over. I was disgusted at her cold manner and was most relieved when Sarah returned. Though, however unpleasant the suction was, it was something that I had to get used to.

I think the worst thing about being in I.C. was the knowledge that I was so completely helpless and utterly vulnerable. I was trapped: a prisoner without any control over my body; fixed to a bed with a variety of attachments. I could not open my mouth. Moreover, my mouth was now full of metal. The surgeon had wired up my jaw. Miss Evans the Locum Associate Specialist, from the Oral Department, had inserted a metal arch bar in my mouth, after major surgery: to secure my broken jaw.

I also apparently had a pharyngostomy tube inserted into the left side of my neck, in readiness for subsequent feeding in a few days' time. Something else I had not bargained for! Staff wanted me to sip water through a straw. I had very little sensation at all, everything in the region of my mouth felt so numb, so grossly swollen and totally alien to me. It was impossible to swallow even a sip of water, the effort required was too much and it was painful to even try to swallow. Totally impossible!

Chapter 21
Back on 2B

What tremendous relief I experienced when Friday morning finally dawned. I knew that I should soon be returning to my own room. In preparation for my return, I was transferred to the end of I.C. opposite the exit. The oxygen mask was removed, for I no longer needed assistance with breathing.

That morning Jane Reams, a different physiotherapist visited me. She did not rush away like her colleague had done the previous day and I made sure that I understood exactly what she meant. I liked Jane immediately. She was very caring and most importantly, was so reassuring. Jane explained the necessity of breathing deeply from time to time, to expand the lungs and promote recovery. I had to breathe in deeply and hold my breath for five seconds, before expiring it. This was to be repeated twice. I then had to make a huffing sound in my throat before coughing and spitting to try and shift all the trapped mucus, which had accumulated during surgery. I was to do this every half-hour. I had to have my arms folded across my chest as I did this, to monitor my chest expansion. Jane stressed the importance of sipping to build up the reflex action of swallowing and to keep my throat moist. It was possible to take a tiny sip now, but it took ages to actually swallow it.

So from 10.30 onwards, I tried to put this breathing exercise into action. I dreaded doing it, because I knew that the awful mucus would rise up into my throat and mouth and have to be disposed of. Quite tricky with a swollen mouth, full of metal, which I could barely open! Jane had laughed at my initial huffing attempts. I certainly felt very foolish at times but it had to be done. I did not manage to do it every half-hour though (by Saturday 31st October, it was down to every hour and this ritual continued for days).

Michaela Smith, a student nurse, came to collect me. She had a lovely bubbly personality, just what I needed to help cheer me up. How wonderful it was to be wheeled back to 2B and my own room. Instantly, I felt so much brighter, once I was amongst all my cards, flowers and other personal things and of course back where there was a much livelier atmosphere. That really was the turning point. I began to feel positive again. I knew that I had survived the worst bit! Although I now realised very soberly, that it was going to be a very long, slow haul. Yet, I had already taken a few minute steps towards recovery. I had to trust that God was going to get me through the rest.

The surgeon visited that morning. He was pleased with my progress and instructed Michaela that the catheter could be removed. This was removed at 3pm. It was inserted before surgery to ensure an accurate record of urine loss to check against dehydration. From then on, the contents of the bedpan had to be measured. As I was not allowed out of bed, I had the delights of this apparatus! I was now able to press the buzzer if I needed anything and someone always came immediately. Everyone was so pleasant and extremely cheerful, which helped me enormously. Michaela was assigned to take special care of me for that first day back on the ward.

I continued to have morphine for pain relief. In I.C. it had been via a drip but once back on 2B it was administered by injection into a thigh muscle and it hurt! Obviously I was unable to take anything orally, because the pharyngostomy tube was not yet in use. The phlebotomist came to check my blood. It was tested daily in those early days.

During that day, Mum came to see me. In fact Mum visited most days. She never let her feelings show, but it must have been a terrible ordeal for her. Her oldest and dearest friend May Oglesbee was very poorly and Mum was very concerned for her. Usually, after visiting me, she went along to see 'Oggy'.

As in I.C. a nurse cleaned my mouth out with a pink sponge brush, to clear away the debris left after surgery. By Sunday, I was supposed to do this for myself every two hours. I remember feeling very surprised that they assumed that I could manage this task myself. Yet, it gave me something positive to do and though it took me a long time, I was at least doing something for myself. It took days to remove all the tiny fragments.

At about 5 o' clock that Friday evening the surgeon arrived to tell me that he had just received the results from the Pathology

Laboratory. The cancer had been completely removed, a clear margin was evident all round the tumour and there were no sinister side shoots to warrant further treatment. It felt strange, hearing this 'wonderful news'. Although I was obviously very relieved to hear it from the surgeon himself; since the operation, I had not given a single thought to the possibility that the cancer had not been completely removed. I remember thinking, *you're telling me something that God's been telling me all along; that I would be completely healed from the cancer.* Whereas John, from the time of my operation up to the time of hearing the results, had spent the most anxious time of his life! It confirmed my view, that it must be far worse to be the one looking on.

Later on that evening, John brought Charlotte and Thomas to visit me for the first time since surgery. I was being treated when they arrived, so John escorted them to the Day-Room. Thomas was apparently very upset, on entering the ward. While they were waiting, a very pretty young lady dressed in jeans and jumper, entered my room and greeted me very warmly, asking how I was. I was obviously supposed to know her but I did not recognise her. I responded as if I knew who she was. I have always had an excellent recall of names and faces but this time I had failed. When I explained that my children were waiting to see me, she said that she would return another day. I was left puzzling about her.

The children's first visit was quite distressing. Thomas, then only ten, hardly spoke and would not come near me. Though I did manage to catch hold of his hand briefly before he went. In contrast, Charlotte acted very cheerfully and was extremely chatty. Much later on, she admitted how she had hated visiting me in hospital and that she had forced herself to put on such a brave front. Indeed with the muscle pedicle and so much swelling to my right jaw and cheek, I must have looked quite monstrous. I later realised how difficult it must have been, especially for my children, to come and see me in such a hideous looking state.

Friday night back in my own room, proved to be another very long restless night. However difficult it was, it was not as bad as the night spent in I.C. I watched television until very late, hoping that I would be able to sleep but I could not. I was still too keyed up; too weak and dreadfully uncomfortable propped up with so many pillows. I needed frequent suction to my throat, which made it impossible to relax. I did not want to fall asleep with a throat full of mucus, fearing I might choke.

At about 9 o' clock on Saturday 31st October, I experienced the registrar's ward round for the first time. I found it to be a most intimidating experience: to have suddenly in my room, about half a dozen white coated young doctors, all focusing on me. I felt very much a spectacle; as I suppose I certainly was! One of the doctors seemed unusually friendly towards me. It came as a pleasant surprise when she introduced herself. Adrian Cozma had often spoken about her. She had been in the same staff residence block. That very tenuous link with Adrian was so comforting.

My neck drain was removed that morning. This had been to prevent blood collecting underneath the wound. I was allowed out of bed to use the commode. I recall how I tottered round to the other side of the bed, feeling very weak and wobbly. My drip had to be manoeuvred very carefully on its stand. I also realised that I had an additional problem to cope with. It was not trauma from the catheter; my period had started early. As if I had not enough to contend with!

That Saturday, feeding started. The tube in my neck was connected to a cylinder of pale coffee coloured feed, Osmolite: a high protein and high calorie liquid food. Later on during my stay, I progressed to Ensure Plus, which had a much higher calorific value but was far too rich to begin with. I was fed for eight hours and then had a four-hour break. At first, I had fifty millilitres per hour and this gradually increased to seventy-five millilitres hourly. By Monday 2nd November, it had increased to one hundred millilitres hourly. This made using the commode even more of a manoeuvre! Just as well that I could not taste what I was having, it looked very yukky to say the least. Nevertheless, I was relieved to have progressed to this stage. My last proper meal of Tuesday tea-time seemed a life-time away. My stomach was so empty.

Once the feed became properly established, my hunger pangs very gradually diminished. An unfortunate side effect, was the feeling of nausea that I experienced in the early days. This, in conjunction with the hollow feeling in my stomach and the trapped mucus in my throat, was extremely unpleasant. Injections were given for immediate relief of nausea but it never took it away completely. It was something else to endure.

On the second night of being on the feed (Sunday 1st November) I had actually been asleep, when I suddenly woke up feeling very nauseous. An injection was swiftly administered and I settled down again. The only occasion that I actually vomited, was one afternoon during that first week. I was doing my mucus shifting, when I felt the need to vomit. Of course, I could not open my mouth. It was a nasty experience and I panicked. Fortunately, that was the only time. From then on, I always had a vomit tray and tissues to hand.

The feeding machine would emit an ear-piercing sound when empty and occasionally at other times. It seemed very temperamental. There was often a problem with trapped air and off it would sound. Once or twice it woke me up in the night. Thereby, proving to me that I did sleep sometimes, as it was very hard to believe. Initially, it seemed so odd to be connected up to a feeding machine. It became so routine, that towards the end of the second week, I was encouraged to disconnect myself: to enable me to visit the loo, go for a walk round the ward or visit the hospital chapel with John.

The sign outside my door stated: 'Nil By Mouth.' I was allowed drinks orally but everything else was via the tube. Every morning, afternoon and evening, I was given iron tablets. These had to be dissolved and the browny-orange liquid poured down the tube. Abinadex mineral drops were also added to this mixture. At night dissolved Mogadon (a bright green mixture) was likewise administered. It gave a weird cold sensation to my stomach, when they were poured down. Once the feeding tube was established, I could now have my pain-killers via the tube instead of by injection. The tube end in my neck regularly became gunged up and had to be carefully cleaned. It dragged and pulled quite hard at times but really there was so much indescribable discomfort all over that area, that it made no significant contribution. I was supposed to support the tube but as often as not, I forgot. With all the dissolved pills and medicines going down the tube and the occasional drop of lemonade poured down to clean it; I must have had quite a cocktail inside me!

Once I became accustomed to the feeding machine and had overcome the nausea, the hollow ache inside my stomach grew less intense. I switched off from wanting real food. I could even browse in the hospital shop among all the chocolate goodies (always a weakness) without longing to be able to eat them. I knew that it was a physical impossibility to eat and just accepted it.

As I have already mentioned, by the third day (Saturday), I was doing my breathing and throat clearing sessions hourly. These often seemed to be necessary when I had company. It was quite disgusting but something that had to be done. If people were present, I would delay it as long as I possibly could; before the build-up of mucus rattling loudly around in my throat, became too unbearable to ignore. Unfortunately people just stayed where they were, which I found embarrassing. The first time it occurred was when Neil, my vicar was there. I asked him to look at my cards, while I had my spitting session. Obviously I had to get used to this. It went on for ages and was so disgusting. What enormous relief when about ten days and umpteen boxes of tissues later, I had cleared it completely. It was another step along the road to recovery. I had found that to be the most unpleasant side-effect.

I was also trying to sip drinks through a straw. It still took an incredible effort to actually swallow the tiniest of sips and the exercise took ages. John had brought in a variety of small bottles of drink for me to try; once I was allowed fizzy drinks. This craving for pop, passed as soon as I had sampled some because it was still such a difficult chore, to try and swallow anything. My thirst could not really be satisfied.

On that first Saturday, from my propped up position in bed, I had a superb view of the main visitors' car park. I noticed how quiet everything was outside, compared to the frantic search for car parking spaces, so evident on a weekday. That day, for the first time, I really appreciated being able to gaze out on such a beautiful autumn day. To see the trees in their golden splendour, was wonderfully uplifting.

Neil visited that afternoon. He commented on the improvement in my speech. Today, I was much happier at seeing him, than when I had seen him in I.C. He stayed for a while. I was literally sighing with relief; as I flopped back, absolutely exhausted after his visit: when Maureen Edenbrow, one of my old school friends arrived. Naturally, I rallied myself again, because I was thrilled to see her. Though, it was really too much for me, talking was so uncomfortable and of course I so much needed to talk! Instead of flowers, Maureen had very thoughtfully brought me a large bottle of bubble bath: something I was later to enjoy using.

One of the nurses had mentioned that I could attend the Sunday morning service. In reality, this was not feasible because they could not release a nurse to accompany me there for the whole hour, with all my paraphernalia. When Sunday dawned, I realised that I certainly did not feel up to going anywhere, even if a nurse had been available. Mum came for the service in chapel and then afterwards Michael took a short service at my bedside for Mum and me, which meant so much.

From time to time since being back on ward 2B, I had been rather concerned about my drip. Knowing that it was to prevent dehydration, I fretted when I knew that it was almost empty and needed replacing. Patience has never ever been my strong point. I easily become het-up and frustrated when things take longer than I want. During that first weekend in hospital, I found it so hard to wait for someone to come. I was at the mercy of the buzzer and although in those early days someone came immediately: sometimes it was to say, 'I'll come back soon.' This I hated. I felt that it was urgent and became quite paranoid; it was certainly testing my lack of patience! I could sense myself getting all knotted up inside and it was not doing me any good. I knew the nurses were extremely busy and would come as soon as they could and not to my dictate. Fortunately, some common-sense thoughts came to mind and I could see the silliness of my concern. *God's hardly going to let you die of dehydration when He's just brought you through cancer.* This had a considerable calming effect.

That Sunday afternoon, John's parents came to visit me for the first time. How delighted I was to see them, especially pleased that his father had come as well because he is usually very reluctant to visit people in hospital. Afterwards, I had a welcome quiet afternoon, semi-dozing. It was still very awkward to sleep, though, I now felt slightly more relaxed. I was beginning to get used to this strange existence!

John visited me every evening. This gave me something to look forward to at the end of the day: before the long night began. I tended to watch television very late, until my eyes were so heavy; desperately trying to make the long ordeal of a sleepless night, that much shorter. Pauline Telford, the nurse who was always on nights, very kindly gave me my bedtime drink and two Mogadon tablets, much later than the other patients. I rarely put my light out before 11.30pm. I dreaded the nights, for I was convinced that I did not sleep. It was far worse to be clock watching at night; unlike daytime, when there was so much activity on a busy ward, to help pass the time.

On that particular Sunday evening, at about 11pm, when I felt more than ready to settle down, Pauline realised that my drip was not flowing properly. It needed transferring into another vein. She bleeped for a doctor and informed me that she had received rather an off-hand reply. However, the doctor who arrived one hour later, was extremely pleasant. She had quite an onerous task to locate a suitable vein for the trocar with its cannula to be inserted. For by now, after more than four consecutive days of having the drip transferred from one wrist to another, in search of a clear vein: the area of my upper hands and wrists was a swollen purplish mess. It was so painful to have the needle-like point inserted yet again. It was almost 1am by the time that the doctor had sorted it out. I lay back absolutely exhausted, hoping that at last I could escape into sleep.

Chapter 22

New Experiences

Monday 2nd November proved to be most eventful. It was to be a day of new experiences. Early on that Monday morning, the identity of the mystery visitor of Friday evening became apparent. Instead of jeans, she now wore a student nurse's uniform. I had to own up that I really had no recollection of whom she was. She reintroduced herself as Joanna Townend and informed me that she had met me on the Tuesday afternoon prior to surgery. She had escorted me to theatre and had been allowed to observe the operation.

Jo offered to take me for my first bath. It was to be my first walk. For up until then I had only vacated bed to use the commode. What a long trek that was; as very shakily, I slowly shuffled past the nurses' station, to the bathroom furthest from my room. As soon as we arrived, I collapsed weakly in a chair. Jo investigated the lift contraption. She was rather unsure about its reliability. I was certain that I was not going to risk sitting in it: so rather gingerly with Jo's assistance, I managed to climb into the bath. Before this, we had a laugh, because my drip had become entangled with my hospital nightie and Jo had to fetch sister to help extract it. Of course, with my muscle pedicle, I could only have a shallow bath but it was absolute bliss to luxuriate in perfumed bubble-bath. Afterwards, I felt much more human again!

Once back in bed, I lay exhausted; longing to be able to sleep but knowing that the usual busy morning stretched ahead. Again, at approximately 9 o'clock I experienced the ordeal of the ward round. Today, my details were explained to the gathering of young doctors and my chest wound was observed as being dry and intact. After checking my mouth, the registrar informed me that I had thrush. Dismay must have shown on my face, as I thought, *oh no, nothing else please!* The registrar quickly reassured me that it was not unusual in the circumstances and that something would be given to clear it up. An anti-fungal substance called Nystatin was prescribed: bright yellow syrup to be taken orally. At first I was anxious about taking it because I thought that it might increase the nausea. It was very sweet but just about palatable! It was left with me to take three times daily, roughly to coincide with meals (ha! ha!). The nurses would ask me if I had remembered to take it. I usually had but at times chose to forget it, to avoid feeling sick.

Jane the physiotherapist, usually came fairly early in the morning. Sometimes her visit coincided with the doctors' round. On this Monday she checked up on my breathing and seemed pleased with my progress. She had brought me a heat pack, which she wedged across my chest: to help ease the soreness of the chest wound. I found that very soothing. From then on, I had a daily heat treatment. I always enjoyed Jane's visits. She was so warm and friendly and I found her very easy to talk to. Her lively sense of humour helped keep my spirits up. As well as giving me necessary practical advice, most importantly, Jane spent time talking and listening to me. When I was into my second week and able to get out of bed for more than just the commode: I was encouraged to try and spend at least ten minutes daily on various shoulder exercises to strengthen my muscles. Again it was something positive that I could do and it was all helping towards my recovery. Although it became yet another task to fit into my hectic hospital schedule.

To my great relief, my drip was removed that morning. I made more of an effort to sip through a straw, the varied drinks at my bedside. I had started to drool about drinking hot cups of tea and coffee, especially when the drink trolley clattered past my room.

That Monday, Sue Winfield the dental therapist visited me. She was a very likeable, chatty person. Sue advised me about the regular mouth care that I had already begun: to use dry brushes to clear away the debris and brushes dampened in mouthwash to freshen the mouth, also to use a toothbrush dipped in mouthwash to clean my teeth. She provided me with a tiny headed brush with which to clean the wiring. As instructed, I had to go through this elaborate procedure every two hours. There was discussion about the need to get me a hand-mirror to do this. I had managed without one up to now and really did not want one. I did not wish to see what I looked like.

Later on that afternoon, staff nurse Cicely Courtney-Day finally located a mirror for me. I held it so that I could only see my mouth. What an ugly sight greeted me and what a shock I got, on seeing that my teeth were really quite black; something I had not reckoned on, even though Sue the dental therapist had forewarned me! Blackened teeth, as if I had chewed liquorice endlessly! Sue, had assured me that the stain could be removed quite easily later on. She had told me that the Betadene mouthwash that I had been using regularly since surgery, had stained my teeth. Of course when I had been given the two different bottles of mouthwash with the instructions to use them alternately, nothing had been mentioned about my teeth becoming stained. Therefore, I resolved to use the bright pink mouthwash, called Oraldene, as much as possible after that.

In breaking the lower jaw-bone (mandible) centrally, the surgeon had decided to remove the most crooked of my rather squashed up, irregular bottom teeth: the result of persistent thumb sucking as a young child. He thus removed one of the right incisors, which was leaning inwards towards my tongue. He thought that this tooth had not done me any favours and could possibly have contributed to the development of my tumour. He had wired the broken jaw together and this light wire frame, I could now see. It stretched across the mouth cavity above my lower teeth. Therefore I could not open my mouth, being barely able to part my lips; making it virtually impossible to do my mouth cleaning, within such a restrictive space. In addition, I could also see the metal arch bar that Miss Evans, the Locum Associate Specialist had inserted. This bar of approximately three millimetres width, encircled the front of my lower teeth and was anchored at intervals by fine wire. The bar secured my broken mandible very tightly: thus ensuring the best possible jaw alignment and the correct bite. This final part of major surgery had taken about twenty-five minutes.

Cis (Cicely) suggested that I look at the muscle pedicle. I really did not want to but finally decided to let her hold the mirror and show me. A mere glance was all that I could manage to endure. Utter revulsion welled up inside me and I felt physically sick. What a hideous sight I looked. My right cheek was incredible. I could not have envisaged that it could have been so swollen. I appeared absolutely gross. The muscle pedicle was so thick. It came as a dreadful shock to see what a monstrous sight I was and to realise what my family and friends had to focus on. I never ever regarded the pedicle again and I certainly did not consciously touch it! I continued to use the hand mirror to check my mouth and later when I was able to get up to the wash basin I always positioned myself so that I only saw the 'normal' part of my face.

By early Monday evening I was eagerly anticipating seeing Charlotte and Thomas. Both were now back at home and at school after the half-term holiday. Mum had also moved in, to be an extra pair of hands and so enable John flexibility to visit whenever he wanted. The visit seemed easier this time, even Thomas came a little closer to me. They had not been there long when I knew that I had to have another spitting session. Although they waited outside in the corridor while I did the necessary, they were still distressed by what they heard. From then on, if this occurred during their visit, John took them immediately to the Day-Room. Tonight before departing, John and Thomas visited the hospital chapel. Thomas lit a candle for me and they said a simple prayer. Thomas was now at the stage of finding church extremely boring, but nonetheless lit a candle after each visit.

After such an eventful day, I was very unsettled during the night and needed to have frequent suction applied to the back of my throat. I started a temperature and was very miserable during yet another interminably, long night.

Tuesday 3rd November, was the twenty-fourth anniversary of my father's death. A day or two earlier I had realised that the date was imminent and had intended to say something to Mum but had forgotten to. Though, when the actual date came round, it turned out to be such a difficult day, that I never gave it a thought. A few days later when I did remember to say something to Mum, she had been so absorbed in the demands of the present that she had completely forgotten that it was usually a very painful time of the year for her.

That Tuesday morning, the registrar informed me that because of my temperature, I had to be on antibiotics. These I had via the pharyngostomy tube in my neck. This, coupled with the fact that I had spent such a restless night meant that I was at my very lowest in all aspects: physically, mentally and spiritually, since that awful day and night spent in I.C. Tuesday 3rd November was a very black day for me. Suppressed feelings of anger, fear, frustration and all manner of confused emotions, seemed to well up from deep within me and spill over that day. I felt very depressed and extremely sorry for myself. Here was I stuck in hospital, like a prisoner, virtually immobile, instead of being free at home doing what I wanted, when I wanted. Despairingly, I thought of the endless variety of activities that I could have been doing at home. All those tedious household jobs were suddenly preferable to what I had to do now. I was doing absolutely nothing and time dragged by so slowly.

Something else happened to intensify my negative feelings: a nurse whom I had never seen before answered my call-bell. She seemed so different from the other nurses, who were all so openly warm and friendly. In contrast, her manner seemed very cool and unfriendly. At the time, I was sat out of bed because the bedding had just been changed. I requested a blanket to wrap around my shoulders. It seemed as if she did not understand my request, because she appeared to dither. By her lack of response, I sensed that what I was asking her, was going to be ignored. Indeed, as my anger swelled up, I got very close to snapping at her, 'Oh, if it's too much trouble, don't bother!' However, I behaved myself and she eventually brought me a blanket. Something else she did also enraged me.

Subsequently, on John's arrival that afternoon, I was in tears as I poured it out to him. He was even more upset because of the effect on me. Though I did not want him to, he insisted on diplomatically putting the ward manager (sister) Karen Woulds, in the picture. Karen explained that the nurse was new to the ward and that she would have a tactful word with her. I really was at my lowest that day and for the first time that I can recall, since being in Intensive Care, became tearful. In retrospect, I think that because of the way I was that day (in a bloody bad mood, putting it mildly!) I misinterpreted the nurse's diffidence for a lack of concern. She may indeed have experienced problems in relating to my condition. After all, I did look repugnant!

It seems very odd to consider that nurses may also, like many of us, have difficulties in dealing with cancer patients. Amanda, a student nurse, admitted this fact to me. She tended me, after the pedicle had been removed; when I looked almost human, apart from a grossly swollen right jaw and cheek. I had asked her to make me a milk shake. She had not blended the ice-cream properly. Something that she very hesitantly voiced, made me realise... here was a problem. I managed to say something, which encouraged her to speak more openly. Amanda admitted to feeling at a loss as to how best to respond to me and was interested to know how the other staff had reacted. I was quite amazed by this but very pleased that she had spoken so honestly. We ended up having a really good talk and I shared with her many of my sentiments and experiences of having had cancer. Amanda commented that she had found what I had said to be very helpful.

After that awful Tuesday, the nurse whom I had been swift to condemn, was perfectly alright with me. She was just much more reserved than the others. Although, she was far less chatty, she did show an interest. I remember how delighted I was when she noticed my children's photograph and enquired about them. I experienced guilt that I had misjudged her.

John also came in for his share of niggles in those early, testing days, after such traumatic surgery. Once or twice, I became very snappy at his seemingly unnecessary questions, such as, 'where do you want your clean nighties putting?' I could not be bothered to answer such silly questions and I know that I took out some of my pent-up frustrations on him. He was being wonderfully helpful and supportive and did not deserve his head being 'bitten off'! I know that this upset him.

However, there was one good thing that happened on that Tuesday and that was the removal of the alternate metal clips, (staples) from the chest wound. I could not have wanted for better care and attention, as student nurse Michaela Smith, painstakingly removed them while Jo Townend kindly held my hand. My wounds were apparently healing up very well and the clips were removed earlier than originally intended. The remaining clips and sutures were removed on Thursday 5th November, eight days after surgery. This included the clips along my right jaw. The relief at the removal of these neck clips was tremendous. My neck had been so tightly restrained and it had been very uncomfortable. I still felt quite restricted but it was nowhere as uncomfortable as it had been. When the nurse that I had originally disliked, came to remove the last of my sutures, I remember clearly thinking, *now I'm in for it!* Of course, she was just as careful as the others had been.

The afternoons were the times for the removal of sutures and for dressings to be changed. The muscle pedicle was cleaned and dressed daily. The first time that Michaela did this, it took ages. It was such a weighty and very chunky muscle for her to handle. I could vaguely see it swathed in dressings, as it hung from below my right collar-bone (clavicle). Michaela had difficulty in removing the initial dressings. In spite of thoroughly soaking the gauze, it was almost impossible to remove. She ended up carefully cutting much of the gauze away. We had a laugh over this, for she thoroughly drenched me! From then on, it was a standing joke, that I would be avenged. Nevertheless, getting soaked was well worth it. Having the muscle cleaned and then re-dressed was so wonderfully soothing.

Chapter 23

Hospital Routine

On Wednesday 4th November, the registrar made his routine morning call. He appeared most concerned that I was feeling low. I responded very brightly, 'Oh that was yesterday, I feel fine now.'

The bulk of my visitors usually came in the afternoon. There were often between two and four at any one time. Sometimes one set would go, immediately to be replaced by another set. Very often there was a mixture of old friends from school days and those from more recent years. I loved seeing people but it was so exhausting. I wanted to converse with everyone who came to see me but I was not supposed to talk for long. Although, some of my older visitors insisted that I listen while they talked; somehow it did not work out that way. At times there was a considerable racket coming from my room. People passing by always glanced in. As pleased as I was to see folk, I was just as pleased to see them go. I would lie back utterly drained, hoping and praying that I could have an uninterrupted rest. Once, during an unexpectedly but very welcome 'visitor free' afternoon, I was enjoying a rest; when Tracey Holland, one of the very friendly health care support workers who often used to come and chat to me, arrived. Tracey had noticed that for once I had no visitors and she wanted to keep me company. Touched by her thoughtfulness, I could not bring myself to tell her that all I really wanted was a rest. After that and as I became more agile, I would close the door and the curtains, to try and escape!

In addition to the company I expected, there were others whom John knew but I did not. This was such a contrast to when I had an eye operation, when only John and my Mum visited. Then there was no vicar to visit me. This time I had visits from five different clergy.

Mornings soon became very busy, trying to fit my chores in around the visitors. Once it had turned 11am, I knew the chances of a rest were very remote. I found it quite remarkable that everyone who came to see me, had such a warm friendly greeting: with either a kiss, hug or handshake. I was regarded as if I were quite normal in appearance. I detected no sign of repugnance to look at me at all. I found the fact that my visitors were prepared for physical contact, when I knew how grotesque I appeared, was the best thing that they could do to reassure me that I was still 'me'!

On the Thursday afternoon, when I was having the last of my sutures removed, someone had arrived to visit me and was shown into the Day-Room. Resting afterwards, I suddenly remembered the visitor. Kathy Russell had been waiting at least half an hour. It was not entirely my fault but I felt very guilty that she had been kept waiting longer than necessary. She had brought me a huge basket of toiletries from the M.U. and a card signed by all the Frampton members. This made a lovely change from all the bouquets and baskets of flowers that I kept receiving.

My room resembled a florist's shop (I have always adored flowers, they are a wonderful tonic). People often paused in the doorway to admire the floral display. Well, they were certainly not admiring the occupant of room 5! I even received orchids from Singapore. My old friend Mick Cockerill (Kathleen's husband) on one of his business trips, had brought some back for me. I had never been given orchids before. They were beautiful. I was able to take the last few home with me and press them. It became a standing joke on the ward regarding the amount of flowers and cards that continued to arrive. The surgeon used to joke about his daily visit to Covent Garden Market.

In striking contrast to my previous three stays in hospital, this time I never had any contact with other patients. Towards the end of my stay I could manage to greet someone in the corridor, but for a long time I avoided meeting another patient's glance. Once or twice, an elderly patient mistook my room for theirs and quickly muttered an apology. Occasionally, I thought how strange that it was, not to be mixing with other patients. Yet in reality, I was so thankful for the privacy of my single room. After all, I was receiving so much attention from staff and visitors that I was hardly solitary for long.

On my final day in hospital, I took the last of my flowers to an elderly lady, endeavouring to chat with her. For the first time since surgery, someone kept saying 'pardon', in response to what I was saying. I did not consider whether the lady had a hearing problem or not but found it an extremely upsetting experience, for everyone else gave me the impression that they could understand what I was saying; even though to me, my speech sounded so dreadfully slushy.

Kathleen Cockerill, one of my oldest school friends, now living near Bourne, surprised me by coming to see me soon after my surgery. I had never considered that she would get over to see me, even though her elderly mother lived in Boston. A few days later she came again, because her mother had been admitted into Pilgrim. For me the timing was perfect, as Kathleen was able to visit me many times.

Knowing how much concern there was for my healing was very humbling and at times quite overwhelming: especially when the well-wisher was someone that I hardly knew or had never met. One morning when Michaela had brought in yet another batch of cards, I opened one showing swans on a pond. I often used to get slightly watery-eyed when reading the messages but this time it was evident to Michaela who was still present. I just found it so moving that the parents of a neighbour should be so concerned as to send me a card.

It really did come home to me that as Christians we are called to be a caring family, giving support when needed. John and I both felt that we were being held up by a strong wave of prayer. It was a real source of inner strength to know that people in so many different places were praying for me. My name was put on prayer lists in many different churches. It was especially wonderful to learn from our friend Dr. Adrian Cozma that candles had been lit for me in Romania.

I felt that I was in a very privileged position because so many people were lavishing attention on me. At times I experienced considerable embarrassment and even guilt at all the care that I was receiving.

The mobile trolley phone was usually parked outside my room, so I could not help overhearing conversations. On one occasion, I tried not to listen to a young distraught female trying to arrange a lift home from hospital. It made me feel sad. This patient had earlier caused considerable fuss, frequently ringing her bell for attention, as she had been so frightened.

It struck me that there must be so many others in hospital without the loving support of family and friends. I was most fortunate to have this tremendous support but more significantly, I had my strong belief in God. In recent years my faith had formed a relevant part of my daily life. Well before the shocking news of the cancer diagnosis it had become so important to me. Now in hospital, recovering from serious surgery; I wholeheartedly acknowledged that my Christian faith was the most vital aspect of my life. What on earth would I have done in my given circumstances without faith in a caring and creative God to keep me sane? Undoubtedly, I would have been metaphorically climbing the walls and probably wishing that I could end it all.

Fitting my chores into the hectic hospital routine, became increasingly more difficult. In my second week, as I became stronger and as soon as I was sufficiently 'with it': I tried to have a few minutes of prayer and a daily reading of a few Bible verses. If I managed this, I knew that I had begun the day properly. At first I attempted to use my 'Daily Light' readings but it proved too much for me. In the very early days it took all my effort to glance at some of the many helpful prayer cards that I had been sent. During the second week, my friend Pauline Wright, brought me a book of daily meditations by Corrie ten Boom (Dutch survivor of a German concentration camp). This was ideal, consisting of one verse of Scripture and very often only two or three lines of comment. From then on I used the book daily: finding it very inspirational and so relevant to my needs.

During those early days, after the initial flux of visitors, John tried to dissuade people from staying so long, because the staff had complained that it was proving too tiring for me. He even printed a notice, which he put up on my door, requesting a time limit of ten minutes! Karen the ward sister thought this was an excellent idea. The notice seemed to ease the problem for a few days but generally people did not realise that talking and listening were tiring!

Strangely enough Sunday afternoon was always very quiet for me. Actually, on two Sunday afternoons no one visited me. On one occasion I was expecting John's parents and when they did not arrive I was so disappointed. On the other afternoon, I was hoping that my daughter Charlotte and her boyfriend would come. They did not and I was quite upset.

From Wednesday 4th November (a week after surgery) I was walking almost the length of the entire ward for my daily bath. That afternoon Lucy Potter, one of the health care support workers, suggested that I have a proper walk. Lucy was such a lovely warm motherly person and during my stay she was very good to me. So that afternoon we set off: Lucy supporting me on one side; while I was pushing along my feeding tube trolley on the other side. We managed a half circuit of the ward. I walked so slowly. It took enormous effort for me to walk unsteadily along with her. I returned to my room feeling as if I had done a marathon, also very satisfied that I had achieved another 'first'. From then on during the afternoons, whenever someone was available to accompany me, I would have a 'walk about'.

By now the craving to drink tea and coffee was getting too much. Sister said that it was perfectly alright to have beverages, as long as the drink had cooled down. Quite anxiously, I lifted my first cup of tea, to my extremely swollen mouth and was pleasantly surprised that I could still drink with very tiny sips. Of course, I had let the drink get stone cold, so it was not quite as good as I had imagined! After a few days of very cool tea, coffee or drinking chocolate, I felt comfortable enough to progress to much warmer drinks. I certainly looked forward to these drinks, even to the point of having the nurses chase up the drink trolley if I thought that they had overlooked me.

During the second week, the traumatic events of surgery were no longer uppermost in my mind and the next operation seemed happily far off. With some astonishment, I realised how at home I felt. I was now quite familiar and entirely at ease with hospital routine. Most importantly, I had come to terms with having to be in hospital. The initial frustrations that I had experienced were changed, by reading a book 'Readings in Sickness' by Norman Autton. Bob Adcock our elderly organist at St Mary's church had sent me the book. I read only a few of these very short readings but they had such a profound impact that I now refer to them. Apparently, Bob had found this book a great help when he was in hospital recovering from a brain tumour. (Happily, he had made a full recovery and lived until the ripe old age of eighty-three. His death in January of 1995 saddened us all. For he was a well-loved member of the community). The first significant extract being:

'A lay-by on the road is a place where the tired driver can pull in and rest... he can think about his journey to this point and that which lies ahead. That done, he and his engine will both leave the lay-by better for their stay. Your present lay-by in bed offers similar constructive opportunities for your whole self, and it is most important that you should recognise and make the most of them.'

(A Religious of C.S.M.V.)

I began to realise that I had been given a 'present' of time. Instead of chafing about all the things that I could not do; it was far better to accept my situation and concentrate my energies on what I could do; within the confines of my hospital bed, busy routine and very limited concentration. At last the luxury of time to just read (I have always loved reading) without feeling guilty that I have not done this or that. Time now to listen to music, to think, to pray, to talk to people, whether they be hospital staff or visitors. Most significantly, I could within obvious limits, at long last just please myself! I was no longer having to meet the demands of family life. Time at last to be myself. I found those thoughts very exhilarating.

Another reading really spoke to me and which I underlined:

'When suffering hits us, it is natural enough to ask the question "Why?" Jesus did. But it is more important to ask the question "How? How will God make this thing, which to me is so negative, into a plus in his hands? Is it possible that I am on my back so that I may learn to look up?" That might be the most wonderful thing I could do.'

(Donald Coggan)

Lastly, I include the extract which convinced me so strongly that God had a purpose for my being in hospital:

'In entrusting us with a load of pain God is often giving us a power to help others greater than that possessed by the most eloquent of preachers or the wisest of teachers. To carry with us that which automatically brings out the best side of other people, that which sends them away with fresh courage and renewed cheerfulness, that which brings them nearer to each other, and to goodness, and

therefore to God, what more lovely ministry could any of us desire?'

(G.E. Childs)

There was such a wonderful caring atmosphere on Ward 2B. They were a lovely group of nurses and health care support workers; so friendly and caring and I enjoyed their company. We would laugh and joke together. I became very fond of them. Of course, some were easier to relate to than others.

One particular nurse, Pauline Telford, only worked nights and was a great comfort, chatting to me on many a sleepless night. Although I was not really in pain, I still chose to take pain-killers just in case. It was so indescribably uncomfortable, always propped up with four or five pillows, attached to a feeding machine and in need of suction from time to time. At a much later stage, Pauline had even suggested that I tried the suction for myself but I could not manage it. I had expected that the sleeping tablets would knock me out solidly until next morning. Pauline explained that they were not strong enough to do that; they were to help me relax sufficiently to fall asleep. Shortly after taking the tablets, I always became very sleepy and was no longer able to focus on the television. After two or three hours' sleep, I would be awake again and then start to toss and turn and ring the bell for attention. Anything, to pass the time away! Pauline would surprise me by telling me that I had been fast asleep. I was convinced that I was awake most of the night. I certainly never slept solidly at all. Consequently, when morning came I would be very reluctant to wake up. As time progressed and I got to know the staff better, they would leave my curtains shut for as long as possible and I would manage a lie-in.

On a few mornings at about 7.30am: Sister Jennie Starkey (a friend of Jack and Edna Kirk at Woodhall) came to see me. She worked nights in the Accident and Emergency Department. In fact on Jennie's first two visits to me, I never met her, for I was still sound asleep. On her third visit I was awake. Jennie always prayed with me and I really appreciated her concern and support. It made a lovely start to my day.

During the struggle of those early, long sleepless nights, I knew that my faith was really being tested. With so much activity in the day, accompanied by the overwhelming support I was receiving from family and friends, nights were to be such a stark contrast. In the middle of the night, when you are supposed to be sleeping and cannot (for whatever reason): then you can feel so totally abandoned and desperately alone. There was no escape from reality and the trauma of my situation. My nights became a time of deep crisis, as I grew utterly dispirited; especially because it was occurring night after night, without respite. It was dreadful. As my sleeplessness continued I became more and more distressed. By now I would have expected that I ought to be zonking out as soon as my head touched the pillows. I had not had a good night's sleep for over a week and I was utterly exhausted and totally ... off! I began to dread having to face yet another awful night: clock-watching was surely going to send me crackers!

On one particularly difficult night, Pauline reminded me of all the positive steps that I had taken so far; also stressing that I really was over the worst. In spite of the monotony of endless days and nights, I was growing stronger even if nothing new appeared to have happened in my recovery. Her words helped me enormously. They coincided with my change in attitude towards being in hospital, after reading Bob Adcock's book.

Quite amazingly, from then on, sleeplessness no longer worried me. I knew that I could sleep in the daytime (visitors permitting) or when awake at night, I could play the tapes John had prepared for me. Needless to say, I only had to resort to this diversion once.

I became so acutely aware of God's greatness to me and I experienced such thankfulness, that I had some valuable time (albeit when under normal circumstances I would have been asleep) to think and to pray. Incredibly, the nights were marvellously transformed; so that instead of tossing and turning restlessly in a desperate craving for much needed sleep: I felt an overwhelming awareness of God, such an intensity of spiritual feeling that I had never known before. Obviously, words cannot adequately describe what I experienced in my hospital room but it was truly wonderful. I felt supercharged with this tremendous sense of God's presence and purpose for me. I was at peace mentally and above all, spiritually. Suddenly long nights became full of meaning. I was content to lie there, in my propped up position. I had so much to do.

Over the years, my prayers have always been silent, apart from the occasional spoken arrow-prayer such as, 'God help me!' Now, it was simply a case of recognising that God was with me in my plight and of letting my thoughts unfold... It seemed that there was a constant dialogue going on between God and me... It became a most precious time.

Chapter 24

Human At Last!

I took the opportunity to say a little about my faith to a few of the nurses, if they commented on how well I was coping, or how brave I was. That in itself was a complete innovation. For never had I been able to talk about my Christian faith: other than with very close and like-minded friends. I had always been too embarrassed.

Jo Townend and I got on really well together. I found her so easy to relate to, especially about spiritual matters. I was able to share some of my deeper thoughts and feelings with her. Jo was very concerned about her exams the following week. I tried to explain how I had coped during important examinations at school and college, all those years ago! Jo was pleased when I said that I would pray for her. John printed out some prayers. However, thanks to 2B's internal mail, she did not receive them until after her exams! Nonetheless, she was very touched by the thought. However, I did manage to get her name included in the prayers in the hospital Sunday service.

During one of my late night chats with Pauline Telford: I was relating to her the details leading up to my hospitalisation. At some point in this conversation Pauline stated, 'You must have been very frightened.' I recall saying, 'Well, no not really.' I told her that it was only my firm belief in God's great love and His continuing care, that was sustaining me.

Months later, as I pondered this conversation, I was astonished at how inaccurate my answer to Pauline had been. At the time that she had questioned me, I certainly was not frightened, the worst was over. Nevertheless, I had known real fear: during the first few hours of being diagnosed and the night before admission into hospital. Fortunately, these feelings had not lasted long and were superseded for the most part, by a calm very positive 'let's get on with it' state of mind. To tell Pauline that I had not been frightened, when that day and night in the I.C.U. was the most terrifying and horrendous experience of my entire life, was quite baffling: especially as it was such a recent event. I believe that when I answered her in that glib manner, I had already blotted out those ghastly memories.

The surgeon and his team were most impressed by my progress. My speech was noticeably improving as some of the swelling slowly subsided. Truthfully, it sounded horrible and dreadfully slushy to me: like I had still got a mouthful of gob-stoppers! My visitors would comment on its increasing clarity. Of course that did encourage me and made me very thankful that desperate prayer demands about my speech, had been granted. At the end of my hospital stay, Cis commented on how good my speech was and added, 'It's because you had the right spirit about it all.'

Christine Ash, the speech and language therapist, was very reassuring, giving me much needed moral support: as well as being responsible for practical advice to improve my speech and to re-establish efficient swallowing. She visited me six days post-op. on 3rd November, to measure the extent of my mouth opening. It was a mere two centimetres. Christine showed me a diagram representing my face. Tapping very gently by fingertip, I had to indicate the areas of greatest numbness and semi-numbness. On her diagram, the totally deadened areas were marked by - signs; whilst the areas of normal sensation and semi-numbness were indicated by + signs. Virtually the entire part of my lower right cheek was without sensation. The greatest degree of numbness being the entire chin area, from below my lips to the central point where the lower jaw had been broken. A slightly less numb area being along the lower jaw-line, extending in a broad band as far as and including the lower right ear-tip. This lack of overall sensation over the entire part of the lower right half of my face, was really weird. The strange, often very hard-as-rock, unfamiliar feel of my affected face caused me a great deal of concern. The diagram took two visits to complete.

On her next three visits, Christine showed me some mouth and tongue exercises which I had to repeat several times daily: opening and closing my mouth, giving a big smile, moving the tongue in and out, to each side, up to the roof of my mouth and down. These exercises were important to enable the developing scar tissue to be stretched to its furthest extent and therefore be more mobile. Thus, ensuring that the tongue did not heal in a restricted way. For the improvement of oral and facial sensations I had to massage and stroke the side of my face, using different textures and temperatures. She recommended that I swish a mouthful of fizzy drink around my mouth before spitting out or swallowing. Towards the end of my stay, she suggested putting a polo mint on a piece of string and to practise moving it from one side of the mouth to the other. I never attempted that, I was too bothered about losing it in my mouth.

As I have already written; a week after surgery I was managing a daily walk around the ward. When I grew stronger, it made sense to ask for my feeding tube to be disconnected during John's evening visit: so that he could escort me on another walk about. It made a welcome break from looking at each other and the four walls of my 'cell'. Having done this once or twice, staff nurse said it was okay for me to leave the ward. Descending in the lift, acutely aware that I looked a shocking sight, I tried to be as unobtrusive as possible. I was most careful to stand facing the lift wall, especially if there were children present. Although aware of stares, it was not really a concern.

How peculiar it was to be in different surroundings. I felt very light-headed and wobbly. Very gingerly, I walked into the main reception area. I tried to show an interest in the shop, as John bought me some small bottles of fizzy pop but by then my head had started to swim; it all seemed too much to take in. We sat in the deserted foyer and it was lovely being on the ground floor, close to the outside world. How attractive it looked, illuminated at night. John suggested a visit to the chapel. We sat there in the darkness for a short time. He lit a candle for me and said a prayer. It was soothing to be in such a peaceful place. From that night on, we made a nightly pilgrimage to the chapel, to light a candle and say some prayers. We gained great strength and solace from doing this and I know it brought us very close. As well as for ourselves, we prayed especially for Brenda and her family. John had spoken to Trudy Elliott, my old college friend, informing her of my successful operation but we were horrified to learn that Brenda's tumour had proved inoperable. Other treatment would be tried but it was only a matter of time…

On Sunday 8th November, I was allowed down for the 10am service. One of the chapel helpers collected me by wheelchair. It was the first time that I had ever been in one. I had prepared myself carefully for this special outing. A final trip to the loo: for the days of the commode had long since gone, thank goodness! I managed a thorough deep breathing and spitting session. I was somewhat apprehensive. My constant companions: a box of tissues, a vomit dish and a bottle of water, were pushed underneath the chair. I sat at the back, hoping that I would remain comfortable enough not to have to make an exit. The chapel helper sat near me, with my mother and Thomas next to her.

For once, Thomas did not fidget. He seemed absorbed by the occasion and for that I was so thankful. It meant a great deal to me that in spite of all his moans about church being boring, he was prepared to join me. Of course, afterwards he had a good candle lighting session! It was a communion service. I obviously could not take communion, but Michael gave me a blessing. At this I became very emotional, especially when the Peace was exchanged. Here was no awkward reserve as people shook hands (as can often be the case in our churches), instead a wonderful feeling of warmth and a genuine concern for those of us who were suffering so much. Prayers were said for many people. My family were all mentioned by name. Finally, a prayer was said for the parents of a still-born baby, Thomas Edward; my own son's names. At that, I could contain my tears no longer.

On Monday 9th November, one of the health care support workers, accompanied me for my daily bath. When she commented on my suntan: asking where I had been, I casually replied, 'Oh, we went to Portugal this year.' At her words, 'That's nice, I haven't been abroad,' I was very conscious, of a sudden overpowering sensation of guilt. In the past few years, we had enjoyed holidays abroad and I had taken it all very much for granted. I realised what a relatively easy time I had known up to now. I did not have to struggle to make ends meet. Moreover, I had the choice of going out to work or not. Later on, as I pondered more deeply about this; I came to the conclusion that at the ripe old age of forty-three, I had enjoyed a good quality of life: whereas, countless people find life to be a perpetual hard grind. I could thank God, that I had already experienced a richness of life. If I had died, or were to die in the near future, I had something precious which so many people however long they live, never have. I realised that it was the quality of life that matters, not quantity.

Thus, I did a great deal of soul-searching during my hospital stay. When I considered all the petty obsessions and concerns of the past few years; that had consumed so much of my time and energy: I could see how utterly futile they had all been. For none of these issues mattered now. How I had been brought down to grim reality! Circumstances had certainly made me put my life into perspective. I knew that I now had to focus all my attention on God and His will for my life: no longer on what I thought was best.

On Monday 9th November, all my positive thoughts were being overtaken, by the growing anxiety within me about my impending second operation. I began to feel quite downcast by niggling worries and uncertainties about what was in store for me. The operation was for the division of the pedicle: as the surgeon had so flippantly said, 'The sausage would be divided and discarded, having served its purpose of maintaining a blood supply, to the grafted tissues of the tongue.' By contrast, the operation was relatively straightforward and would last approximately forty minutes. The problem of working, within the confines of my small mouth (which was still grossly swollen and now had the extra restriction of the metal arch bar) to do the division and the necessary tidy-up work, had been mentioned to me by the surgeon. Both he and the nurses had spoken the dreaded word 'tracheostomy' as a possibility: an opening would be made in the trachea (windpipe) and a tube inserted to ensure an air supply. I had disliked the idea of this. In a chat with the registrar, he had said something about a nasal tube being an alternative way of maintaining an air supply. To me, that seemed the best choice out of two evils. At least I would be able to talk afterwards! All in all, I was not getting a definite answer. This lack of communication made me extremely frustrated. I was also very worried about whether I would have to go into I.C. again. I could not bear that. I got opposing views about this. There really did seem to be some confusion and that did not help my peace of mind.

Early on that Tuesday evening, the surgeon visited me. To my consternation, he explained that he would most probably have to do a tracheostomy. My mouth could not open wide enough for a tube to be put in and he needed what little space there was inside, to complete his work. I really had not bargained for this little 'extra'. It meant, that I would be unable to talk afterwards, because the tube would stay in after surgery. Horror of horrors! I was alone and quite near to tears, after this bombshell, when Michael, the chaplain arrived. It really was perfect timing. He was as wonderfully comforting as ever. He discussed this minor 'hiccup' with me and I began to feel slightly better. On a positive note, I was looking forward to the pedicle being removed, since the last day or two, I had been far more conscious of it and it had been itching.

That evening there was to be a Julian Prayer Meeting held in the chapel. Pat Hedgecock and Hilda Kendall from the M.U. at Wyberton, had arranged to collect me. John also joined us. The meeting consisted of a reading, followed by a long period of silent meditative prayer. I had plenty to pray about and I found the time of silence, very valuable and deeply calming. Afterwards, over coffee (by then I was able to enjoy it reasonably hot) many friendly people whom I did not know, came to speak to me. That night, Pauline told me, that after surgery I would be back in my own room. Oh the relief!

Wednesday 11th November was the start of an exceptionally long day. Today, I was last on the list, as opposed to the surgeon's only patient of two weeks earlier. John had arranged for our old friends, Mike and Linda Johnson from Scothern near Lincoln, to visit me that morning. I had not seen them for over a year, so we had much to catch up on. Mum had come along too and we were chatting most animatedly: Mike having the weirdest sense of humour!

Our light-hearted banter was abruptly interrupted, by the anaesthetist's arrival. The manner in which the anaesthetist breezed in and questioned me about the instructions that the surgeon had left, regarding my forthcoming operation and the possible tracheostomy (as if I were an authority..!) was extremely disturbing. My visitors and I, were quite taken aback. My fears about the impending surgery, instead of being lessened, were simply magnified: as in dread, I wondered just what lay ahead of me in the operating theatre.

Early afternoon, by my request, Neil Russell came and spent a short time with me and I was so glad when he offered to say a prayer before he left. I was still far from happy about the idea of a tracheostomy. Later on, John was with me, when an unexpected visitor arrived. We had not seen Heather Judge since the charity dance she had organised for the Romanian Relief Fund. At about 3.30pm they both left, so I could change into my hospital gown and have the pre-med. injection. At long last, I felt calm and was content to doze in bed. Time still passed slowly. About 4.30pm, I remembered that the debate regarding the ordination of women priests in the Church of England, was being televised. I watched the end of the debate and the voting. Excitedly and with some emotion, I heard the happy outcome of this, before I was collected at 5.10pm. By now the calming effects of the pre-med. had worn off and I was very tense and anxious. This was in stark contrast to how I felt when facing serious surgery.

I was further unsettled when the anaesthetist had difficulty inserting the trocar with its cannula, into a vein in my left wrist. The subsequent attempt on my right wrist was also unsuccessful. Finally, after the third attempt, (now back to the left wrist) it was inserted. However bad this seemed, the worst moment was still to come. In absolute terror and sheer panic I realised that the anaesthetist's words that morning, 'I'll have to keep you dry,' meant that the method of anaesthetising me for the tracheostomy to be done, was to use a face mask. I had always hated them. Instead of calmly drifting under, I was fighting the mask and gas. My staring eyes were fixed on those around me, while I tried to take deep breaths as I slowly lost consciousness. Those frightening moments seemed to go on forever. My eyes must have looked terrible.

I came round about 7.30pm to find John at my bedside. I felt completely dejected and thoroughly miserable, having the awful tube in my windpipe and being unable to talk. For the very first time since being in hospital, I literally clung to John. I could not bear him to leave me. The memo-board that he had brought me ages before, had to be used seriously for the first time. Until now I had managed to make myself understood, even in my very slushy voice.

Pauline had her work cut out that night, trying to cheer me up. She of course, was unable to tell me how long I would have the tube in. She did explain that sometimes a voice-piece is inserted, to enable speech. I did not like the sound of any of it. I hated being unable to talk. I cannot describe what it felt like. Something vital was missing and I found it utterly unbearable. I spent another agonisingly, restless night. I had to have an oxygen mask over the 'trache' tube. To my annoyance, the mask kept slipping and I was forever adjusting it.

By morning, I had my questions written out, ready for the registrar's visit at 9am. He alarmed me by saying, 'We may leave the tube in until the metal arch bar comes out.' I was horror-stricken and just could not believe what I was hearing: because I knew that the metal arch bar was not scheduled for removal for some time (when the broken jaw had mended). I spent my time in frantic prayer. I was scared and I could sense panic surging up within me. It was a strange, stifling feeling, having this alien tube sticking out from my windpipe. I knew that I could not cope with it much longer. I was very near to losing self-control. I could scarcely wait for the surgeon's visit.

He came before lunch and I was so elated to hear him say, 'Yes, everything's fine, it can come out this afternoon.' Apparently, the nurses were very surprised at this early removal: it is usually done forty-eight hours after surgery. I discovered afterwards: it was because there was less swelling (oedema) than usual. The thought did cross my mind (knowing how busy they were) that it could well be an awfully long afternoon and that I might have to pester them! Far from it; I managed to absorb myself in a book and was actually surprised when Karen (sister) entered my room at 3pm, to remove the dratted tube! Jo, the student nurse, held my hand, as very slowly, Karen removed the 'trache' tube. I was amazed to see that it resembled a very fine wire. Tiny particles of blood showered over us, as it was finally withdrawn.

At a much later stage, Jo was to admit how upsetting that it had been for her: watching me go through this procedure. So much so, that she had left the room for a few minutes, in order to recover. Of course, I had been unaware of how anyone else was feeling; I was totally absorbed in how I was and so greatly relieved that this dreadful 'hiccup' was over. A padded dressing was fixed over the wound and I was instructed to apply direct pressure on this, whenever I spoke: otherwise my voice would come out in a very wheezy manner. Even with this odd sound, it was great to have my voice back. I was not supposed to do much talking but I ignored this instruction: I was so pleased that I could talk again!

How I thanked God that He had recognised my limits of endurance in this matter and had readily answered my specific prayers. It was wonderful to be freed from the pedicle. I felt human again, at long last. Although, the lower right side of my face was still immensely swollen: I could now bear to look in the mirror. Great celebrations: after days of looking forward to the event; at last I could have my hair washed. Alison Brown, one of the health care support workers had this dubious pleasure!

The following day Friday 13th November, Jo came to say goodbye, for she had completed her three-week stint on 2B. To my surprise, Jo handed me a gift bag with two foil wrapped presents inside, together with a card. She had written some lovely words and I was flabbergasted at what she had put about me and very moved. In fact we both became emotional. I told Jo, that I would like to keep in touch and that I would write to her once I was back at home. She had become a real friend to me and I knew that I would miss her.

That night, Pauline also said goodbye: for when her next set of night shifts came round, I would be home. I now knew that there was possibly only another week to go. I was very sad to say goodbye to Pauline. I had grown very fond of her and she had been a great help and comfort to me during many tedious hours. Funnily enough, Pauline was the only nurse who ever called me Mrs. Marshall. All the other nurses used my Christian name and I much preferred this (I always think of a school situation, when referred to in a formal manner). She had shared personal things with me about herself, as had some of the other nurses. I felt privileged that they felt able to confide in me. This brought home to me, that even though I was a patient, in need of considerable care; I could still be aware of other people's problems and be there to listen.

Chapter 25

Real Food!

On Saturday 14th November, the staff wanted me to try some 'real food'. So that afternoon, Lucy fetched me a chocolate mousse from the ward store and I tackled it with a straw! I could not manage more than a few sips, because it was very firm in texture and took so much effort. Later on that evening, I tried a small carton of ice-cream. I let it become quite soft and then very slowly and noisily sucked it up. It was delicious! I had not attempted to use a spoon, for I was too scared. I was terrified of not being able to control the food in my mouth and of being unable to swallow it! Though I knew that I had to be able to swallow again and I was only putting it off.

During that weekend the uncertainty over the removal of the metal arch bar was bothering me. The thought of another general anaesthetic was utterly unbearable. I was aware that I had surprised many (especially myself!) by the way that I had coped throughout. However, I realised that I did not feel brave about the idea of yet another general anaesthetic; not after the unnecessary trauma of the second operation. I prayed hard that if I had to endure it again, that at least I could go home for a while first. How I desperately needed to return home, before enduring anything else. In spite of recognising that this little operation ahead of me, was absolutely nothing in comparison to what I had been through: I had a strong conviction that if I had been faced with yet another 'theatre trip' that week, I would have gone to pieces. I began to realise just how long I had been away from home in this strange environment. I mentioned my worries about the third operation to the nurses and a message was left for Mr. Glendinning concerning them.

On Sunday morning for the first time ever, the breakfast trolley stopped outside my room. I attempted Weetabix dissolved in milk (it resembled a very gritty liquid) and afterwards a mashed up banana. Very tentatively, I used a small spoon and to my utter amazement found it easier than I had anticipated. Breakfast took absolutely ages but I managed the lot. The nurses told me that I must now start eating properly; otherwise I would be kept in hospital longer than was necessary. By now, I was making extremely good progress in all aspects of my recovery. Re-establishing 'normal eating' and rebuilding my strength, were the last hurdles. I certainly could not leave hospital until my food intake was satisfactory. Nevertheless, I had grown so dependent on being fed via the pharyngostomy tube, that I was rather reluctant to take foods orally again. One of the nurses had assured me that the tube which was still my main source of food intake, would not be removed, until a normal feeding pattern was well and truly established. I was content that day, to try a small amount of food orally: but when it became too much like hard work, I abandoned it.

Having spent a quiet Sunday afternoon, that evening I was eager for some company. John did not arrive until almost 9pm. I knew that he was taking an evening service at St Mary's and would be a bit late... Consequently, I was in a very angry and tearful state (feeling so sorry for myself), when he finally rushed in. John had recorded the service for me and afterwards listening to it, recognising a few familiar voices, I began to overcome my self-pity. I knew that I would soon be back among them all and that was something to really look forward to.

Sunday 15th November marked the start of 'Prisoners' Week.' A few days earlier I had picked up a poster from the chapel. In almost ghostly effect, it depicted a prisoner sat head in hands, with the words underneath 'Out of sight... out of mind.' I stuck this on the inside of my door. Kaye Willoughby, one of the health care support workers, commented on what a sad picture it was and I said, 'It's to help me not to feel sorry for myself.' At that she replied, 'You've not been like that at all.' The poster did help me though. How could I feel sorry for myself? Thoughts of the Yugoslavian concentration camps and other equally grim human rights' issues filled my mind and made me thoroughly ashamed of the self-pity that I had indulged in. In spite of having at times felt like a prisoner; especially when I was trapped by all the paraphernalia of drips and the like: at least I had been a very 'privileged prisoner', experiencing a high standard of care, in a most humane manner.

That Sunday evening I considered that I had done extremely well with regard to feeding. I had managed: two Weetabix, a banana, a carton of ice-cream, a mousse and a yoghurt. Consequently, during the night I felt bloated, so the feeding tube was disconnected.

On Monday 18th November, just before 8am, I was in a really messy state; having just spooned up my liquid Weetabix and now earnestly tackling a mashed up banana: when Mr. Glendinning surprised me by turning up at my bedside. He said that an appointment would be made for me to attend his out-patients' clinic, a week after my hospital discharge. How relieved I was to hear this. I could go home before any more theatre! I was less happy when he said, very matter-of-factly, 'I'll do a general anaesthetic.' I could face that. At least I would be going home before that ordeal.

However, the niggles about another general anaesthetic persisted, so that morning I told Lucy, all about my unhappy experiences, leading up to the second operation. She advised me to mention it to the surgeon. Until then, it had never crossed my mind to do so.

During the registrar's morning visit, I described my entire food intake; since the commencement on Saturday, of 'real food'. How pleased I was at my progress. That Monday was the first day that I had actually chosen from the menu. Nothing had really appealed to me, but I had chosen macaroni cheese. When faced with this compact mound of pasta, by now of very rubbery consistency; I knew that it had been a mistake and that I should have ordered the fish and creamed potatoes instead. I tried to swallow one or two mouthfuls but it was hopeless. Fortunately, soup had been the first course and this helped to sustain me. Ice-cream was my choice of dessert and this time I used a spoon! Tea consisted of soup, followed by a fruit yoghurt. They had sent me a most unsuitable one, it was full of seeds which took ages to shift. So I was far from impressed. Since I had been sampling proper food, my oral hygiene took much longer. The surgeon had instructed me to swill my mouth thoroughly; in order to dislodge any possible pieces of debris, trapped on the right of my tongue. This I did fastidiously, before cleaning my teeth and using the mouthwash. Thus, it took ages to clear my mouth completely.

That afternoon, Susan Summersgill, a dietician visited me: to discuss the sort of food that I should be tackling at this very early stage. Susan was very helpful and gave me a useful booklet; for those on a soft diet, having difficulty in chewing and swallowing. There were many useful suggestions on how to still eat a variety of foods, albeit in a different form: liquidised, puréed, or soft. Susan ordered liquidised meals for me. Each course was like having a bowl of soup!

Early that Monday evening I noticed the surgeon and staff nurse walking past my room. I could hear Cis telling him about my food intake that day. I felt rather put out that for once he had not bothered to come and see me for himself. At about 6.30pm I had settled in the chair and was engrossed in a novel that Neil had lent me: when to my astonishment the surgeon and his registrar entered my room. I was quite peeved for they were interrupting me at an enthralling part of my book, which no doubt showed! This was the first time that they had both been to see me together. However, a further surprise was to come. The surgeon informed me that he had heard that I was not eating very much (I thought that I was eating quite well). He then stated, that the only way to get me to eat more, was to take the tube away and that it would be removed that night. He joked that he would allow the existing cylinder of food to be used up, for he did not like waste. I managed a half-hearted smile at this comment. I was not at all amused. Cruel man, I thought crossly. I certainly had not expected that step so soon. Though, he was quite right, of course.

While they were both present I thought that I should take the given opportunity to tell them about the lead up to my second operation. They listened attentively and with considerable concern, as I described my unfortunate experience. The surgeon quickly reassured me, by promising that he would ask Mr. Glendinning to remove the metal arch bar by local anaesthetic. How relieved I was that I had told him.

The feeding tube was removed for the last time at 9.30pm. From then on, it was completely up to me. It took me ages to spoon up my soup and liquidised main course which did not satisfy me for long. I was permanently hungry. Luckily, in between meals, I was allowed snacks from the nurses' store (Build-up soups and desserts). Earlier on in the week, Lucy had offered to make me a milk shake using Fortisip (a high protein and high energy drink), combined with ice-cream. It was delicious, so I used to request one of these most afternoons. I also had some goodies (chocolate mousses and fruit corners) brought in. I kept these in the nurses' personal fridge and helped myself. Now, into my fourth week I was well and truly at home! I felt a bit stronger and more like pottering around. How conscious I was of my thin legs, the muscles were very small and flabby through lack of use. My weight had decreased to seven and a half stone: whereas my normal weight was eight stone with a slight fluctuation of a pound or two. Now, no longer at the mercy of the bell: if I needed something, I would go and pester!

The hunger pangs were so hard to ignore. One morning at 4am, I just could not sleep, on account of being absolutely famished. The nurse brought me a couple of Weetabix. Needless to say, I was still ready for my proper breakfast at 8am! The night staff were very thoughtful and on a few occasions I had cups of coffee in the early hours.

My 'trache' wound was being dressed daily and the wheezing effect when I spoke, was gradually lessening. At the age of fifteen, I had developed an allergy to sticking plasters, the result of leaving a plaster on for too long over the site of a smallpox injection. Therefore, my 'trache' wound was covered with a micropore dressing because of the allergy. Nurse Linda Bowen, thought that the micropore dressing was not giving the best seal. Linda wanted to experiment, to find out if I was still allergic to plaster. We were joking around and so foolishly I agreed. Sleek, a form of plaster, was used over the 'trache' site. To complete Linda's crazy experiment, two different types of sticking plaster were also put on my arm. By the following afternoon, a rash had developed on all three sites. My patience was tested to the utter limits. Staff seemed even more rushed off their feet than usual and I had a very long wait before they could change the dressings. The itching nearly drove me mad! I tried to concentrate on some reading, in order to take my mind off the irritation. It was another great lesson in patience! The rash took a few days to clear up, by which time I was back home. Dabbing myself with calamine lotion, I just had to see the funny side of it. So much for Linda's experiment!

One evening during that last week, Miss Evans, the Locum Associate Specialist who had inserted the metal arch bar, visited me.

To my surprise she chatted for nearly half an hour. In fact, I was extremely grateful to her, for what she had to say. Miss Evans was the only person throughout my hospital stay, who actually discussed the possible connection between worry and stress in the development of mouth cancer. I have always been a 'worry-guts' and this thinking was new to me and quite sobering. Miss Evans expressed concern as to my mental and physical state. We discussed in depth, how John and I were coping emotionally. I was most impressed by her obvious empathy of what we were both going through.

During that final week, preparations for my hospital discharge were underway. Melanie Wright, one of the Macmillan nurses visited me. Sue Winfield the dental therapist, cleaned as much of the black stain from my teeth as she could (the metal arch bar still being in situ). I was much happier knowing that my teeth looked clean.

Throughout my stay, Jane Reams, a physiotherapist, had been working with me. On 19th November (my penultimate day in hospital) I was taken to the gym. How weird it was to put on clothes again, after more than three weeks of being in nighties. My legs looked like matchsticks in black leggings and I pulled my long jumper down even further.

I had heat treatment applied to my chest wound, for a lovely soothing ten minutes. Next, a few tasks to be repeated umpteen times to strengthen my various weakened muscles. The most exhausting exercise was having to go on the bicycle for a solid ten minutes. That was agony. I quite enjoyed my journey to the gym: being pushed through the hospital corridors (albeit rather drafty) made a welcome change. On returning to the ward I felt absolutely shattered, as well as ravenously hungry!

Friday 20th November was my very last day in hospital. I still could scarcely believe what I had been through before arriving at this day. Indeed, the thought had struck me on more than one occasion, *this isn't me coping in this way.* I had always been the world's worst worrier. It was as if the Holy Spirit had entered my body and taken over; and I was merely an onlooker, looking on at someone else in the most horrendous situation. This is very hard to explain but I had the strangest feeling that I had been carried through something terrible: like a passive observer of a horror film, as opposed to being the main character of the plot.

Christine Ash, the speech and language therapist visited me. She listed the mouth and tongue exercises that I should continue to do at home. She also talked at length, about the variety and forms of food I could try and tackle. For greater oral agility, Christine suggested that I chew gum or small boiled sweets or polo mints. Licking ice-cream, lollies, even stamps and envelopes was also advised.

Although, I appreciated all the practical advice that I was being given; nevertheless, it was a dreadfully daunting prospect, acknowledging that I had to learn to eat normally again. I was aware that I still had such a long way to go, to full recovery. Not only had I to recover from the trauma of major cancer surgery: in my case I had the added complications of re-establishing the process of normal eating and speaking. What a mind-blowing experience it had been and indeed still was! Just as well that I had not understood what really lay ahead of me, from that dreadful day when I was first diagnosed with cancer. Thank goodness, I had only been given sufficient detail at each stage, rather than the full picture from the word go.

On my final morning in hospital: Amanda, (the student nurse who had initially been apprehensive about talking to me) escorted me down to the surgeon's clinic. How strange to be walking along corridors amongst normally clad people, whilst in my dressing gown and slippers. It was my longest walk since surgery. The surgeon surprised me by saying that he was now going to remove stitches from my tongue. I grimaced at the attending nurse before he took them out; but it was really nothing. He thoroughly examined my mouth and then I had to try and move my tongue. I managed to move it quite easily to the right but there was very little movement to the left. He told me that he wanted to see me at his Combined Clinic on the first Thursday in December.

On my last afternoon, I had another physio session and Jane requested that I continue them twice weekly, for the next four weeks. Susan Summersgill brought me a large supply of Fortisip, to increase my calorific intake. She suggested that I supplement my ordinary diet with three Fortisip cartons daily. In fact, the only way that I could tolerate the taste, was by blending them with ice-cream.

I had advised John to collect me after tea on Friday evening. From what I had gleaned from overhearing various conversations: I knew that there could be many last minute details, to be arranged before discharge. Thus, I thought that it would be easier to have my evening meal in hospital and let the family have theirs before I came home.

About 6pm, when the surgeon and staff nurse walked past my room: I called out high spiritedly, 'I'm still here!' Back came his reply, 'If you don't hurry up and go, I'll keep you in another week!'

Chapter 26
Home

I had extremely mixed feelings about going home: especially in anticipation of the continuing problems with my daughter. Moreover, I felt very sad at having to say goodbye to the staff on 2B, of whom I had grown so fond. After all, the ward had been my home for three and a half weeks (25 days). I was reluctant to leave such a safe, controlled environment for the difficult realities of my world outside. The novelty of being fully dressed and with everything packed had long since passed: by the time John arrived at 7.20pm, I was rather on edge and close to tears.

Staff nurse Rachel Frecklington (the nurse who had admitted me on 27th October) did the necessary paperwork. It seemed that the ward had not heard personally, from the district nurse who would be responsible for visiting me daily, while the 'trache' wound needed dressing. As a result of this lack of contact, Rachel informed us that the district nurse might not call until Monday but that the dressing would be alright until then. Needless to say, I felt a bit put out by this indefinite arrangement and it did not seem a satisfactory note on which to leave the ward.

It was so strange, walking out of the hospital doors and being driven home in the dark. My emotions were a confusion of sadness and happiness. Charlotte and Thomas had made me a lovely 'welcome home' card. I had hardly been home many minutes before Charlotte was chafing to go and see her boyfriend. I found this most upsetting but when they both returned shortly afterwards with flowers for me, then I understood.

I could not sleep at all that first night. My mind was far too active. I sensed that things would be so different now that I was back home. I was convinced that it would be a difficult time.

On that first morning at home (Saturday 21st November) the uncertainty over when the district nurse would come to change my dressing, really agitated me. John contacted our own clinic at Kirton, to explain the situation. The problem was cleared up and the relief nurse on duty that weekend called before lunch. We fixed an earlier time for her Sunday visit, as I anticipated attending church. By the time Boston Health Centre rang up that afternoon, to say someone would be calling, I was able to say that we had already sorted it out.

Even on that first morning, I managed to potter about. I insisted on making cauliflower cheese for lunch. I did seem rather wobbly, measuring out the ingredients for the sauce but I took my time and really enjoyed the end result. I only ate a tiny portion and froze a few portions for later use.

Charlotte and Thomas seemed somewhat reserved but as they had seen very little of me, during my hospitalisation, I accepted that it was inevitable. Charlotte was very pleasant and my first day at home passed quite well. I had a long rest in the afternoon and realised that it had absolutely shattered me just unpacking and doing little tasks. I realised that I did not feel strong enough to go to church.

That Sunday, John had invited Pam Mellor (a Christian Youth Worker) to visit us. Pam told us that if we needed some 'breathing space', in the early days of my being at home, then she would willingly let Charlotte stay with her. We were very grateful for this offer but I immediately dismissed it as unlikely to be taken up.

By late Sunday evening Charlotte's bedtime routine (which in the past had become a nightmare) was once again causing us hassle. I retired to bed most upset. During the Monday morning pre-school routine I was trying to rest in bed, wishing that I was still in hospital. Things seemed just as bad as they had ever been before my surgery: the battle over the hairdryer, being late leaving the house... I was so wound up that I snapped at John, 'It's no good, I can't bear this, she'll have to go to Pam's!' So an equally despairing John rang Pam up and arranged for Charlotte to go there that same evening.

I was broken hearted and hugged her when I said goodbye; it was especially upsetting because she appeared to be very bright, even saying that it would be for the best. Indeed Charlotte seemed to look on staying with Pam as quite an adventure. I felt dreadfully low: the change in Charlotte's behaviour which I was convinced would happen, as a result of my illness, was not apparent. Little did I know that it was not to be as straightforward as this.

However, I was soon enjoying the new-found peace of our home. Thomas seemed much happier. I realised that I was not missing Charlotte at all. By Thursday evening, I began to dread having her back for the weekend. In spite of the absence of Charlotte, those first few days at home were an awful trial. In those early days of readjusting to home life, I often longed to be back on ward 2B.

Mum and John obviously did things differently to me. I became very frustrated seeing what needed doing around the house, knowing that I could not do much and would not be able to for some time. I would start to interfere or try and do little bits out of sheer cussedness and then have to stop because I was exhausted. I certainly was not being a perfect patient at home! I remember clearly one morning during that first week at home: suddenly anger and deep frustration welled up inside me. The utility room was a bit cluttered and a few things were out of place. Only my nearest and dearest have been privileged to witness my fiery outbursts of temper! In the past, door slamming has been a favourite release of tension for me: hence the number of weakened door frames in our home! Suddenly I snapped, screaming, 'It's not bloody fair!' as I banged and slammed doors, throwing what shoes lay around and even flung some grapefruit onto the floor. John came dashing down demanding, 'Whatever's the matter?' He was angry at my loss of control. He did not appear to understand what the rage was about. Mum said nothing: I knew that she understood.

During that first week at home, the visitors and phone calls continued. The very first time that I left the house, was to go with John for a short walk around our estate. We went at night because I did not want to be seen by anyone. Then, on the Thursday of that week, I ventured out in daylight. We walked (albeit still very slowly) much further than I had intended and I was exhausted afterwards. It had been a very damp, cold November day. I was having to accustom myself to the weather again.

On the Tuesday following my hospital discharge, I attended physiotherapy. I felt a nervous wreck because John insisted on dropping me off outside the physiotherapy entrance; while he parked the car and then went to visit someone. I was really uptight about being reliant on him to collect me and wondered what on earth I would do if he did not arrive back on time. I felt so weak and lacking in confidence and I did not want to walk anywhere on my own. John's support throughout had been tremendous and I still needed that. Happily, John returned before the session had ended, so my fears had been groundless. Afterwards, I was utterly drained of all energy and starving hungry. On subsequent visits over the next four weeks, I became more relaxed and more confident. Sometimes John went 'walkabout' but usually he stayed with me.

Charlotte returned for the weekend and at first was much more polite and considerate. By Sunday she was back to her normal standard of behaviour. That Sunday (29th November) I attended St. Mary's Frampton. How wonderful it was, to be back with my church family again. On the prayer-board, which I had instigated ages ago but which had never been properly utilised by others, as I had hoped; I saw that my friend Carole Hampson had put up a prayer for our family. With a lump in my throat, I read the prayer which Thomas had written out, 'Please pray for my mum Heather Marshall.'

Monday 30th November, was the day for my appointment with Mr. Glendinning. I was under the impression that he would see me at his morning clinic and then in the afternoon, would remove the metal arch bar from my mouth. I had even taken along my overnight bag, just in case. At the consultation, he informed me that he would use a local anaesthetic and sedation when he removed the bar. Everything was recovering very well and as I was coping with the impediment in my mouth, he would leave it in for the full six weeks. In jubilation, I exclaimed, 'You mean you are not going to do anything to me today!' He looked most amused. Quite elated at my reprieve, we went along to chat to Michael Johnson, the hospital chaplain.

On Thursday 3rd December, I attended the surgeon's Combined Clinic. John accompanied me. I was extremely tense. I had not known what to expect but experienced great dismay on entering a room full of people, including the surgeon, several doctors and nurses. I recognised a few faces. Everyone was smiling encouragingly but it was such an ordeal. I had wanted to ask the surgeon what was really on my mind. Had he done a thorough check? Was he sure that there were no more cancerous cells lurking about? I could not ask such questions in front of all these relative strangers. It was a most intimidating experience.

That coming Sunday, I was scheduled to do a reading in church. The rota had been made out months earlier. In hospital, I had discussed the possibility of doing this with Christine Ash, the speech and language therapist. She had thought that because I would just have had the metal arch bar removed, it would be inadvisable: my mouth and voice would need time to get over the trauma of yet another operation. Although I had real difficulties over certain sounds (double 'ee' and 'ch' for example) I readily admitted that my speech was not as slushy as it had been. In all honesty, to me, my speech sounded terrible... but everyone else was assuring me that it was not so. I could hardly accuse medical people of telling me lies: whereas friends out of misguided kindness, might not be too honest! However, so many people were complimenting me on the standard of my speech that I had to believe that it must be reasonable. Therefore, I knew that I had no choice but to practise my reading.

John agreed that he would do it for me, if I really could not manage it. Before the service, he checked the lectern because I did not want anyone to suspect that I was going to read; in case I chickened out. Though deep down, I knew that I had to. I had to show my church family how wonderfully their prayers had been answered. Above all, what better way did I have of thanking God, for restoring to me the gift of clear speech, that I so desperately had wanted to continue to use?

Accordingly on 6th December, five and a half weeks after major oral surgery, I read in church. I felt that it went well (even before anyone could tell me) and I really believe that God used that reading for His glory. Joan Mills told me afterwards that she had wanted to applaud. Thank goodness she did not. Another lady said that she had tears streaming down her face. Fortunately, I was unaware of people's reactions.

Isobel Ladds and Sheila Burton, the two district nurses who attended me, were very supportive. I used to look forward to their daily visits. I had known Isobel previously; for we had both been on the Middlecott School P.T.A. After I had told Sheila on one occasion, about the impending removal of the metal arch bar by sedation, she had described most graphically, her experiences of having sedation. I had listened politely but with considerable scepticism; as in glowing terms, Sheila had told me how wonderful she had found sedation to be.

In the early days, as well as dressing the 'trache' wound the nurses also applied calamine lotion to my plaster rash. Of course, I had scratched the rash and made it far worse. A week after my hospital discharge the rash had cleared up.

The nurses were encouraging me to take Fortisip three times daily because my food intake was very low. I could only swallow soft foods, being unable to chew, with the metal arch bar in situ. Swallowing the tiniest amount of food was so time consuming, so tiring and so thoroughly disheartening. I was virtually in a permanent state of hunger. I tried to eat 'little and often' but it was such a laborious chore and I knew that my hunger could not be satisfied. I could not snack on quick and easy fillers: such as bread and biscuits, neither on chocolate and cakes, nor on my favourite food of fresh fruit. It really frustrated me.

On 28th November, a small area of flesh was over-granulating on the 'trache' wound (a small protrusion of flesh had developed above the surface of the wound). I had to see my G.P. before Isobel could apply silver nitrate to the area. This appeared to stop the growth. Subsequently, the area healed up and by 11th December a fully formed scab had dropped off the 'trache' wound. The daily visits ended. A week later, when Isobel saw me, the 'trache' wound was again over-granulating and a new scab was forming. Applications of silver nitrate were given on 18th, 19th and 20th December. By 22nd December the area was much smaller. On 30th December, the 'trache' wound had completely healed up and I was discharged by the district nurse.

Being aware of how restricted my mouth opening was: I could not bear to imagine, how on earth Mr Glendinning was going to manoeuvre this metal contraption from my mouth, without my yelling the place down! Having been through so much, I considered that I could not be brave any longer.

In reality, it all worked out perfectly well. On Tuesday 8th December, I attended the prayer and healing group led by Neil

Russell. Sadly it was to be the group's last meeting, for Neil's departure date for Stamford was fixed for January 1993. Prayer was said for me. I experienced tremendous peace and an awareness that I was now ready for the final hurdle.

Thus, on Wednesday 9th December, exactly six weeks after major surgery, John and I retraced our steps back to ward 2B. The registrar and the young doctor who was acquainted with Adrian, were talking at the nurses' station. On seeing me, the doctor rather bluntly said, 'Oh there's no room for you here, you're on the short-stay ward.' This was contrary to my admission letter. The registrar quickly softened her rather unfriendly words by greeting us warmly and commenting on how well I looked. He asked if he could inspect my neck wound and was most impressed by its appearance. We then made our way to the short-stay ward.

Michael prayed for me during his visit that morning. I felt extremely calm and composed. I had another long wait, for I was last on Mr. Glendinning's list. I busied myself, reading and writing letters. Today there was no pre-med. However, I was utterly relaxed when the porter wheeled me away: so much so that I even managed a light-hearted joke with the accompanying nurse, about her taking my place. It seemed as if I were making the third appearance in a stage play. It was all so terribly familiar. This occasion was a much pleasanter experience than the last one. A nurse commented on how much better I looked, than when she had last seen me.

Mr. Glendinning was beside me, grinning broadly; as the anaesthetist explained that he would keep topping me up with gin, as required! Sedation was given via a vein in my left wrist and local anaesthetic given by two or three injections in my mouth. I knew nothing at all of the latter, nor of what subsequently happened. I was far away in dreamland. I took absolutely ages to come round afterwards. Yes, Sheila Burton had been correct. Sedation was wonderful! I was conscious of being so sleepy and utterly relaxed. How blissfully happy I felt, knowing that at last my surgery was finally, yes finally over. What an incredible journey God had brought me through!

Chapter 27

Normality?

As I have already intimated, those first few weeks at home were immensely difficult. What I had endured in hospital seemed almost preferable to the mental and spiritual anguish that I was now experiencing. Occasionally, I even wished to be back in hospital undergoing it all again, rather than bear this different kind of torment at home.

I was still numbed by the dreadful shock of having my entire world turned upside down dramatically and so drastically, with only two weeks from diagnosis to major surgery. Now came the grim realisation of what actually lay ahead: a laboriously slow return to 'normal life', a recognition that my life had been changed irrevocably; a gradual acknowledgement of having to adapt to a new normality, with a different range of expectations. There was no wonder that my future seemed terribly bleak!

Under normal circumstances I would have been busily preparing for Christmas; doing extra cleaning and baking in readiness for the holidays. Instead, I was spending most of my time sitting around resting, trying to come to terms with what I had been through, feeling extremely weak and still in a state of great shock at what had happened to me. One of the worst aspects of my continuing trauma, was the constant hunger. I could not satisfy the emptiness. I became sick of the sight and taste of Weetabix, soup, yoghurt and rice-pudding (all easy fillers)! I felt so dispirited, imagining that I was destined to exist on this soft diet for the rest of my life.

As someone who has always consumed a huge amount of fresh fruit and salads, preferring crunchy and rather dry textures, hating anything remotely mushy: this was such a disgusting come-down. Yet, I simply had no choice in the matter. When you are starving hungry, as I was permanently; even a bowl of mush is most welcome! At least it was better than being fed by pharyngostomy tube. Patience has never been my strong point. In those early weeks of re-establishing normal eating, I frequently wallowed in the depths of despair. It could not have happened at a worst time, with all the tempting Christmas delicacies around.

Christmas could not be ignored. We still had presents to buy. I was dragged most unwillingly into Boston. I found it a real ordeal standing round, whilst John compared prices for a music system for Charlotte. On one of these shopping trips we lunched at Oldrids. I tackled soup and afterwards lemon meringue pie. The latter was delicious, simply dissolving in my mouth. I recalled the surgeon's words, pre-op. 'You will be able to dine out in restaurants again.' At the time, I had not taken his words at all seriously. Eating out was the least of my worries! Although eating quite messily, I was nevertheless managing a simple snack in public. That occasion boosted my self-confidence enormously.

My twice-weekly physiotherapy sessions lasted for a month. The exercises were very helpful in rebuilding my weakened body. I conscientiously followed the exercise programme at home. Jane the physiotherapist, always had time to talk to me. I was very impressed by her concern. I found these chats so encouraging. Jane obviously cared about how I was feeling and not merely about my physical well-being. One afternoon she pointed out that our carers' needs often have to be met before our own. This was new thinking for me. Yet, I was to identify with this. My mother stayed with us right up to the New Year. In one sense it was far too long. I would have attempted to do more if she had not been there. However, her dearest friend 'Oggy' had died the week after my hospital discharge. I am certain that tending me, helped her at such a very sad time.

Charlotte only stopped at Pam's for two weeks. She was due to go for a third week but Pam was unwell. By then, we had realised that her staying elsewhere was not the answer. I had to try and switch off from the outrageous behaviour, allowing John to manage her.

The 14th December was to be John's Police Christmas Dinner. Weeks ago, this had been ruled out but a few days before the event, John thought that it would be good for me to attend. The only drawback as far as I was concerned, would be the main course. The restaurant staff were put in the picture. Very obligingly, they offered to serve me plaice with cheese sauce.

It was wonderful to dress smartly. I enjoyed the most marvellous meal in ages. Along with everyone else, I easily managed the soup. I ate no bread. It was something I had not yet attempted; fearful of being unable to manoeuvre soggy bread, in my mouth. Most impressive, was my main course. Everything was presented in individual shiny silver dishes. It was a banquet to someone who up until then, had only eaten blended 'mushy' meals. Delicious plaice which really did melt in my mouth and proved effortless to eat; along with creamed potatoes, mashed carrots and cauliflower, accompanied by plenty of cheese sauce to help moisten each mouthful. To me it looked far more appetising than all the Christmas fare that the others were tasting. A choice of dessert and again I could manage the soft cheesecake.

Many people spoke warmly to me. John's boss, at the beginning of his speech, commented on my remarkable recovery and I was given three rousing cheers! It was a superb evening. We joined in with most of the dancing. I was determined to enjoy it to the full. I even surprised myself by asking John's boss to dance, while John was dancing with someone else.

By the lead up to all the Christmas events, I felt a little stronger. I was still needing a rest most afternoons and only rising after a long leisurely breakfast in bed (mushy Weetabix, a mashed up banana, still no bread).

One evening, Mum and I attended Kirton Parish Church for the Primary School Concert. This was the first time since surgery that I had been in such a crowded place. The church was packed with staff, pupils and parents. I felt extremely conspicuous and was pleased that we sat in a side aisle. The staff were delighted to see me. They had already sent me cards and flowers much earlier and prior to this concert; I had received a lovely poinsettia from them. By now, I had managed to walk on my own to the village, to do a little light shopping. So many people seemed to know about me. It was very humbling to be shown such concern.

On another occasion, John and I were invited to a party with some of the students from the German evening class that I used to attend. It was a lovely evening and most stimulating to meet different people. How refreshing to discuss other subjects: other than what we had focused on for the past two months. I chose not to indulge in any of the party food but ate my two chocolate mousses. Something else I was tiring of! We played Trivial Pursuit in German. My German was sadly very rusty but I had to take my turn in reading the questions. Once or twice I even managed to respond in German. That was another boost to my ego. I could communicate not only clearly in my own language but in German. Nothing was said directly to me about my operation. Though afterwards, John informed me that the tutor had been very impressed by the clarity of my speech. The evening did us both good. I had been able to join in and even socialise with a few new people. It helped me realise that I was not a freak at all. Compared to my gross appearance in hospital with muscle pedicle, I now looked quite alright. There was still some swelling on my right jaw but it was greatly reduced, to what it had been.

Towards the end of December, I had a most pleasant surprise. David Langley, a member of St. Mary's congregation, invited me to be in the Candlemas Pantomime, to be held the following February. I knew that it was time that he very furtively selected his cast and had anticipated that it might well be John's turn again. I was staggered at David's obvious confidence in my ability to communicate clearly. Indeed David had given me the most enthusiastic welcome in church on our first meeting, post-op. Apparently, he had expected to see me looking grey and gaunt and was amazed by how well I appeared and had wanted to jump for joy. For years David had been most complimentary about the way that I read in church. Taking part in the pantomime was exactly the challenge that I needed and I was immensely grateful.

As was our custom, the nine of us from the ex-Bishop's Course Group held a Christmas get-together. Throughout, they had all given me such tremendous support. I was further surprised, by being presented with a beautiful Christmas table decoration. Bob Hiron rather awkwardly, obviously trying to pass it off in his usual matter-of-fact manner, said something complimentary about the way that I had coped and of being terribly brave. I know that without the love and encouragement shown by so many dear friends; the situation would have been much harder for us. We had our usual mad session of 'letting our hair down'. John had been invited too and was just as bad as the rest of us!

The prospect of how to spend Christmas, was solved by my sister-in-law Carol offering to come and cook our Christmas meal. So Carol, nephew Mark and niece Sarah, spent the day with us. I was still only swallowing soft foods therefore I chose to have my Christmas dinner blended. It was far easier than attempting to chew for the very first time, especially with so many people present. We thoroughly enjoyed our day.

After Christmas we viewed a really hilarious film called 'Shirley Valentine.' It told the story of a housewife who abandoned her family to go away on a foreign holiday. Afterwards, it brought to mind my desperate longings of early 1992: when in an extremely depressed state, I had envisaged how blissful it would be to escape from my life and its problems and to 'just be myself'. It suddenly dawned on me that those wishes had been granted but in the most bizarre way possible. Three and a half weeks stuck in hospital after major surgery for cancer has not quite the appeal of being wined and dined abroad. Nonetheless, I had like Shirley Valentine, been given a most precious breathing time to rediscover myself. The overall attention lavished on me in hospital: served an even greater psychological need as well as the more immediate necessity of having my physical needs met. It brought home to me how much I was valued as an individual and not merely as someone's wife or mother.

The 1st January was to be the final breakthrough for me. We spent the day at John's parents. I consumed roast pork with all the trimmings (a much smaller portion than I would have tackled pre-op). At long last I actually dared to chew. I ate tiny morsels very, very slowly... I was actually chewing and swallowing! It was such a relief! It took me ages to demolish the meal but it was a fantastic sense of achievement. In retrospect, I am sure that physically, I could have tackled chewing slightly earlier; thus, minimising the hunger pangs. However, mentally I could not even bring myself to try.

Bread was the ultimate hurdle. It proved to be one of the hardest and slowest things to eat. In fact, two and a half years on, when this was originally written, it still is. I did not even attempt a bread crumb until well into January 1993. Once I had succeeded I was ecstatic. Foods that I had drooled over as being totally unmanageable, were once more possible. How marvellous, to have an unrestricted diet again! For years our family have only eaten wholemeal or granary bread. Soft white bread only being eaten when out. The latter, I quickly discovered was to be avoided at all cost. It stuck to my palate and had to be literally scraped away. Chocolate, biscuits, cakes, pastry and scones caused similar problems.

The 11th January, was another significant date. John and I ate fish and chips at Tate's Restaurant in Boston. I managed to consume half of a meal that I would normally have completely eaten. Obviously, it would take time to eat larger quantities of food again.

My weight gradually increased. By mid-January, I was back to my normal eight stone, having regained the half stone that I lost post-op. Never one to eat gravy, I still ate plain meat and vegetable meals dry. However, I soon found that smaller pieces of meat, (rather than whole slices, chops or steaks) in a sauce, were much easier and more palatable to eat. Fortunately, I have always enjoyed cooking a variety of mince and casserole dishes: so initially I tended to concentrate on these. Fish, of course, was much simpler to eat.

By the end of January, I was tackling a normal range of foods again, with some essential differences. Fruit had to be peeled, (even grapes!) otherwise the skin would remain in my mouth. Ever since I had my upper six front teeth crowned, I had never dared to bite into a whole apple. Now, all fruit was chopped up finely and I only put tiny pieces into my mouth. Eating, especially main meals, took an eternity. It did not exactly help, that my family used to devour their food like starving beasts! Previously I had always eaten very rapidly. It was now at snail's pace. The family were ready for their dessert, when I was barely a quarter of the way through my main course. It was less stressful to eat alone, whenever I could. In those early days, I very rarely finished my meal. I used to give up, tired out by the exertion of slowly chewing and swallowing, before I was really satisfied. Fortunately puddings were much easier to devour. Annoyingly, not long after having eaten a meal, I was still hungry.

Easy fillers, especially breakfast cereal and bananas were very handy. I always carried a few biscuits with me, wherever I went, as emergency rations; in my determination not to fast unnecessarily. I continued to use Fortisip build-up drinks, for the first half of that year. I needed a fortifying milk shake, very often mid-afternoon with biscuits, to stave off hunger pangs until my evening meal.

Feeling hungry so much, was to become one of the main negative aspects of the post-op. stage. Indeed, two and a half years on, I still tend to eat smaller meals little and often. The effort of eating and swilling afterwards, depending on what has been eaten, can be extremely time-consuming.

I soon discovered that having a permanently dry mouth, (including dry lips) was another definite side-effect. Even while drinking, my mouth felt so dry. Two and a half years post-op., at a dental clinic; Miss Evans suggested the use of Salivix dry mouth pastilles, as an aid to stimulate saliva . These gave some relief although I never used the maximum daily dosage of eight. They were ideal to carry in my handbag, whenever a drink was unavailable.

Six years post-op. the dryness persists. Counteracting the perpetual dryness of my lips, can be an irritating and time-consuming chore. The most effective relief is to be found from a generous application of Vaseline Pure Petroleum Jelly. When out, I use a lip balm. In addition to the pastilles, my handbag now contains a tiny plastic miniature Gin bottle. This 'emergency water' is also invaluable for swilling away debris from very dry snacks, such as scones, biscuits, cakes and sandwiches. The surgeon has since explained that the extreme dryness in my mouth is due to the removal of the right submandibular salivary gland. The lips are dry because the nerve supply to the oral cavity and the surrounding area has been interfered with.

Eating and drinking post-op. was a very messy affair. I needed a bib! I just could not drink cleanly. There was always some spillage on the container or on me. With any crumbly foods, there were more crumbs around my mouth, on the chair or floor than in my mouth! Initially when out, I was so self-conscious of the debris that I was causing; always requesting a saucer for my drink or a plate for food. One always knew which drinking utensil I had used; not by the lipstick stains but by the drops of tea or coffee spilt on the side. This was due to my jaw alignment being different; which has altered my lip contact. In time it became less of a problem, no doubt because I had become accustomed to it.

On Thursday 5th January, 1993 I had my hair trimmed and permed. That made me feel so much brighter. At least my hair looked decent! With great apprehension, I attended Combined Clinic. I was most unhappy at the prospect of a consulting room full of people.

Prior to that, I had an appointment with Christine the speech and language therapist. She remarked on my speech improvement. That was my main concern at this early stage. In spite of many people commenting favourably; I was still dissatisfied. To me, my speech sounded gross. Christine explained that as the swelling subsided and as tongue mobility increased, my speech would improve. I read a few extracts aloud and then worked through some word lists. Christine noted the sounds that I needed to practise at home.   These being: words with 's' endings, words with combination endings, e.g. a consonant followed by an 's'or 'z' sound such as the 'ks' in books, words with a double 'ss' in the middle e.g. misses.

Christine also advised me to practise reading aloud, isolating any difficult sounds and then working on them. My speech was of an acceptable level but there was reduced clarity in polysyllabic words (words of many syllables); in tongue tip sounds such as 't' and 'd'; in words with two or more consonants together e.g. 'spl' as in splash; in words with the same set of consonants at the start; middle or end of a word; such as though, clothes and mouth.

As well as this practical help, I discussed with Christine how I was really feeling, explaining how difficult I had found Combined Clinic. She suggested that I have a quiet word with the nurse beforehand. As usual, I was slow on the uptake and by the time my name was called, I had said nothing. Feeling quite peeved with myself, I was ushered into the crowded consulting room. Somehow, it was not as bad as before. The surgeon thought that my operation had taken place much earlier. When I reminded him that it was only ten weeks ago, he commented that my recovery was quite remarkable for such a short time. I asked one or two general questions before saying that there were a few things that I wished to query with him and would it be possible to make a separate appointment, because I did not want to waste his colleagues' time. With that, he obligingly offered the use of the adjoining room. I was able to ask what was really bothering me and to be greatly reassured by his answers. I also queried what I had only recently become conscious of: the immobility of the right side of my lower lip; most noticeable during speech and when smiling. I was worried that people on meeting me for the first time would regard me as an ugly freak! The surgeon looked terribly apologetic about this one permanent effect of his surgery, as he quietly said, 'I am very sorry about it but it's better than having cancer.' That certainly put it into perspective. He seemed to understand when I pointed out how intimidating I had found the previous clinic. I was much happier than when I had arrived, having had my real concerns answered.

In mid-January I had an appointment to see Mr. Glendinning and the hygienist. Expecting a mere check-up, it was an awful shock to be told that my back teeth on the right side of my mouth, needed further smoothing down to protect my tongue. This was an extremely tricky manoeuvre. A nurse kept my tongue as far away from Sue's instrument as she could. I tried to reassure myself that this was nothing at all in comparison to what I had already been through. Nonetheless, it was most unpleasant especially because my mouth would not open very far. In addition Sue cleaned the remaining black deposits of mouthwash from my teeth. The gap where one of my lower incisors had been removed during the splitting of my jaw-bone, had closed; making a false tooth unnecessary. My very irregular set of lower teeth now looked more evenly spaced. An unexpected bonus!

John took the opportunity to speak to Judith Woodham, the senior dental nurse who had been present at the biopsy. He described our feelings regarding the lack of immediate support, after the shocking diagnosis. He mentioned the helpful BACUP literature that a friend had given us. Judith agreed that something more should be done. John promised to send the Oral Department some BACUP information. We then revisited 2B and were most warmly greeted by Sister Karen Woulds and nurses Cis Courtney-Day and Linda Bowen. We informed them of our willingness to speak to any in-patients or relatives, if they thought that it would help. Sister said that she would inform the surgeon.

Afterwards, we joined Michael Johnson and Jenny Dumat for the midday Wednesday service. I took communion for the first time since surgery. (I could only manage a tiny fragment of the wafer). How appropriate that this should take place in the hospital chapel.

Chapter 28

Picking Up The Pieces

Rehearsals for Aladdin were great fun. John had the leading role. He was the narrator and Genie. I played a Chinese lady-in-waiting. My few lines had to be uttered in a sing-song voice. On the night, I looked extremely glamorous: whitened face, oriental eye make-up and vivid red lips. To complete the ensemble, I wore a black wig skewered with knitting needles plus huge red bow. I was dressed in lilac silk pyjamas. What a contrast to the monstrous image seen in hospital. How thankful I was that God had delivered me safely through such a terrible ordeal. Now He was enabling me to regain my confidence and be able to participate even in the non-essential but enriching fun things of life. At fourteen weeks post-op. I was getting back to 'ordinary life'.

Household tasks were now tackled in short bursts. I still relied on John to do the big supermarket shopping, or to accompany me. I had not even attempted to drive. I knew that I could not delay much longer because it was so impractical. My first drive was to hospital, for my February Combined Clinic appointment. It was exhilarating to be at the wheel again and I sped down the new A16! This time there were fewer people in the room and I was much more relaxed. Everything was absolutely fine. The surgeon did his usual thorough examination of my mouth and neck. That afternoon at Pilgrim, I experienced an overwhelming sensation of really being back in a place which was so familiar and comforting to me. I felt strongly drawn to the hospital. Doubtless, all the reassurances from the surgeon and the speech and language therapist about my excellent progress, contributed to this state of well-being.

My first solitary shopping trip to Somerfield was rather an ordeal. I felt mentally and physically drained before I was even halfway through the shopping. At the February half-term I managed my longest drive. Mum, Thomas and I, visited the Cockerills at Bourne. Kathleen then drove us to Peterborough Ice Rink. We skated for an hour. Thomas whizzed round with her boys. I was utterly content to skate slowly round, marvelling in being strong enough to do this activity. Another first!

By now I had begun to chafe about returning to swimming. It seemed peculiar that I had been denied my favourite pastime for so long. Pre-op. we tried to attend the weekly sessions organised by the Police Social Club at Boston Swimming Pool.

My chest wounds were well healed. I was extremely thankful that the lineal scar which extended five centimetres from my right armpit (axilla), across the upper margin of my right breast, down towards the mid-line and continued for approximately five centimetres along the inframammary fold; was neatly concealed by my bra. Therefore, I felt perfectly confident about wearing a swimming-costume. This being in spite of the fact, that on my final day in hospital I had such a terrible shock: on noticing that my right breast was slightly higher than the left one. The surgeon explained that in removing the pectoralis major muscle, from behind the breast, the latter had been elevated. He thought that it would become less in time but that the right breast would probably always be higher. I was put in touch with Margaret Dooley: who was then the stoma nurse advising ladies undergoing mastectomies. A prosthesis (false piece) to wear inside my bra was ordered but it made no difference. She thought that a more supportive bra was all that was required. As I was not well endowed and certainly not one to sunbathe topless, it was not a problem! Clear pronunciation mattered far more to me than a slightly lop-sided look when unclothed.

The scar which did perturb me, being visible above my swimwear: was the seven centimetre long scar along my right clavicle. It was a weirdly shaped scar, extending in width for approximately five centimetres. The stitches had been done in a higgledy-piggledy fashion. To me the scar resembled a large spider with its long legs splayed. This, apart from appearing quite bizarre was incredibly sensitive to touch.

I found the sensation immensely repugnant. I believe that it triggered off unpleasant memories of how gruesome I had looked. Underneath this wound there was a very small raised pad of firm flesh, which was a remnant of the removed muscle: a contrast to the even leaner layer of flesh that now covered my ribs on the right side.

I have always been conscious of having prominent ribs and shoulder bones. Nonetheless, it would not deter me from indulging in my favoured hobby. In March, at Combined Clinic, the surgeon said that it was perfectly alright for me to swim. I swam for the first time, eighteen weeks post-op. I managed four lengths. I was to enjoy two further swims that month.

Christine the speech and language therapist, pointed out that it had been to my advantage to have previously enjoyed a high level of speech clarity. She considered that as a French teacher, I had certain skills in monitoring and reproducing specific sounds, vital for teaching purposes. These same skills had been of paramount importance in re-establishing my high level of speech, post-operatively. Christine recognised that I had the necessary motivation to regain this quality. What an understatement! Recovery of speech to **my** acceptable high level, was of prime concern; almost to the extent of it being an obsession. She assured me that I was still at the top end of the high quality range for normal speech, although now there was a slightly lower ceiling. These were early days but I had achieved a very good result in a very short time. She explained that the position of the tumour: on the right lateral border of my tongue, with its subsequent removal, was the least detrimental to speech, compared to if the tongue tip had been affected. For loss of the tongue tip would have a serious effect on the agility of the tongue and the range of sounds possible. Working on my sounds, reinforced this sobering fact. Relief that the most important part of my tongue had been spared, was tremendous. I practised my words lists frequently. Charlotte and Thomas used to delight in saying the hardest words that they could think of, for me to repeat. It was a great game!

In March I attended a ceilidh at Kirton Primary School, with three friends. The last time that the staff had seen me, was at their Christmas concert. They were thrilled with my progress. I had not given a single thought as to whether I should ultimately return to supply teaching. I was far too preoccupied, coming to terms with what I had been through and of how I was on a day to day basis. My energies were naturally focused on building myself up to normal health and strength again. One or two staff joked about me being ready to return to teaching. I chatted to Gill Wright the head teacher, mentioning that I had started some writing and that I felt extremely drawn to the hospital. Much to my surprise, she informed me that she had taken my name off the supply list. I had a strong conviction that because someone else had taken that decision for me; it was God's way of letting me know that I was not to continue teaching.

The writing which I commenced in March 1993; had actually originated in hospital. Along with the few personal items that I had taken in, was a red hard-backed exercise book. Once I had accepted my stay in hospital more positively, I found the book invaluable to record details of dates, treatments, comments on my daily progress and frame of mind. After my discharge from hospital, I continued to note further information that I gleaned at my numerous out-patient appointments. In fact, the Revd. Neil Russell, on one of his early hospital visits to me, when I had mentioned my notes, had said, 'Perhaps, if you wrote about it, you would be an encouragement to others.' Doubtless, these aspirations had lain dormant in my mind. Val Halgarth our church magazine assistant editor, had suggested that I write the opening letter for the April issue. In our interregnum, several people were taking a turn in writing what would normally have been the vicar's letter. Val thought that it would be most fitting for me, to share my personal testimony of suffering at Easter.

I quickly realised that I could not possibly write it as a letter. It had to be a straightforward account of my diagnosis, leading up to and including my experiences in hospital. This writing became a most significant undertaking. It developed into a sixteen-page account. The first four pages were included in the April and May editions of our magazine 'The Spires.' As much as I had felt compelled to write; I was extremely apprehensive about revealing such personal details. At that time John and I believed that possibly a booklet could be printed off and money raised for DOCATEF (the Detection of Cancer and Treatment Equipment Fund). Indeed this was what Val included in her introduction to 'Heather's Story.' John had helped me choose the title, 'Safe In The Shadow Of The Lord' *(See Chapter 3).*

Towards the end of March, during a weekend away; we arranged to meet Trudy Elliott. It was lovely to see her again after nearly six years. Our conversation focused on Trudy's friend Brenda, who had only a few months to live. Unfortunately, we were unable to meet Brenda's husband Olly and their three children. In spite of not knowing them personally, they had been in our prayers since the previous October.

After church on Sundays, I was always full of good intentions to keep my cool, regarding Charlotte's annoying habits! It was a futile exercise because I never did! On Mothering Sunday, having made my habitual inward resolutions; I returned home, dreading what inevitable chaos and muddle would trigger off my bad temper. Much to my annoyance, Charlotte was still in the bathroom.

Entering the kitchen, instead of the usual messy half-hearted attempt at clearing away her breakfast dishes: was an immaculately tidy room. On the kitchen table lay a baking rack, with home-made biscuits and a lovely note from Charlotte. I felt so ashamed. It was totally unexpected and such a very rare event to see a thoughtful side to her nature. The occasion merited recording, so I took some photographs. The biscuits were delicious. It was a recipe that Charlotte had done previously at school. Although, they were supposed to be for me, she ate most of them. I did not mind at all. After all, it was the thought that mattered and hopefully a lesson that I had learned!

In April, three of us from St. Mary's attended a Deanery Study Day on Christian Healing, at Pilgrim Hospital. During the introductory session, the chaplain Michael Johnson, informed us that in the afternoon we would all share in a service of Holy Communion, with the special laying on of hands and anointing with oil. He mentioned a text, saying that someone would be reading that out. Immediately, I knew that I had to do the reading. During coffee, I was deep in thought, when Michael approached a circle of people asking for someone to volunteer for the reading. As a shy very retiring person, I could never push myself forward, preferring to be asked, rather than to volunteer for anything. I would then experience deep frustration because someone else would inevitably, unreservedly take the given opportunity and as usual I was overlooked.

On this occasion no one else stood a chance. I volunteered at once. I found the morning stimulating, although extremely difficult to listen to at times. My experiences of healing were so real! At this early stage, I was focusing primarily on my physical healing. For the first time ever in such a large gathering, I knew that I should say something but my shyness or may be my emotions held me back.

After lunch we met in the chapel. I felt very honoured to be contributing to the service by doing a reading. Obviously, not many people present were aware of the significance of this for me. It was a beautiful service. Being anointed with oil again brought back memories of the first time that I had experienced this. John and I received Holy Unction the night before major surgery. That, being a tremendously moving occasion.

At our concluding session; everything suddenly welled up inside me and I hastily retreated to the loo, for a good howl! There obviously had been a good reason for my being the last to arrive that morning and so have to take the seat nearest the door! Acutely conscious of being red-eyed, I eventually joined everyone for tea. Joyce Fairweather, the churchwarden from Kirton, came over. She told me that the most meaningful part of the entire day for her, had been hearing me read. It had brought to mind the occasion when she had visited me in hospital, with the Kirton vicar. It was the awful morning when I still had the 'trache' tube in. I was unable to speak and in a most distressed state of mind.

At my April appointment, the speech and language therapist measured my mouth opening. It was approximately four centimetres; double the width when an in-patient. By now I was conscious of deterioration in my speech. I seemed to be hissing certain sounds. Aware that I had made excellent progress in my speech, in only a short time: it came as a terrific shock as well as being extremely puzzling. Christine explained that healing in my mouth went in fits and starts. Speech would improve dramatically, followed by a few steps back and then further improvement. My tongue was still settling down after surgery, the dynamics of the post-operative stage. The sounds may be worse than before because my tongue was still changing shape and may not be touching the same contact spots. My post-op. tongue does not have the complete range of movement, ease and speed of mobility compared to my pre-op. tongue. It is smaller and scar tissue reduces its speed. According to the surgeon, a third of my tongue has been removed. All has been replaced but it is not an exact reconstruction; the tongue being fractionally 5% narrower. The tongue may not be touching the contact spots necessary to produce certain distinct sounds. This changing relationship of tongue to mouth cavity affects the amount of air escaping as a sound is produced. This explained the hissing sound (sibilance) that I noticed especially with words ending with 's' and 'z'.

That Easter, we travelled to Devon. My brother Alan and his fiancée Lynne were to marry on Maunday Thursday. Alan did not say anything specifically to me about my illness; though, I did get a very good hug from him. Lynne, as usual was much easier to talk to. It meant a great deal to me, when Alan asked me to be his witness at the short civil ceremony. Naturally, I was included in the photos. I was even more self-conscious than ever, with my crooked post-op. smile.

On Easter Sunday, I read in church. It filled me with immense joy to be participating on this most significant day in the Christian year. What a marvellous feeling of utter thankfulness exuded from me: that in spite of such traumatic major surgery, I still had a very clear voice that God intended me to use for Him.

Throughout those difficult months of 1993, the situation with Charlotte had not noticeably improved. Once, when feeling particularly depressed: I snappily told Charlotte that I just could not cope with anymore worry because the stress and anxiety that she had caused me previously, might possibly have contributed to the development of my tumour. It was wicked of me: as soon as the words were uttered, I knew that I had sunk so very low. Inwardly, I admitted that I had lashed out in a nasty loss of temper. I had never experienced any bitterness that I had suffered cancer. Indeed, I had accepted this only hours after the diagnosis: fervently trusting that God would use the cancer and bring something positive out of it. Yet, I was utterly distraught over the continuing battles at home. I could not comprehend why things had not radically improved. After all, I had done my bit; I had endured all that terrible suffering.

Wasn't that what it was all about? To resolve the mother and daughter problem? How much more I had to learn...

Charlotte was naturally terribly upset at my outburst. It obviously did not improve our relationship. Feeling extremely guilty, I realised that I had to make her understand that she was not to blame. Yet inexplicably, I blotted the whole incident out.

In 1994, Charlotte was quizzing me about my diagnosis. 'Do you still blame me?' she asked. I was absolutely horrified. Had she been feeling guilt-laden all this time? I could no longer ignore the issue and I gave a very long, overdue apology and attempted an explanation for my words and subsequent behaviour. The relief she expressed simply reinforced my shame. All I could do was to ask her forgiveness and to ask God to forgive me for venting my anger on her. I had to leave it there and pray that I never stooped so low again.

Once I had resumed the responsibility of doing the weekly shopping at Somerfield; it became quite a meeting place. While people pushed by with laden trolleys, I would be talking about my hospital experiences and my faith. My writing also proved to be a topic of conversation. A few people from church commented that the four-page extract had been very moving and they were keen to read more. Strangely however, the majority chose not to comment. At that time I found it hurtful.

I also noticed the reluctance of many people, amongst them some very old dear friends: to talk in depth about what I had gone through and most importantly to discuss the reality of how I was right now. Usually, after a brief enquiry as to how I was, that was as much as they wished to discuss. I am certain that for most people, once I was discharged from hospital, that was it...end of story! I was better! No need for further concern or support.

Apart from John, my mother, the children in their very limited way and possibly a couple of close friends: no one realised the inner turmoil that I was enduring after such a traumatic experience. In my hurt, confused state, I took this at face value. People don't really care. They think I am back to normal and that everything is as it was before. It struck me as highly insensitive, that virtually as soon as I was out of hospital; my name was removed from St. Mary's prayer list. Admittedly, life at church was now more difficult with Neil

Russell's impending departure and the unwelcome prospect of a long interregnum. This disappointment in the lack of prayer support in my own church, was heightened; by meeting up with the Revd. Andrew Burnett at Neil's induction service at Stamford. Andrew had visited me in hospital. After warmly enquiring about me, he stated, 'Good, now I'll put you on our thanksgiving list.'

Once Christmas was over, visitors became few and far between. This coincided with a period of feeling generally so miserably low and dispirited at what I now had to battle through. In reality, life was still very much a continuing nightmare. From the almost 'over-the-top' response during my hospitalisation: it seemed like total abandonment. I was spending a great deal of time on my own because John was naturally back at work and the children were at school.

I saw local church friends at services and other activities, so they were in touch. However, there were two friends who faithfully continued to pop round. Carole Hampson came regularly, as did Val Wilkinson. I had only got to know Val properly since my diagnosis. She was the only one to whom I could speak so openly about my high and low times. Val was still undergoing her own treatment for cancer. We had so much in common. She understood much of what I was going through. Many occasions when Val just happened to call round: her timing was perfect. It was as if she sensed that John and I were in need of special support at that particular moment.

Chapter 29
The Way Forward

During that spring, I had numerous doubts about whether it was right for me, to detail a most traumatic experience so graphically. I certainly could not write it in any other way. Deep down I knew that I was doing what I had to. I began to feel that God was trying to tell me something.

I now realised that my original sixteen-page account was grossly inadequate. I attempted no further writing for two months because I was extremely uncertain as to how to proceed. In May I began to rewrite it. Instead of commencing with the shocking diagnosis, I described how I was feeling early in 1992. As I did so, I recognised pointers (scoffers would derisively dismiss these as mere coincidences); which convinced me that God had been preparing us for this shock for many months and maybe for a few years. Many significant events have occurred throughout my life. I would definitely not call them chance happenings but God's mysterious and amazing way of working. The most chilling pointer being the article that I had read on mouth cancer, two or three years prior to my own surgery. It had really terrified me. Yet strangely, once the initial fear had passed, I had completely forgotten the article: that is until my writing began in earnest.

John was most impressed by what I had written and thought that it should go into print. He too had recorded his own brief account. It was intriguing how his version of what had occurred, differed from mine.

It was not until I had cancer, that I was able to talk openly to non-Christians about faith. Now, whenever I began to discuss my experience of coping with cancer; I constantly referred to the significance of it.

I soon realised that my writing might take a long time, but if it was meant to be; then it would be, in spite of life's ordinary and frequent distractions! I have always been content to spend hours on my own and have never been at a loss over what to do when not teaching. As my written work developed; I was also becoming aware of my great need to talk. I would even look forward to visiting the local shops. There would always be someone I knew, with whom I could chat. If I spoke about cancer I experienced a boldness to witness about my faith. John would say, I would really glow. Val Wilkinson said, 'I'd blossomed.' Whatever the explanation, something so remarkable had happened to me that I had to share it, whenever the opportunity arose. I was never at a loss for words either: they just flowed! I firmly believe that the Holy Spirit took over. I was also being given the opportunity to listen. Nothing strange in that: for years I had thought that I was a good listener. Married to John, how could I be otherwise!

One evening a friend Linda Hiron, telephoned to ask a favour. Would I pray for a friend who was very ill with lung cancer? Apparently, as soon as she had learned the bad news, Linda had felt compelled to contact me because I would understand what he was going through. Pre-op. I would have been completely floored by such sad circumstances. We talked at length and I offered to accompany Linda when she visited, if that would help. She seemed pleased at that. Sadly, in a few days, her friend died. I had prayed for him and his wife and in spite of having never met him, I was very saddened. Afterwards, Linda admitted how much it had helped to talk to me.

It seemed that everywhere I went, there was always a hospital connection: as if for some reason, I was not to be allowed to forget the place! I used to have regular chats with Judith Woodham, the dental nurse at Somerfield. Once, while buying skates for my son Thomas, of all the unlikely people to meet: was the registrar, who had assisted at my operation.

I thus spent considerable time pondering over my hospital experiences. As I write this chapter, approximately two and a half years afterwards, the memories are intensely vivid. Whether because I am still making sense of it, or getting over the shock, I do not know: or whether it is the compulsion to write which necessitates keeping those memories alive, for the purpose of accuracy. I only know that I have to record what happened.

The 12th of April finally arrived: the day John and I had been eagerly anticipating Dr. Adrian Cozma's return. It was a wonderful reunion. The timing was perfect. Adrian was able to join us for John's licensing as a Reader in Lincoln Cathedral, on Saturday 17th April. It was a tremendous occasion. We were so proud of John. The transformation in his life since becoming a Christian, had been truly outstanding. The family and a few local friends travelled by minibus. Other friends joined us for the two-hour service, including Revd. Neil Russell and his wife Kathy. After all, he was to blame for all of this! How we all missed them. Our loss was Stamford's gain.

After the weekend, Adrian travelled to London to take the P.L.A.B. test. If successful, he would be able to work and complete further study in a British hospital. We were absolutely gutted on learning that he had failed. It seemed that he would have to return home. The Romanian relief fund had already invested a considerable amount in his further medical studies. To keep him here until he could re-sit the test in six months' time, was totally unaffordable.

I had kept in touch with Joanna Townend, the student nurse, whom I had met on 2B. On Thursday 29th April shortly after Adrian had returned to Pilgrim; we all arranged to meet in the hospital social club. Jo was most impressed by how well I looked. The last time she had seen me was the day following the removal of the 'trache' tube. A few of the doctors known to John and Adrian were also there. Dr. Abe Syed an anaesthetist, spoke very warmly to me. I had not seen him since he had visited me in hospital. Jo drove us to The Ball House. Initially, the four of us were discussing Adrian's future.

Up until then, Adrian had only made a few general comments about how well I looked. He had not asked me anything about my operation. I had expected him to have bombarded me with questions. I felt extremely puzzled and a little disappointed at his apparent lack of interest. Of course, John had written to him in great detail. So he did know what had occurred. Out of the blue, Adrian suddenly embarrassed me by blurting out, 'Heather, you are the bravest person I have ever met.' I turned a deep beetroot colour, much to his amusement. He continued by saying that before my surgery; while looking at a photo of me, his mother had remarked that I was going to get through okay.

Jo and I had so much news to share. In fact she made a thought provoking statement, regarding my teaching. 'Perhaps, God has shut the door on it!' The week before my diagnosis, I had done a solid week of teaching and had thoroughly enjoyed it. Indeed, I was actually looking forward to the few days, that were booked for the same class, right through from late October until the following February. It was obviously not meant to be. How glad I was that my final week of teaching had been such a happy and fulfilled one. Better to go out on a good note than a bad one. Jo was the first person to voice the thoughts that by now, I had already been considering. Yes, it may be that God had finally closed the door on my teaching career. I could accept this possibility but it certainly went no further. At this stage, I was not consciously wondering, *what new door is going to open for me?* I recall telling Jo that I felt very enriched by what I had experienced. Furthermore, I had met so many people that I would not have normally come into contact with.

On 26th April, I was very disconcerted to discover a tiny white spot on the right side of my lower lip. Straight away, my stomach churned in dread. John thought that it was an ordinary ulcer. These I had never experienced. By the following day it was so painful and it hurt to eat and drink. I felt very low, trying to believe that it was a mere ulcer but nevertheless... a tumour has to start somewhere. I was worried. I applied Bongela and after a few days the ulcer disappeared. In its place I could see a tiny dent in my lip, presumably caused by contact of an upper tooth. Five days later, another tiny white spot appeared. Fortunately, the next day was Combined Clinic. The surgeon reassured me that the ulcer was not cancerous. The dent was caused by a tooth coming into contact with part of my lower right lip. This has been rendered immobile because of irreparable damage done to the mandibular branch of the facial nerve; which in my case is an inevitable side-effect in the surgical approach to cancer. This was exactly what I had figured out. I was much relieved. Furthermore, the surgeon explained that my tongue and mouth were still in a state of change, due to the dynamics of the post-op. settlement of tissues. He would write to Mr. Glendinning so that the tooth could be filed. He stressed that in future; if something was worrying me, I had only to telephone and he would see me as soon as he possibly could. I was most impressed by this concern for my well-being.

To celebrate John's fortieth birthday; we held a joint party with Tony Hales, who was fifty the following day. It was to be a 'Tramps' Supper.' Jane Hales, a born party organiser, did most of the hard work, for which I was very grateful. We hired St. Michael's Church Hall and hosted about seventy guests between us. A good proportion dressed up. I was in my element: a real scruff, daubing mud from the garden onto my face and arms. Charlotte's rig-out was more of a tart than a tramp, though she looked good! It was a lovely evening. The after supper entertainment: was of John and Tony, sat on a makeshift privy. They were privy-builders and their hilarious dialogue had people in stitches! It was a party with a difference.

Tuesday 4th May, was John's actual birthday. We took Adrian out to Stockwith Mill. Over lunch, they discussed the various options facing Adrian. I felt excluded and was tempted to walk off and leave them to it! There seemed to be a barrier between Adrian and me. For I still could not comprehend his reserve. I wanted to talk to him in depth about all the past events but our conversation was purely on trivia.

The following weekend Adrian accompanied us to church. I decided to update him on my recent consultation, regarding the lip ulcer. I also informed him that the surgeon had joked about my visit to the hospital social club. Adrian merely laughed, saying that everyone knew about my being there.

Later after lunch, Adrian and I were chatting light-heartedly in the garden. All of a sudden Adrian blurted out, 'I've got to tell you, everyone is amazed at your wonderful recovery!' Being extremely surprised but highly delighted at this comment; I queried to whom he was referring. He mentioned the names of Dr. Abe Syed and Dr. Shanti Shah. Adrian explained his reluctance to enquire about my surgery. He was not sure if I would want to discuss it. I assured him that I was only too pleased to. How relieved I was at this breakthrough. We were finally communicating. I informed Adrian that I knew why I had made such a good recovery; not that the doctors would necessarily accept my Christian viewpoint. Again, Adrian mentioned that the surgeon was most gifted in his area of specialism (Head and Neck Surgery) and had a very good success rate.

The technique of using a pedicled flap for intra-oral repair, was developed in the U.S.A. in 1979. In 1981, a few doctors in this country began this procedure; my surgeon being one of them. How wonderful to hear that. It reinforced my belief that so much had been in my favour, prior to going into hospital!

I repeated to Adrian what I had told Jo, about cancer being an enriching experience; adding that I was now beginning to feel that I would not have wanted to have missed it. I was now seeing life from a totally different perspective. One example of viewing life very differently, was confirmed during a local shopping trip. I was chatting to someone who complained that shopping was a real drag. I replied that I used to feel like that, but now I was so thankful to be able to manage such routine tasks. Indeed whenever facing boring household jobs; I have only to recall that dreadful Thursday endured in Intensive Care!

Before my surgery, if I was to be at home all day, I often found it hard to motivate myself: I had all the time in the world to drift round doing housework. What a contrast now! Although, still reluctant to actually vacate my bed: once up, I am better able to do essential tasks and hopefully by mid-morning; I can concentrate on two or three hours of writing! I then quite happily tackle the remainder of my domestic chores for that day.

By now I was beginning to think that I should develop my writing; to include my father's death and that of other people who had suffered from cancer. On 11th May, I contacted Jennifer Neil, the friend whom I had taught with at Woad Farm. I needed a few details about our headmaster's death from cancer. Jennifer queried whether I had contemplated going into hospital to talk. This was the first mention of that from anyone. I wondered if it was another pointer.

It was not until November 1993 that I began to write about Dad's illness and death. I had a vivid recollection of it all, in spite of the time span of exactly twenty-five years. Setting it down on paper, was an incredibly distressing and highly emotional experience. My grief was overwhelming: as if Dad had only recently died. In considerable astonishment, I realised that for me, the grieving process had been incomplete. Had I been too busy to mourn properly? Had it all been suppressed during those hectic college days? If so, I was certainly making up for it now. Countless tears have flowed, in the writing and redrafting of this difficult period of my life. It came as a considerable shock to realise that after all those years; I had never really got over Dad dying so early in my life. Sadness at all the events that I had been denied a father's involvement. The greatest sorrow I shall always bear, is that John, Charlotte and Thomas never met him.

Regrettably, there was so much about my father that I never knew or simply could not remember. Occasionally, when Mum and I used to visit his old friend Jim Medley, I would glean more about Dad's character. Jim firmly believed that after his own retirement in July 1969, as head of the Establishment Section of the Treasurer's Department; my father would have been promoted to take his position.

While clarifying several facts for my writing; Mum divulged something that she had only shared with her dearest friend May Oglesbee. On one occasion early in 1968, Mum had visited the doctor for a routine test. On that particular day our family G.P. was absent. The locum enquired whether her husband was Albert Edward Spencer. He then explained that her husband had a very small tumour in his bladder. Surgery was impossible, due to the tumour being in such an awkward place. He informed her that the only realistic option was radiotherapy. The doctor stressed the importance of not telling her husband. After father died, I became aware that our own family doctor had never acknowledged to my mother that her husband had suffered cancer. His lack of openness made her feel quite resentful.

My reaction to Mum's revelation was of extreme shock and incredulity. It was distressing to hear how the doctors had handled my father's illness. The position Mum had been put in was dreadful. What a stark contrast to the direct and informative approach that I was to experience, twenty-four years later!

For years I had marvelled at the way Mum had coped on her own. Likewise, when I was diagnosed with cancer: she had shown great strength of character and had been tremendously supportive of all the family. However traumatic this piece of writing has been, it has had to be included because it deals with the most tragic event in my life and my first experience of cancer.

Understandably, there was so much whirling through my mind: regarding the possible extension of my writing. Yet one particular doubt persisted. How could I be so conceited to write all that personal stuff down and imagine that it might interest or encourage someone else?

On Saturday 15th May, something in my daily Bible reading notes struck me. 'A year ago, I was in Intensive Care recovering from a heart attack. Friends made many encouraging comments but the people I really wanted to hear from, were those who had suffered a coronary themselves. After all, they would know exactly how I was feeling and could no doubt go into great detail about their own experiences too.'

Monday 17th May was Thomas' eleventh birthday. I had awoken, having had a strange but extremely vivid dream about Neil Russell. It brought home how much I missed talking to him about spiritual matters. Sadness filled me as I wondered who could take his place.

That morning, I had a hospital appointment to have the offending tooth filed down. With hospital parking being so tricky, I departed early, intending to visit one or two people prior to my 10.30am appointment. Before even entering the building, I bumped into the Revd. John Moore, who was the vicar of St. Thomas'. Here was a captive clergyman! I had not spoken to him properly since before surgery. We talked for at least ten minutes. He was extremely interested to hear how I was and to learn of my writing.

I wanted to see Melanie Wright, the Macmillan Nurse, for advice about the chest scar, which had blistered and bled, at three small points. She was bleeped and on meeting me, her first words were, 'What a coincidence! Before they rang up to tell me about you, I had just read what you'd written in your parish magazine.' Isobel Ladds, the district nurse who lives nearby had sent her the second part. At that, I quietly replied, 'I don't think it's a coincidence.' Melanie made no comment, so I boldly asked for her opinion. She remarked that she had found the account very moving and that it gave a real insight into how it is for a patient. She thought that it was a valuable thing to do. I felt that she was confirming something that I should already know. We chatted for a while. I had not seen her since the awful Combined Clinic in December. Melanie praised the excellency of my speech and the fact that my face was symmetrical again. She too referred to the image of 'The Elephant Man.' For, weeks after my surgery, John had confessed to me that my grotesque appearance had brought to mind the deformity of that unfortunate man. (Joseph Merrick is believed to have suffered from Proteus Syndrome).

After my dental appointment I went along to see the Revd. Michael Johnson. I spoke of my growing conviction of wishing to be involved at the hospital. Michael outlined a few ideas: one of these being to join the Chaplaincy Team, which assisted at Sunday worship and collected patients for chapel. That had no appeal whatsoever and I said as much. Michael mentioned the possibility of talking to the nurses. He had some input into their training and there might be an opportunity there. That definitely was more me!

In spite of not having yet read the extract, Michael was most interested in my writing. He remarked that the writing in itself was cathartic. I sensed his meaning, although it was a word that I was unfamiliar with:

Catharsis; a cleansing or purification: in psychology, it is the purging of the effects of pent-up emotions, by bringing them to the surface of consciousness.

He thought that the idea of a booklet or book was good. I was thrilled when Michael remarked that writing about my hospital experiences could well be my ministry. Michael was the first person to say this and I knew at last that it all made sense. I declined his offer of borrowing the booklet, that a young doctor had written before her death. I did not want to be influenced in anyway. Likewise, a few months earlier, when John had brought me the hardback version of Lyn Ellis' book which I had read two or three years before; I had given it to Mum to keep. Later out of curiosity, I had dipped into it. It was astounding because mere names in a book; had now become actual people to me. Nevertheless, I resolved not to read it again properly until my writing was finalised.

I drove home from the hospital on cloud nine. What a memorable day it had turned out to be! I was overjoyed. Prayers of many years had finally been answered. All the uncertainties of the past few weeks had definitely been clarified. It was as if God was saying,

'I've been dropping hints to you for ages... at last you've got the message... now get on with it!'

It was marvellous that John too, shared my enthusiasm. When I told the children that my work was now my writing, Thomas hooted with laughter. He would delight in winding me up. 'Why can't you get a real job like other Mums do?' When Charlotte was being sensible, she was extremely perceptive. To my surprise, after she had read the magazine extracts; she made none of her usual scathing remarks about personal faith. I think that she was moved at the way that it was written. Thomas of course, read it without comment. Charlotte did voice something that had been troubling me, 'Won't people think you're copying the lady who wrote that book?'

Charlotte even admitted that I had changed. She was pleased that I was no longer teaching. Her peers could no longer moan about her horrible Mum being a teacher! How I regretted doing that term of full-time teaching. Was that what lay behind the extreme anger and rebellion which had developed since secondary school? In spite of believing at the time that it had served the purpose of involving the school in the Romanian relief work: had all the repercussions, proved it to have been a dreadful error of judgement?

Chapter 30
Unexpected Healing

A few friends had commented that I was much more confident and far more at ease than I ever was pre-surgery. Surprisingly as I took stock, I came to realise just how happy I now was. I firmly believed that I had been granted a new lease of life: a chance to do something intensely meaningful. I had been cured from cancer and given the opportunity to make a fresh start from all the failures of the past. God had transformed me into a different person and there was a reason for it. It was awe-inspiring the way that God had delivered me through the terrible ordeal of cancer and restored my health and quality of life. Best of all, was the realisation of God's will as it was gradually being revealed. Those past few years of muddling along: searching for an additional purpose in life, besides that of wife and mother. I had finally received answers after years of waiting. God had wonderfully restored my feeling of self-worth; which had been so badly eroded during the trials of family life. The latter had all been taken very much to heart, along with a load of guilt over my mismanagement of the mother-daughter relationship.

A most unexpected aspect of my healing, was being set free from my obsession with Charlotte. Her problems still concerned me but I could see them more in perspective. After all, I did have my own life to lead. On a school morning, I was eager for the children to leave; so that I had the house to myself to write. If John was asleep after a night shift, that was still conducive for writing because I had to have solitude. When he was around during the day, I was content to do other jobs. Naturally, with any work attempted at home, there were frequent distractions. Therefore, my writing developed very slowly. It was wonderful therapy. I hated being disturbed. Initially, I even kept the curtains closed and John's 'Shift worker asleep - Do not disturb' sign up, to deter would be visitors and often ignored the telephone. However, I soon stopped those extreme measures.

No way could I return to a classroom full of children. There was far more important work for me to do now. I had certainly moved on.

Physically, mentally and spiritually, healing had taken place. I was different. Whilst the emphasis was naturally on the physical healing process in early 1993; as the year progressed, I experienced a far deeper form of healing. I was amazed at how positive I was, towards a black period of my life.

The desire to share my experiences grew even stronger. As an extremely sensitive person; I continued to feel very hurt and let down by the attitude of most people towards me. Perhaps it was unrealistic of me, to expect others to be able to talk about the profound issues that I was now totally absorbed in. I found this apparent lack of interest quite insensitive. As a result, I grew closer to those with whom I could be more open.

Reading, thinking and writing about cancer, was taking up most of my waking hours! At school, I had done only a limited amount of Biology. I had never been interested in the subject, nor in medical matters. Moreover, I was extremely squeamish; always averting my eyes when the television screened an operation! Now, I was absolutely fascinated. I wanted to know as much as possible about my surgery. Jo had loaned me some medical books. I had bought my own Baillière's Nurses' Dictionary, which proved invaluable for my writing.

In addition to my writing, I was now keeping a daily journal. I recorded a detailed account of each day; especially noting answers to prayer and significant conversations; of which there were many. One tremendous answer to prayer being the one concerning the funding for Adrian Cozma. On Thursday 20th May, a most despondent Duncan Howells rang up: the Romanian fund had insufficient funds to allow Adrian to stay until he could re-sit the exam. Unless Pilgrim Hospital could finance him, Adrian would have to return home. By now there was less interest in Romania and fund-raising was more difficult. I hated the thought of saying goodbye to Adrian, perhaps forever. The following day, I was feeling particularly cross and niggly over some minor problem with Charlotte and school, when Duncan rang. That very morning he had received a cheque for £1500 from Pilgrim Hospital Trust. Adrian could stay! We were absolutely ecstatic. All petty irritations just vanished.

During the previous week on Wednesday 12th May; instead of rushing away from the table after our evening meal, Charlotte began to question me about the discovery of my tumour. She wanted to know all that had been said by our G.P., my dentist and then by the consultant. It was the first time that she had wanted to know specific facts. Ironically, in spite of having recorded it all in minute detail, my oral account seemed rather blurred. I wondered if it was because I was uncomfortable speaking to my own daughter on such an emotive subject. Charlotte admitted how she had thought that I could not possibly have cancer. We then talked at length. At one point, Charlotte flung her arms around me saying, 'If you'd died…!' She then burst into tears. She confessed how much she had hated being banished to Pam's for that first fortnight after my hospital discharge. Her bravado exterior had merely been an act. Her friends had told her how awful she had behaved and she really felt that they had all turned against her. Whereas I had plenty of support; Charlotte felt that she had none. It had been very hard for her. The inner turmoil that I was up against in those early weeks, was my sole concern. I was totally oblivious to the fact that Charlotte was struggling through troubled times of her own. It made me feel very wretched and extremely guilty hearing what it had actually been like for her: especially to realise how much her needs had been overlooked.

Mercifully, there was great relief that we were now communicating very honestly. From subsequent little talks from time to time, I sensed that we were closer. That in itself was a tremendous blessing. Furthermore, Charlotte comprehended my desire to be involved in the hospital and to undertake my writing. Whereas Thomas' reaction was to ask, 'Why don't you get a proper job like other Mums?'

On Tuesday 15th June, Charlotte and I managed another serious talk. It was an extremely emotional time: we both shed quite a few tears and felt compelled to hug each other tightly. She showed me my photo cut from a family snapshot, taken on our 1992 Portuguese holiday in Cabanas. She had kept it in her wallet ever since my diagnosis. Charlotte admitted that the gravity of my condition had not really registered with her, until long after I had left hospital. In fact the night I did return home, she could hardly bear to stay in:

feeling *this isn't my Mum!* Apparently this strange feeling persisted until the Sunday evening: when I reprimanded her and she knew, *this is my Mum!*

In complete contrast to Charlotte's openness: Thomas was becoming increasingly hostile at listening to so much hospital-based talk. Regrettably, I was very slow to view things from his perspective and to realise that for a ten-year-old; it must have been absolutely horrendous to see his mother in such a frightening situation, appearing so utterly grotesque. He obviously did not want reminding of those shocking events. I had to make a conscious effort to avoid such unwelcome conversation when in his earshot.

In spite of the occasional 'heart to heart talks' and the gradual realisation that God, to a degree anyway, had answered my pleas for an improvement in the mother and daughter relationship: Charlotte's unsociable behaviour and rebellion resumed unabated. The summer term marked a new and more serious concern: with Charlotte being frequently late for school. Aware of my recently acquired relaxed attitude towards Charlotte: I knew that I was once again in danger of becoming obsessed by her difficulties. At all costs, I must not follow that destructive path. In addition, Thomas's hostility became more apparent: he started to swear and behave badly at the dinner table. Resumption of battle stations!

Early in June, John was to attend a Readers' Service and Social at Chapel St. Leonards. I went along with mixed feelings. It would be good to see the Revd. John Duckett again but I really did not feel like doing my usual 'wifely bit', standing by John's side all night, whilst he led the conversation. This had happened for years. I found it hard to join in conversation: especially with strangers, or when discussing unfamiliar subjects. People obviously varied as to their sensitivity and patience in trying to draw out a diffident and sometimes quite difficult person. In John's words, I could be 'hard work!' To be honest, it was not only shyness that held me back: occasionally, it was sheer laziness or cussedness on my part. If I sensed that I was being excluded, I would frequently withdraw into my own, far more absorbing world. Accordingly, it was most unsatisfactory, very unsociable and at times, quite embarrassing for John. Deeply frustrated, I used to seethe inwardly. I loathed myself for being so acutely shy and lacking in self-confidence.

It was a Service of Holy Communion. At the communion rail, I knelt beside Mr. James Knowles, who was the other Consultant E.N.T. Surgeon at Pilgrim and also a Reader at Boston St. Botolph's. I thought, *there's no getting away from the hospital is there Lord?* Jenny Dumat, the assistant chaplain at Pilgrim, was also present with Reader husband, David.

At the buffet, someone called Rob Rae introduced himself, enquiring how I was. He mentioned hospital, adding that he expected that I was glad to put it all behind me. That was my opening! I launched into my favourite topic. 'No, I don't want to forget about my hospital experiences. Far from it, I'm busy writing about it all.' His wife Trish, was sat nearby in a wheelchair. As we were introduced, I marvelled at the way her face radiated such intense warmth and joy. They invited me to join them. I fetched my coffee, from where John was sitting at another table. How surprised he looked! I was able to talk so openly and easily to Rob, Trish and another lady in their group. It was quite an innovation for me because I was doing most of the talking. That night I acknowledged thankfully, that a tremendous burden had been lifted from my shoulders. I had been liberated from the dreadful shyness that I had suffered from, throughout my forty-four years!

Chapter 31

A Minor Setback

An extremely fine white lineal scar extends downwards underneath my chin, for approximately six centimetres, from where the central point of my jaw-bone was split into two. The scar then continues along my right jaw-line and as far as my right ear. It is barely noticeable.

Six months after surgery, the clinic nurse was enthusing about how good the scar looked. I joined in; saying how thankful I was that he had done my surgery so skilfully and unobtrusively. The surgeon seeming almost embarrassed, shrugged his shoulders dismissing it by saying, 'Just good luck!'

As I have already written, I was more self-conscious about my mouth. At times, John had to remind me not to cover my mouth up, when I spoke. I had never attempted to conceal the 'trache' wound, always choosing to wear open necked shirts or blouses, rather than hide it under high collars.

In March, after I had resumed swimming, a tiny blood blister formed on the inner scar line of my right breast. It had gone unnoticed until my third swim; after which it burst. Initially, the surgeon thought that a stitch could have been the cause. He probed about but found nothing. Silver nitrate was applied, to dry it up. In May, two others blisters appeared on its upper scar line. At the June clinic, I informed him that the blister had reoccurred, in addition to two more. Having just stated that he could improve on my 'trache' wound, though at a later date because I had already been through enough: I was quite astonished to hear him now offering to resuture the chest wound. Assuming he meant under local anaesthetic; I agreed that I would like it done as soon as possible: in readiness for my summer holiday.

When the admission letter arrived for the resuturing of my chest wound (known as 'Toilet of Chest Wound'): I was dismayed to read that it was to be done under general anaesthetic. I felt somewhat shocked because the surgeon had stated that it was only a very minor resuturing job. There had been no mention of it having to be done under general anaesthetic. 2B were unable to sort it out for me, as the surgeon was away for the intervening two weeks. They assured me that a doctor would see me on the admission morning and it would be sorted out then.

After all my ravings about what a positive experience hospital had been (for the most part), I realised what an utter fraud I was; for I dreaded the prospect of another general anaesthetic. The horror of last time was still so vivid. However, I made myself focus on the one advantage about staying overnight after general anaesthesia: the possibility of seeing Pauline Telford. She was the only nurse who I had been unable to see since my discharge from hospital. Pauline had been such a tremendous help to me throughout my stay. She only worked nights and although I had enquired about her, I had not actually seen her. I also consoled myself, with the thought of a peaceful night away from Charlotte. Furthermore, if I were to stay for the night, I might be able to get some of my questions answered. I still had many queries, regarding my treatment.

The weekend prior to my Monday admission, was fortunately very busy for us. Thomas was packing, in readiness for his first school trip, which was also his first time away from home. He was looking forward to his five days staying at Staithes in Yorkshire. We were sure that it would be beneficial for him.

Our old friends Mike and Linda Johnson from Scothern, spent Sunday with us. Their children are of similar age to our two. It was a lovely warm day and we enjoyed a leisurely lunch-time barbecue. Linda and I had a really good talk about my writing and my feelings towards the hospital. After having read the magazine extracts, she urged me to continue. Later that day, I had a similar conversation with Mike. He was full of praise for the amazing way in which I had coped and recovered. Moreover, he added that all my friends at John's fortieth party were of like opinion (I assumed that he was referring to my old friends from Holy Trinity because they had all shared the same table that evening). This was news to me. I was so surprised and it was flattering to hear his comments. Maybe I had proved to my old Boston friends, that I was not such a drip after all! It was most embarrassing because Mike certainly laboured the point. All I could think of to say was: 'God gave me the strength. I know he carried me through.' Mike was most complimentary about my writing, saying that he would want a signed copy. I felt very happily boosted up, ready for further surgery.

Monday 21st June, Thomas departed for Yorkshire. He did not cling or get upset, as I had half anticipated. He was definitely a big boy now, as he very matter-of-factly said, 'Hope you get on alright, have a nice time.' Then quickly corrected himself, 'No, that's not the thing to say.' A quick kiss before John drove him to school.

We gave Adrian a lift to hospital and he disappeared without even wishing me well, which really upset me. In spite of it being a most minor op. I still felt apprehensive about having another general anaesthetic. John said a prayer in the chapel. I began to feel quite tearful but had composed myself by the time 2B was reached. It was a strange feeling to be back as an in-patient again. Staff nurse Rachel Frecklington was on duty to admit me, as before. I had the best possible welcome ever. I was shown into room 5 – 'my room'. I was so elated at that. I had spent hours gazing down at the main car park. How different it looked from last October's autumn scene. Now the trees were in full foliage, so that much of the car park was covered by an expanse of green.

We sat waiting for an hour. How despondent I felt. Surely, it was a mistake to return? Things could not possibly be the same as before. I was going to be so disappointed. At 10 o'clock, a student nurse booked me in. I answered her mechanically. I was considerably relieved on hearing that the anaesthetist was Dr. Abe Syed. He would visit me later, as would one of the operating theatre nurses. The student then informed me that the surgeon's registrar might do the operation, under the surgeon's scrutiny. This came as a real shock. I experienced an awful sinking feeling in my stomach.

John left mid-morning. He was commencing a night shift and had a few jobs to do, before having a rest. Carol my sister-in-law, was to stay with the children that night. A health care support worker came to see me. It was her first day on the ward and she felt very apprehensive. Talking with her helped me relax; possibly it helped her too. Suddenly, things felt as they should. Caroline Allen, a nurse who had qualified when I was there before, came for a chat. By the time she left and someone else had popped in to say hello; I felt quite at home again.

That morning I even had a visitor. The Revd. Andrew Burnett from Bicker, came to see me. The week before John had seen him at a Deanery meeting and updated him. I told Andrew about my writing and the need to talk about my experiences. He agreed that writing might well be my intended ministry. At the end of our long talk, he gave me a blessing.

I had a lovely surprise when the recovery nurse from theatre came along. It was Michaela Smith, the nurse who had been responsible for my specific after-care, when I first left I.C. I was so pleased to hear that she had kept my Christmas card to her. We were having a lovely chat, when the surgeon arrived to inspect the wound. I had been right. It was only to be a local anaesthetic. He left to tell the girls that I could have lunch. My great relief at realising that I would be able to see what went on; was quickly overcome by dismay at missing my night in hospital.

Early that afternoon, I was very pleased when Cis Courtney-Day came on duty. We had a good chat. I explained what had happened. She assured me that there was no problem because the room was booked for me. I felt considerably cheered up, especially after Rachel suggested that there would be more time at night for someone to go through my notes. Cis could do that if I liked.

Fully organised for this visit, I spent the afternoon writing about the day's events. It seemed the most sensible thing to do and would certainly save time at home, if I kept my daily journal as up to date as possible. Michael the hospital chaplain, spent a long time with me towards the end of the afternoon. We had a time of prayer and a very good talk. I had not seen him since the Healing Day service. He commented on how much it must have cost me to pluck up courage to volunteer to do the reading. I had not thought that at all. It was something I felt compelled to do. At 4.45pm, I had to send him away so that I could change into my hospital gown. I decided to ring John to put his mind at rest about the anaesthetic. A grumpy John answered: I had disturbed his rest. Furthermore, he did not see the need for me to stay in overnight. That made me feel very glum, as I wondered guiltily whether I was being very selfish.

About 5.30pm, I was wheeled along to theatre. That familiar journey again! It was the fourth time in less than nine months. I was trying to memorise as much as possible: valuable research for my writing being at the back of my mind. I remember noticing in the theatre reception area, the colourful pictures on the walls for the children. I had forgotten all about those. A very pleasant theatre nurse checked my details. I missed seeing Michaela because she had gone off duty.

What memories came flooding back, as we entered the sterile area and then into that long, brightly lit corridor. Today I felt bold, almost relishing the novel experience of being fully conscious in the operating theatre. This time we turned into the first room on the right, instead of proceeding along the entire length of the corridor. Then came the familiar bed changing procedure. While the nurses did their pre-op. checks on pulse and blood pressure, I was wondering where the anaesthetist was. Instead the surgeon appeared, clad in his green gear. He was most apologetic about my long wait. I assured him that I had not minded; I had been busy reading and writing. Immediately, I realised how daft that must have sounded. He joked that the fun part was now about to start.

I was pushed into the operating theatre. How surprised I was on seeing that it was such a small and quite ordinary room. I had expected there to be far more equipment than there appeared to be. Obviously I had a limited view from my horizontal position. Heavy green cloths were masked around the wound. The surgeon stated that I could shut my eyes, focus on the lights, or keep an eye on him. I chose to focus on the cluster of large round ceiling lights when I was injected because initially it did hurt! Then, (far too soon it seemed to me) he was using something like tweezers to dig into my flesh. We had to have a few stops and starts while further anaesthetic was injected. A nurse held my hand throughout. It was a most fascinating ten minutes... with the strangest of conversations! It brought to mind a 'get well' card received last year: depicting an operating theatre, a surgeon with a huge needle sewing up a patient, who was fully conscious! The operating team were staring at a large bone on the floor. The caption read, 'It's amazing what some people will do to get attention!' At first, I had not appreciated the card's black humour. After this minor operation, I sent the surgeon a photocopy with a thank you note.

No sooner had I been wheeled back into my room on 2B, when the surgeon came to check on me. He informed Cis that I could go when they were ready. She replied that I was staying the night. Jokingly, I begged him to tell John what a dreadful ordeal I had been through and that I just had to stay in to recover! Looking extremely amused, he replied that he could not do that but his parting words were, 'Stay as long as you like!' He must have thought that I was the weirdest patient ever, actually wishing to voluntarily stay in! I was then content to lie very still and recover. A cold meal awaited me but initially I had no wish to eat. I felt so calm and wonderfully relaxed. I was totally at peace.

Jo my student nurse friend, visited me about 7.30pm. I was telling her of my intention to stay in overnight, when John arrived. To my relief, he had no further objection. Jo kindly volunteered to drive me home the following morning. John would be sleeping until the afternoon and it would save Mum a journey. John had brought along a food parcel: cold chicken from Sunday's barbecue, cake and yoghurt. It supplemented the hospital ham salad. What a contrast sitting in bed; eating heartily and quite normally, after my liquid meals of the time before.

Cis came at 9 o'clock. She spent at least half an hour talking to me. Part of the time was spent answering queries from my notes but mostly I was listening to her. I could feel tears welling up in my eyes as Cis spoke. I felt extremely humbled that she felt able to confide in me. It was my turn to listen to someone else's problems.

My prime motive for staying overnight, was hopefully to see Pauline Telford. Fortunately she was on duty. It was wonderful to see her again. She was delighted with my appearance and most impressed by my 'amazing speech'. I was touched to learn that she still had the Christmas card that I had sent her. After having updated each other about the state of our family life, Pauline continued her rounds.

As had been the custom during my long stay, Pauline brought me my bedtime coffee much later than everyone else. Of course tonight there was no prescribed sleeping pill for me. At 10.30pm I settled down, extremely content about the day's outcome; for I believed that many prayers had been answered. Ahead of me (this time by choice) stretched another interminably long night, to toss and turn. As if I had not endured enough of those to last me a life-time? I thought, *oh well, there's got to be a down side to today!*

I lay there feeling absolutely great! This time there was no need to toss and turn because I was so comfortable. I was content to lie motionless absorbed in tranquil thoughts. Remarkably, I knew nothing of the night. I slept solidly until about 6 o' clock. I had a further good chat with Pauline, before she went off duty.

I was busy copying from the huge wall diagram of the mouth and tongue, when Jo arrived. Before leaving I chatted to nurse Linda Bowen and we reminisced yet again about her experiment to see if I was still allergic to sticking plaster. Linda enquired whether I had returned to teaching. I informed her that I seemed to be drawn to the hospital. I also mentioned my writing. We laughed about everything on 2B being revealed. I reminded Linda that I would be prepared to share my experiences with other patients, if appropriate. Linda remarked that she thought that I would be good at counselling. No one had ever said that before.

I spent two hours with Jo, chatting over coffee and cakes, before she drove me home. In spite of the twenty-year age gap, Jo and I had become good friends. We related so well to each other.

My day and night in hospital had proved to be extremely profitable. How right it had been for me to return. The very last night that I had spent in 'my room' had truly been a most precious few hours.

Chapter 32

Obstacles!

Reading about other people's reactions to a cancer diagnosis, made me realise how angry many become. When I pondered my initial reaction, I did not consider that I had experienced anger. Shock... bewilderment..., yes and an overwhelming emotion of feeling so badly let down by God. As I tried to analyse my response, I puzzled whether my lack of anger meant that I had merely passively accepted the diagnosis. The fact that I had not ranted and raved angrily: had that shown how lacking in character I really was? These thoughts perturbed me considerably.

About a week later, on Thursday 1st July, I attended Combined Clinic. I had the last appointment because the surgeon had kindly agreed to allow me extra time, in order that he might answers questions for my writing. First of all, I took the opportunity to thank him properly for the successful outcome of my surgery. I also needed to convey how delighted I was with my speech. At an earlier clinic, I had given the impression of being dissatisfied. Nothing could be further from the truth.

I informed him that as weird as it must sound: I could truthfully say that I was glad to have experienced cancer. I had not known such peace or happiness in years. He explained that many cancer patients seemed to find deep peace and strength from their experiences. He listened attentively to my long outpouring of how the cancer had woken me up, transformed me and given me a definite purpose in life. I stated my belief that if the tumour had not happened, then the depressing obsession with my daughter would have continued. I added that most probably I would have ended up on a completely different ward! The fact that I could talk so freely to him was certain proof that I was so different from the person that he had operated on last October.

I had intended to ask for a detailed account of my operation but he made a remark, which utterly disconcerted me. Flicking through my file, he enquired whether I had been put in touch with a Mrs. ...?

'No,' I replied. He then abruptly said, 'Of course not, you had a psychological battle!' Quite forgetting myself and in true Marshall 'school-marm fashion' I snapped, 'Psychological battle, explain!' Unperturbed, he continued by saying that as much as he could not recall all the details of that initial meeting, he could remember the general mood. He felt that I had been angry at the diagnosis, in hospital and possibly afterwards. I assured him that I had most definitely not been angry. He stated that being angry was a perfectly justified reaction to a cancer diagnosis, especially in a relatively young person. Though he readily admitted that he could be wrong. He had joined us after the diagnosis had been given and he had never met me before. I had nothing further to say. I was almost speechless!

He then commented on my speech, informing me that he had expected it to be good but not this good. My voice recovery was much better than he had anticipated. Meanly, to put him on the spot, I asked for his opinion as to why this was so. He hesitated before replying, 'I don't know.' Another pause and then he added, 'Probably because your will was so strong.' He added that he had just done a similar operation on an elderly man. I offered to meet the patient if he thought it appropriate. I had the impression that he was not very keen when he replied, 'We'll see, maybe in a week or two.' He stated, that I was one of his best hemiglossectomy patients and would be doing plenty of talking!

It took me a while to work through the issue of whether or not I had been angry at my diagnosis. I interpreted it as an implied suggestion that I had shown weakness in how I had coped. John thought that as usual, I was 'making a mountain out of a molehill'. I was delving too deeply into things. Yet that was me, my way. I had to understand as fully as possible how it all was. Had I been proudly kidding myself; or even boasting that I was not angry? No, I firmly believed that I had been very shocked and very broken but not angry. To put the surgeon more fully in the picture; at my next Combined Clinic, I handed him the extract dealing with the diagnosis and preparation for surgery.

The surgeon's comments made me re-examine the way that I had recorded my hospital experiences. Perhaps I had been focusing too much on the positive aspects and had neglected the real difficulties.

Had I been painting a rather rosy impression of my hospitalisation? I tried to describe the grimmer aspects more frankly. I rewrote the I.C. chapter: endeavouring to convey the sheer awfulness of it all, rather than gloss over the ghastly details. Much later on, I could accept that the surgeon had done me a favour, in making me think more critically about my reactions.

In my July appointment with the speech and language therapist; Christine and I discussed my growing awareness and concern at the occasional variation in the standard of my speech. She explained that even under normal circumstances, speech can vary in competence. Anxiety, excitement, fatigue, illness and stress can mar it. Within my post-op. speech ability, is a range where clarity may fluctuate according to the above mentioned factors. My brain is having to re-learn these relatively sudden post-op. changes to my mouth, compared to the far more gradual development of early life.

On Monday 5th July, I had a lengthy talk with the chaplain. Amongst many issues, we discussed my possible involvement at the hospital. Michael dismissed the idea of me speaking to groups of nurses, saying that the opportunity would not occur very often. He suggested that perhaps I ought to be looking elsewhere. The chaplaincy team was again mentioned. He had gathered that I was not keen on taking patients to chapel. 'Was that too humble a task for me? Wasn't Jesus a carpenter?' Michael made me feel most uncomfortable. Somehow I waffled my way through. In spite of having gained so much from my own chapel visits, while on 2B: it had never entered my head, that I should become a member of the chaplaincy team.

Before I left, Michael took me along to ward 2A, to meet a young lady called Morgan Woolsey. A few weeks earlier John had brought home a copy of a poem that he had read in the hospital chapel. It was entitled, 'The Journey.' Underneath the poem, it explained that a leukaemia patient had written this on the occasion of being anointed. John had been extremely moved by the poem, suggesting that I include it on St. Mary's prayer board. Having first checked with Michael; I did so.

I rather half-heartedly accompanied Michael to visit Morgan. She was still very poorly and I was apprehensive about meeting her. I was absolutely amazed by what Morgan told me. She described vividly having a plaster cast mould made in preparation for her cranial irradiation. She had to have this bolted onto her face and of course had been terrified at the prospect. It was ghastly to hear her description of it. I knew that I had escaped lightly! Morgan described how it was not as dreadful as she had envisaged. She experienced an almost floating feeling. It seemed to her, that God had lifted her above it. By now, we were all in tears. It was extremely moving to meet someone who had been through so much and was showing such tremendous faith. For the very first time, I shared my wonderful experience of feeling God close to me, as I focused on that ceiling beam (Jesus' Cross) while being anaesthetised. Later on as we parted, Michael handed me a letter saying, 'I don't know whether this is for you but take it home and read it.' I put it away and forgot all about it for a few days.

On Wednesday 7th July, I attended a fashion show at Kirton Primary School. For once, Charlotte and I had actually gone out together. During the show, she commented that someone was staring at her. I assured her that the young lady was probably looking at me, for she seemed vaguely familiar. Sure enough, when we dispersed to try on our intended purchases, I had the opportunity to enquire. To my astonishment, she even remembered my name. It was Mandie Wray, the health care support worker, who had been on duty with Tracey Holland, during my first weekend in hospital. They were such a zany pair and helped jolly me through the grim aftermath of my operation. As it was the first time that I was changing in public since surgery: I chose a quiet corner of the classroom and faced the wall, so that my chest wounds would go unnoticed.

On 10th July, I decided to glance at Michael's letter. I could scarcely believe my eyes! It was absolutely electrifying! The letter outlined the setting up of a Pastoral Visitors' Scheme. A ten week training course was planned for the autumn. The scheme was to be operational by early 1994. Each pastoral visitor would be expected to visit a specific ward weekly: to build relationships with the staff, as well as being there for the spiritual needs of the patients. Pastoral visitors would also be part of the wider chaplaincy team.

My immediate reaction was, 'I've already begun this work!' Suddenly, the significance of that overnight stay in June, sprang vividly to mind: notably the time spent listening to Cis. Similarly, I could identify other times throughout my main hospitalisation, when I had listened to other meaningful conversations. I knew instantly that this was what God had been preparing me for, all along. Things really seemed to be making sense at last!

John seemed only moderately interested when I eventually plucked up courage to show him the details. He immediately pointed out the impracticalities. 'You can't leave St. Mary's for the hospital chapel! How will you get there?' I mentioned the possibility of using Mum's Mini. 'You can't drag your Mum out here, so you can have her car!' John's negative remarks upset me deeply. Here was something that I desperately had to do. More to the point; here was something that God was calling me to do and John was trying to thwart me. Believing John to be totally unreasonable, I enlisted the prayer support of two close friends.

I had a further discussion with Michael. He stressed that the lay involvement on the wards had to be a development of the monthly Sunday chapel work. Of course, I then realised that I could no longer regard wheelchair pushing as 'not for me'. I informed him that John had stressed the impracticalities of my involvement, with regard to his shift work and car availability. Apart from being on a reading list at St. Mary's, I had no other church commitments. Sunday School had ceased and even if it were to recommence, I knew that my days of doing Sunday School were over. Michael said that if I could manage to help with chapel patients once every six weeks; that would be sufficient. I did not admit to him that a big drawback to me, was the very daunting prospect of actually pushing a wheelchair. I had never done that and thought that it would be quite physically demanding. Yet the most depressing thought was my immense fear of lifts. I never travelled in lifts alone: though admittedly, a few times in Menorca, I had actually steeled myself to use the lift when alone. I would not be able to handle patient, wheelchair and lift. It seemed as if the odds were against me in this. Michael stressed that it must be what God wanted. I was to go away and give the matter considerable thought and prayer. I could give him an answer in

September. How I wallowed in self-pity, 'It isn't fair Lord to put all these obstacles in my path!'

In July, John was trying to book our summer holiday. This year I could not bear the hassle of going away. Part of me felt that I did not want to be far from the hospital. However, I did realise how much we all needed a break from routine, especially after the traumatic time that the whole family had been through. We have always been fairly long winded in booking our holidays abroad but this year was absolutely ridiculous. John was becoming very impatient with my lack of interest and my general moodiness. He expected me to snap out of it. He obviously did not understand why I was in such a dithering emotional state. I even began to doubt all the positive developments that I had experienced and shared. One day in tears, I told John that I was a total fraud. I had only been pretending to cope, in reality I had not and I was not managing now. John answered by telling me that I had been an inspiration to him and to many others. At a similar time, John also boosted my flagging spirits, by telling me that Adrian had admitted to him that his faith had been strengthened, by how I had coped. On one particular occasion, Adrian had spoken to me very openly about his faith. He shared something deeply spiritual that he had experienced. Before my surgery, he had been praying for me and the words came to him, 'Don't you know, I always take care of my own.'

19th July, my dithering finally ceased because we booked a holiday on the Algarve. Destination to be revealed on arrival at the airport. We had less than two weeks to go. Having finally committed ourselves, I began to feel more positive and looked forward to getting away.

After months of wondering how Brenda was, I received a postcard from Trudy, promising to ring and update me. That was another answer to prayer.

21st July, I was an invited guest at the primary school's farewell presentation to Mrs. Eve Benson. It was the first time that I had been back properly since surgery. I enjoyed seeing the pupils. A few of the younger ones caught my eye and looked pleased to see me. It seemed to me as if they were probably thinking, *we haven't seen Mrs. Marshall for a long time.* I was reminded of the happy times that I had spent teaching there. It was not all bad by any means. As I sat in the hall, observing the staff supervising their classes; I thought, *this isn't for me anymore.* I no longer wanted the hassle of organising a class of children. I sensed that this was also my farewell.

When Charlotte told me that Trudy was on the phone, I instinctively knew... Brenda had died the day before, on July 28th. It was something that I had been expecting. Although I had never met her, I had somehow been involved in her life since the previous October. Trudy said that Brenda had made her peace with God. She was very sure of his purpose and knew that her healing was not to be here. We were terribly upset as we spoke. I felt rotten! After all I was supposed to have learnt, I was still allowing myself to get bogged down needlessly. Surely, still being able to face all the ups and downs of life: was far better than leaving behind a husband and children. Brenda's death deeply upset me.

Our two-week break in the Algarve proved to be one of our best family holidays ever. We stayed in a luxurious apartment attached to two villas. This exclusive row of three holiday homes, overlooked the main complex. We shared a small swimming pool with the two families occupying the villas. I was really relieved to be sharing the pool facility with only a few people: being acutely self-conscious of my 'loathsome leggy spider' (clavicle scar), which was discernible when wearing swimwear and most off-putting! Fortunately, the long scar across my right breast was within the line of my costume.

The first time that I relaxed by the pool; it was a typical hot afternoon. The sky was a gorgeous deep blue, such a contrast to the attractive white Algarvean villas. All around me were lovely bougainvillea; with their fragile, almost tissue paper petals, in vivid shades of pink and purple. It was a breathtaking sight. Flowers always inspire and uplift me. As I contemplated my surroundings, I bubbled over with emotion. Sheer gratitude for what I had been safely brought through and the fact that I was very much alive and able to enjoy such beauty.

Being in such quiet surroundings was ideal. I wanted peace to sit and think and John wanted to read. Initially Charlotte was disgruntled; for she liked activity and crowds of youngsters! As I have previously written, we all needed a good break. Indeed, we were all blessed in the most wonderful way possible. The family next to us, had a fourteen-year old son called Ross and a daughter Penni, aged seventeen, who had learning difficulties. Ross was a real 'live-wire' and from the second day onwards he, Charlotte and Thomas, had a great time together. Towards the end of our first week, we discovered that their Mum Liz was a committed Christian. It made such a welcome change to talk about faith, as well as the usual lighter holiday talk. It was very rewarding to meet Penni. It was incredible to witness the way her family handled her exhaustive demands. What a lesson that was to me! It put the problems with Charlotte on a different level. God willing, she would eventually grow out of her tiresome ways!

Our apartment was located about two miles from the sea; a drawback because we did not bother to hire a car. Consequently, we only had four day trips to the beach. I experienced the usual magical sensation of the sea but it proved an ordeal getting there. We would bus one way and then trek back in the gruelling heat. We thus spent far more time based around the pool and Ross and Penni being there, made all the difference. It was lovely to watch Charlotte and Thomas playing happily together with Ross. How wonderful to observe Charlotte enjoying a quieter, far calmer sort of holiday than the previous year. She hardly moaned! Ross's Mum Liz was very patient with Charlotte. She spent a long time teaching her to dive. By the end of our holiday, Charlotte was confidently diving alongside the boys.

The third family in our row, consisted of grandparents Pam and Archie Harold, their daughter Angela and her two children Christian (four) and Emily (two). Frequently, there were five children playing together. Sometimes, Penni under close supervision, would join them. At times there was a terrific amount of noise and excitement. It was good to see the varied age range getting on so well.

John as he usually did, was quick to make contact with the Harolds. I held back, preferring my own company to making conversation with strangers. On the Thursday evening of our first week; I went to join John, who was talking to Pam and Archie. By then, conversation had revealed that they too were Christians. I was invited to sit down and did so rather reluctantly. I really did not feel like listening to John. He was speaking in depth about his Reader ministry. All of a sudden, I became aware of how much I needed to speak; but as usual my extreme diffidence constrained me. I sat seething with the inner frustration that I had lived with for so long. At one point, Archie caught my eye. John continued. A few minutes later, Archie quite out of the blue asked, 'Heather, have you thought of counselling?' I gaped at him, 'Why do you say that?' He replied, 'I think you'd make a good listener.' I laughed and jokingly retorted, 'And John makes a good talker!' I found myself becoming quite choked because it dawned on me that God had not only recognised my need at that point but had promptly provided me with the opportunity. I explained that I was at a turning point in my life. I briefly mentioned what had happened and that as a consequence, I felt strongly drawn to the hospital. I referred to the pastoral visitors' scheme. Archie's words were, 'Go for it.' He thought that it did indeed sound right for me. However he urged caution, 'One step at a time and you will soon know whether it's right and then you'll go on in God's strength.' Whilst John gave a detailed account of my operation to Archie, Pam and I talked. She had undergone a very serious operation three years earlier and we shared our common experiences. Pam explained that her feeling of peace and of knowing God's purpose, had only happened in the last two years but it had made her so happy. How I echoed her sentiments.

    The following Saturday, the Harold family were due home. In my final chat with Archie that Saturday morning, I mentioned how supportive of John I had been in his Reader training and ministry. Archie firmly stated, 'It's not enough just to be supportive, you need your own role as well.' At last I knew that this was so! He also told me that my writing was a spiritual gift. How blessed I felt that we had been able to talk so frankly. Michael had urged me to go away and pray about a possible hospital involvement. I perceived that God had used Pam and Archie to show me that the way ahead was indeed what I was hoping for. Another clear indication was the fact that for the first time ever during our holiday; I had been made acutely aware of the substantial number of holidaymakers who were wheelchair users.

On our last day, I wrote to my old school friend Di Pettifer, the only one of my old friends that I had not seen since surgery. I described how I believed that the door on my teaching career had firmly closed. Strangely, for the very first time ever while abroad, I had no desire whatsoever to converse in the language. Previously I used to amuse the children by my feeble attempts. It was immensely satisfying to have a go and the locals always appreciated my efforts. Even the idea of developing my French coaching, no longer seemed important. Such different priorities had taken over.

One morning after our return from Portugal, I had an intense desire to get away from the family. I desperately needed to talk to someone else. I hoped that Margaret Barsley would be at home. To my disappointment she was out. I walked round the estate and called in turn, on three of our parishioners. They too were all out. Dejectedly, I trailed back towards home. I had just noted that Margaret's car was still missing, when as I approached our drive, she drove round the corner.

I spent two hours off-loading to Margaret. Behind it all, were my fears that John was putting obstacles in my path. In spite of the quite remarkable development on holiday, I had avoided further discussion with him and obviously time was passing. Margaret was fully behind me, assuring me of her prayers. I mentioned my dread of lifts. We had a laugh about that. I knew that I would soon have to overcome that particular hurdle.

The following week, I had my four-monthly check-up at the Oral Department. So that week a great deal of concentrated prayer was offered up regarding the wretched lifts! On Wednesday 25th August, after my appointment with Mr. Glendinning, I spent time in the hospital chapel and lit a candle. Then I braved the lift. Amazingly, instead of dithering nervously outside, trying to pluck up courage; I calmly entered, relieved that initially others were using it. In stages I ascended to the top floor and then at similar intervals I descended. On two of my short trips I was completely alone. While waiting on one floor, a lady admitted to me how much she hated lifts. Finally, having reached ground level, after half an hour of using them, I drove home highly elated, aware that I had overcome my fear.

The following day I mentioned to John that I wished to join the chaplaincy team. I explained how I had given the matter careful thought and prayer. Moreover, I had received assurance that it was the right thing to do. On the practical side, I informed him that Mum would help out when necessary. To my astonishment, no difficulties were put forward. John stated that we could work around his shifts. He suggested that the Sunday morning after his Saturday night shift would be the most convenient. For then he would be sleeping and I could use the car. This would follow a four weekly pattern; thus enabling me to join the chaplaincy team on a monthly rota. What a relief to hear that John was not against the scheme but had merely been pointing out the practical issues.

Shortly afterwards, something alarming occurred. On Sunday 29th August, I noticed something white on the upper surface of my tongue. Frantically praying that it was food; I went cold with dread when I realised that it was not. It appeared to be a tiny white strand, which had been pulled up from the very coarse texture of my tongue's surface. I likened my tongue, to that of a loosely woven piece of cloth and the strand to that of a stitch pulled loose. I applied Bonjela and anxiously monitored it.

The following Thursday, 2nd September was Combined Clinic, so at least the surgeon would soon be able to examine my tongue. As the time approached, I became more and more edgy and especially nasty towards Charlotte and Thomas. I could not believe that I might have another tumour developing. *Hadn't I got important work to do now - my writing?* On the Wednesday it was John's rest day. We spent a very pleasant and hot day at Old Hunstanton. All day, I had this awful nagging feeling which was impossible to shift. What would the surgeon say? Time dragged even more the next day because his clinic was running quite late. How relieved I was to hear that it was merely a tiny loop, which had been pulled up from the tongue's surface and would eventually disappear. Indeed it had gone before my next monthly appointment.

Chapter 33

The Wheelchair Push

On Saturday 11th September, Val Wilkinson and I, accompanied by three teenagers from Kirton Methodist Chapel, set out on the Lincolnshire Old Churches' Trust Sponsored Cycle Ride. By noon, the youngsters had cycled as far as they wanted; from then on it was just the two of us. I was determined to follow the exact twenty-six mile route that John, Thomas and I had cycled the previous September. What a blissfully ignorant state I was in then: a month before my diagnosis.

Val and I enjoyed a fantastic day out. The weather was simply glorious: ideal for cycling and talking. Ever since her first visit to our home last October, Val had become our good friend.

At St. Nicholas' Church, I wandered off for a few minutes to stand alone on the river bank. Nostalgia swept over me because this had been where my family had spent many carefree Sundays: cycling, walking and picnicking. There was also great sadness too, as I revisited the grave of a very dear pupil from my second class at Woad Farm School. I then rejoined Val inside the church. We both experienced a great sense of peace in that ancient fishermen's church.

At one of our local churches, a lady commented to me, 'You're obviously getting on well, as you're riding!' I was uncertain as to her meaning and so queried it. She referred to my illness and at that I flippantly said, 'Oh that!' She continued, 'It's obvious by that comment you're getting on very well. You made headline news.' Afterwards, Val explained that the lady's husband was suffering from cancer. I recognised his name, for it was always included in St. Mary's prayers for the sick. How I regretted my flippancy.

During the day, I really wanted to chat to as many cyclists as possible. Being friendly was no longer an effort! Pre-surgery I would have been content to have merely uttered a greeting and left it at that. Yes I had certainly changed!

At night John and I attended a 25th Wedding Anniversary party. I spoke to someone whom I had last seen when she visited me in hospital. She commented on how brave I was to have gone through such an ordeal, adding that she would not have been able to. This sort of remark had already been said to me once or twice. I responded, 'You don't know until it happens what you'll do.'

The following morning, Val Wilkinson joined us at St. Mary's. John was taking the service and Val was to give her Christian testimony. Jim Lewis (my former English teacher) Val and I, read a dramatised version of Psalm 82. I also read the prayers (not Marshall originals but from one of John's prayer books). It was the first time that I had led the prayers since surgery. Two people were very complimentary about them.

On Wednesday 22nd September, I began the training course for pastoral visitors. Apart from Michael, I did not think that I would know anyone else; so I did experience considerable nervousness. Over coffee, prior to the start of the first session, a lady who looked familiar to me asked how I was and apologised for not having visited me in hospital. I was very surprised to learn that it was Penny Church: the Midwife teacher who had shared that very memorable service of Holy Unction on the eve of my operation. There were nine of us in the group. Although they were all extremely pleasant and welcoming; they all appeared to know one another. I was aware that I was very much 'the new girl'. Throughout the evening, I kept thinking in total disbelief, *what on earth am I doing here?*

As we vacated the lift at ground level, I met Lucy Potter, one of 2B's health care support workers, about to commence her night shift. We hugged. Seeing Lucy, simply confirmed the strong feelings that I was where God wanted me to be.

Sunday 26th September was my initiation day for chapel rota. I had a poor night's sleep and even dreamt about wheelchairs! As with any new venture, I get worked up for ages beforehand and this was no exception. My snappishness with Charlotte and Thomas increased as Sunday drew nearer. It was all so silly! When John came to bed at 7.30am after a night shift, I was already up and dressed. He was amazed that I had sufficient motivation to be up early on a Sunday morning. I had never done so before. I love my lie-ins too much. Since being in hospital, I tend to wake much earlier than I used to.

I dropped Thomas off at Mum's before driving to the hospital. I hoped that Charlotte could be trusted to be reasonably quiet on her own, to allow John maximum rest. For this first time, I accompanied Peter Locke, another team member. I pushed the wheelchair whilst he made light-hearted comments, as I clumsily manoeuvred the patient along. I only managed to bash the wall once. Fortunately it was an empty chair at the time! Peter was a great character and quickly made me feel at ease. The service was about to start, as I was pushing our last patient from ward 8A into the chapel. The gentleman realised that he would be unable to follow the service book because he had forgotten his spectacles. Without a moment's hesitation, I dashed back into the lift to fetch them. For me that was certain proof that I had mastered my fear of the lifts.

A young man led the service. I realised that I had heard Pam Mellor and Val Wilkinson mention him. He gave a most moving account of his hospital experience. His legs had been badly smashed up almost two years before in a horrific car crash. He still had a long way to go. As I listened in tears, I could identify with so much of what he was saying. Afterwards I felt compelled to speak to him. He recalled meeting Charlotte during her stay at Pam's. He told me that he and the others at Pam's prayer group had been praying for me.

That night I was boosted up even more, when my old friend Angela Steven telephoned, to finalise details for our proposed visit at half-term. She said that she and Al were thrilled to receive my holiday letter from Portugal. They had found it so joyful, so positive and so full of energy.

The following Wednesday, I was eagerly anticipating our second training session. On my way to the meeting room, I recognised one of my former friends: someone whom I had spent a great deal of time with, both in and out of school. Up to receiving our eleven-plus results we had been firm friends. I found her hostile reaction at that time, extremely hurtful. The last time that I saw her was prior to my marriage. I recognised her but she did not appear to even notice me. In any case I would not have spoken. Many years later I occasionally thought of her; wishing that I could have the opportunity of speaking to her. It felt wrong to have harboured bad feelings for so long. Even when we returned to the Boston area; I thought it most unlikely that we should ever meet up again. Scarcely believing my good fortune I spoke to her. She seemed pleased when she realised who I was. She imparted a few details about herself and I did likewise. From then on I would often see her because she worked at the hospital. I continued on my way almost reeling in stunned amazement... *there's no end to the answers to prayer that I'm receiving at Pilgrim.* To me it was another form of healing, less spectacular but still immensely significant.

At our meeting Michael presented us with four case-studies. As we discussed the fourth person, someone whom Michael had named Megan; I realised that Megan was the leukaemia patient Morgan, whom Michael had introduced me to on 2A. After Michael had read out her poem, 'The Journey,' one of the group commented that people very often write about their traumatic experiences. At that, Michael smiling broadly stated, 'Perhaps Heather will explain why we are both grinning?' I briefly summarised what had led to the development of my compulsion to write.

After our meeting, I had arranged to meet Dr. Adrian Cozma for coffee. On our way from reception I passed Sylvia Stanhope, one of the health care support workers coming onto 2B for night duty. She looked so surprised but extremely pleased to see me. I informed her that I was on a course, adding that she might see more of me later.

On our third session, we looked at visiting and communication skills. We viewed a video showing a chaplain visiting a hospital patient. I found it most compelling but so very daunting. How was I ever going to cope, being a pastoral visitor? Afterwards, the youngest member of our team asked me if I was John Marshall's wife. She turned out to be Helen Staples from Fishtoft. I recollected her name and remembered that I had once spoken to her on the telephone. Helen had done some fund-raising for the Romanian project. On one occasion she had accompanied John, to talk to pupils and staff at Boston High School. A mutual acquaintance had told her of my tumour. Wondering if the Heather Marshall mentioned was indeed John's wife, Helen immediately contacted John and had the news confirmed. From then on she had been praying for us. How fitting that in less than a year, Helen and I should be brought together on such a worthwhile course at Pilgrim Hospital.

Chapter 34

One Year On

With the approach of October, I began re-living the events of the previous autumn. In many ways it seemed utter fantasy. Had I really survived all that? Tuesday 12th October, I went shopping in Kirton, prior to meeting Mum in Boston. It was pouring with rain. Everyone appeared thoroughly miserable. How could I be like that? I was virtually skipping through the puddles, in an overwhelming sense of joy, at the new lease of life that God had endowed me with. It being exactly a year since the biopsy, which was to dramatically change my life forever.

Thursday 14th October, John was away. I kept myself very busy, for I did not want to brood about the shocking events of last year. I called on Val Wilkinson in the morning and after lunch visited Jane and Tony Hales. To me, it was quite miraculous: to have endured such a distressing period in my life and as a result, to have become a far more whole person.

At Combined Clinic on Thursday 7th October, the surgeon allowed me additional time to answer further questions. Most obligingly, he copied from my notes, the exact description of my surgery (*See Appendix 1*). According to him, the dynamics of post-op. changes in my mouth, were virtually complete. He concluded the consultation, by warmly assuring me that everything was fine and that I was doing very well. After a year of monthly check-ups, I would now be seen every two months.

That day also marked the end of my speech therapy. After those early meetings of practising sounds and word drills; Christine had spent a great deal of time, simply talking to me about the implications of surgery on my speech and the healing process now taking place within my mouth. She described where sounds were made in relation to the position of the tongue in the mouth. I found it quite complicated and we seemed to cover the same subject many times. Most importantly, Christine gave me much needed moral support. Frequently, I would discuss with her what I wanted to ask the surgeon. At the end of my first year, Christine and I saw no real reason for continuing to meet. By then the practical work had long since finished and most of my queries had been answered. Obviously she was there if I needed support in the future. I knew that Christine had played a most significant part in helping me come to terms with what had happened. I was immensely grateful for her friendship and encouragement.

It seems appropriate to mention here: the effects of my surgery, which are indeed permanent and to describe how I am coping with them twelve months on. Some of the resultant side-effects of my post-op. state have already been described in detail in the earlier chapter 'Normality.'

The immobile part of the right side of my lower lip is still something that I avoid looking at if at all possible. Putting it into perspective: even with this permanent facial defect and crooked smile; I really do look wonderful, compared to my initial gross post-op. appearance!

There is still fullness underneath the right side of my jaw. Depending on how I hold my head, determines whether I appear to have a double chin! Medical staff have assured me that an uninformed person would be totally unaware and that the feature is really only noticeable to me. Although the pedicle (from the clavicle to the jaw) was removed, after the blood supply was established to the grafted tissues used in repairing the underneath part of the tongue: a remnant of the muscle flap remained inside the jaw. It was supporting the skin flap from below. To remove it would leave a large gap between the floor of the mouth and the skin of the neck. However, the muscle flap has largely withered and in subsequent years will mould even closer to my facial contour. The fullness is caused mainly by oedema (excess fluid in body tissues). Surgery has interfered with the normal drainage of tissue fluid which takes place via the lymph system, thus causing a retention of fluid. There will always be a slight bulk present.

My chin and the area surrounding my right jaw line still feel numb. Occasionally my jaw goes rock hard and is extremely tight and uncomfortable. The surgeon has explained that this sudden involuntary muscle contraction, will occur from time to time.

Breaking the jaw, has resulted in it changing shape by being narrowed slightly. There is nothing detrimental in this and in time I will not notice the muscle spasms.

Approximately six months' post-surgery, when to my mind I was back to reasonable health and strength: I was made painfully aware of the existing weakness in my right arm and shoulder. This lack of strength, being caused by the removal of my right pectoralis major muscle. The latter (one of a pair of main chest muscles) controls the movement of the shoulder and upper arm. Its functions are: to flex, to adduct (draw arm to midline of the body) and to rotate the arm. I went to open our 'up and over' garage door. I stretched my right arm vertically, to give the door a forceful push up. Excruciating pain racked me. For a considerable time afterwards, I had to consciously make an effort to utilise my left arm for this task and for carrying heavy shopping. In time these problems were to disappear. By the end of the year I was able to once again carry heavy loads of shopping in that hand and even wear a weighty shoulder bag without any discomfort. Though, if I moved my right arm awkwardly or overstretched it, then I did experience a painful twinge. Whenever Thomas was proving his greater strength, he always seemed to take advantage of my weaker arm!

My faded scars are now a distinct white: compared to my normal light skin tone. Apart from one, they no longer cause me concern: for after all they are part of the 'new me'. However, the right clavicle scar (my higgledy-piggledy spider) is still highly sensitive to touch. It makes me cringe inwardly because I can detect a tiny remnant of the right pectoralis major muscle. I still feel revulsion; remembering the grotesque sight of the muscle pedicle, protruding from this clavicle incision.

At a clinic appointment in late July, I was wearing a dress with a cut-away neckline. For the first time the surgeon commented on the clavicle scar; saying that he could improve on it at a later stage but not at present because I had already been through enough. I admitted that this was something which I should eventually want doing.

On Monday 23rd October 1995, I was admitted into hospital for 'Excision of Scar Tissue of Right Clavicle.' Using local anaesthetic, the surgeon removed my seven by five centimetre 'spider scar'. He skilfully replaced it by a single line of tiny stitches. My second visit into the operating theatre 'fully conscious' proved to be just as fascinating as when I had part of my chest wound resutured. This time the operation was longer: thirty compared to a mere ten minutes. The resultant lineal scar, was eight and a half centimetres in length by one centimetre at its widest point. I was delighted with my new scar's unobtrusive appearance.

I have become accustomed to having a permanently dry mouth and lips. At times it can be a real drag to have this constant dryness, even while drinking! I have already detailed in the chapter 'Normality' the practical ways I try to minimise the problem.

Throughout the year, I gradually became less messy in my eating and drinking. I tended to use a saucer under my coffee or tea mug, for at least the first year. Then I no longer bothered. A reduction in oral swelling and greater confidence, resulted in a more relaxed attitude, even if I did drop crumbs or dribble. It is the alteration in my jaw alignment, which has caused the difference in lip contact. The fact that I could still consume food and drink orally, was what really counted.

When out socially, I tend to avoid eating white bread and other soft foods because of the embarrassment of food sticking to teeth and hard palate. Again in the privacy of home, I am able to happily munch into a chocolate bar. Yet, I now have the tell-tale evidence of chocolate around my mouth just like a toddler! In fact with whatever I eat; there is usually some residue left which varies in quantity according to the type of food consumed. The children are most contemptuous and utter crudely 'Wipe your gob Mum!' People seem to visit at mealtimes and I instinctively wipe my mouth whenever answering the door. When in company, I frequently dab at the corners of my lips because of minute deposits of white matter, which are particularly conspicuous when wearing lipstick.

Oral hygiene takes ages. I have to thoroughly swill my mouth with water. I find that warm water is kinder to sensitive teeth! Depending on what has been eaten, determines the amount of debris that is trapped on the right side of my tongue, which is now fixed to the floor of my mouth. This can work to my benefit: fish bones and fruit pips are more likely to lodge in this 'trap'; (along with grape and tomato skins, the only fresh fruit I no longer bother to peel) rather than being accidentally swallowed as would have hitherto occurred. After swilling I then set to work with a normal sized toothbrush, followed by a wire brush to clean in the crevices. Finally, as an extra precaution, I use a diluted mouthwash. The wash-basin then requires cleaning. All in all, rather a time-consuming ritual!

I try to chew on both sides of my mouth and I am now aware of a different sensation to the right side of my tongue, due to hard scar tissue. One year on, there is undoubtedly greater mobility in my tongue; including a slight increase in its movement to the left, in contrast to the negligible amount of early post-op. days. Scar tissue tethering the right side of the tongue will have slackened. My tongue can no longer be stuck out straight. Its tip now deviates to the right. Surgical intervention has altered the right side of the tongue, so it now has less muscle, a reduced nerve supply and scar tissue which exerts a downward pull (because it is tethered to the floor of the mouth). Whereas the left side of the tongue has a complete amount of muscle, a normal nerve supply and no restrictive scar tissue. This left side is much stronger than the weakened right side. Instead of working in conjunction with its opposite side, to extend the tongue tip out straight: the left side presses against the weakened right side, pushing it further across than would occur in the pre-op. state. Therefore the protruded tongue tip now tilts over towards the right.

The tongue is composed of different muscles, which are responsible for controlling its shape and position in the mouth. When a tumour and the surrounding tissue margin are removed from the lateral border of the tongue, the muscles on the opposite side compensate for the defect. The length of my post-op. tongue is slightly shorter but long enough to reach all the contact points needed for clear articulation (with practice).

With the exception of uncooked celery, which tends to leave an unpleasant stringy residue; I can tackle the same range of foods as I could pre-surgery but my tastes have altered somewhat. To counteract the perpetual oral dryness, I tend to use more sauces in my cooking. Eating a main meal can still be excruciatingly slow and it is at such family mealtimes that Charlotte and Thomas frequently 'play up'. I often give up before I am satisfied. My reconstructed tongue has impaired chewing and swallowing because the tissue used in the repair acts merely as a filler. It cannot undertake the function of the tongue muscle that it has replaced. Moreover, the removal of the right submandibular salivary gland means that there is less saliva to mix with the broken down food (bolus) for subsequent removal by tongue, before swallowing can take place. Therefore chewing and swallowing is less efficient and at a much slower rate. Eating becomes a lengthy time-consuming chore and the greater effort required can be exhausting. A breakfast of cereal and toast; admittedly with the interruption of organising Charlotte and Thomas for school, can sometimes take a good hour! Occasionally I am too tired physically to tackle foods; preferring the hunger pangs to all the hassle involved!

After the first six months, Nestlé Build-Up soups and milk shakes proved invaluable, once I had ceased having Fortisip on prescription, Bananas are so convenient and are quickly demolished! I eat pounds of them now. Formerly, I never ate a jacket potato but they have now become an easy option, especially with a lubricating filling. Sometimes laziness persists and I choose soft foods involving effortless eating, rather than the more strenuous chewing of chops and steaks (this is certainly true whenever eating out). Firm favourites being cauliflower cheese, fish and pasta.

On rare occasions, I am aware of an accumulation of swallowed debris at the back of my throat. My impaired swallowing does not always maintain a clear passage. This is most unpleasant. Loudly clearing my throat and drinking, is necessary to remove the build-up.

Occasionally I still cringe at my voice. I have imposed a high standard on myself. As a teacher, my speech has always been crucial. I hate imprecise sounds. Although readily acknowledging that I have regained a very high standard of clear speech: I am well aware that in the normal speed of daily communication, certain words may be too slovenly for my liking! I admit that I am too much of a perfectionist in that sphere. At home, If I believe that I have mispronounced a word, I tend to repeat it at least two or three times. In total exasperation, one of the family then assures me that it is alright. Without doubt they are not analysing my diction as my speech therapist or I would!

During my first year of post-op. recovery, I quickly discovered that most people not only shied away from discussing my illness but did not even refer to what I had been through. Hardly anyone enquired about my continuing out-patient care. Generally friends, extended family and acquaintances behaved as if nothing had happened. It seemed like total denial on their part. As this coincided with the many difficulties that I was experiencing, it was all quite hurtful. I really must have exhausted John's patience. He was forever assuring me that people were still concerned because they would ask him for a progress report.

Slowly, I began to realise that whereas I have wanted to talk openly about my experiences and indeed have found it to be hugely therapeutic to do so: many cannot handle thinking, let alone verbalising about such grave issues. Likewise, those who read my initial four-page extract; may have felt unable to comment. Who is to say what painful memory or fear it has evoked? One surprising reaction from a friend, was to simply indicate a spelling error and to query whether our computer had a built-in spell checker! There was no reference to the content.

I could recall instances from years back, of feeling totally inadequate, of not knowing how to respond to someone else's situation. The awful helplessness I experienced, when my brother Alan's marriage broke up; completely flawed me. I just did not know what to say to him. The silence I was meeting now might well be because of deep reserve, or fear of talking to someone who has had cancer because they simply do not know how to respond to me, or how I might react. It took me a very long time to see things from this viewpoint.

My perception is that some people look on me as having had cancer, being cured of cancer... and that is that... resume the status quo. It could not be further from the truth. I tried to explain it to Thomas by saying that if I had gone into hospital with a broken leg: once it had healed, that would have been the end of that episode. When someone has cancer, whatever the outcome; you are a changed person. You see things from a completely different perspective. The knowledge of that cancer (and the healing as in my case), is something that is with you day by day. Having been restored to full health again: I cannot take it for granted. I can now acknowledge that suffering cancer was the making of me. It was the worst time of my life but paradoxically, it was also the most awe-inspiring! Here I am referring to the spiritual dimension. Amidst the horror of the physical and mental trauma, I experienced a new and deeper awareness of the closeness of God; to be cherished for the rest of my life.

I have tried to imagine what it was like for me pre-surgery but I simply cannot. The side-effects have become an accustomed part of the 'new me'. I have never reflected, *how I wish that I was physically and especially facially, as before.* In spite of the constant numbness along my right jaw line and the disadvantages that have been described: I have only to recall how I felt in hospital; then these are mere trifles. In my opinion, there is absolutely no purpose served in contemplating the scars and other side-effects of surgery with bitterness. There is no point in brooding, *if only this hadn't happened.* I can truthfully say that I have never thought this. It happened. I have come out far more whole than I ever was before (S*ee Chapter 30*).

In addition to the physical; I received mental and spiritual healing which made such a huge impact on my recovery and gave me a positive attitude towards the experience of cancer. I am healthy again and able to resume life with a renewed vigour! I have gained far more than I have lost!

Chapter 35
2B Or Not To Be?

At the commencement of our training, Michael had emphasised the need to pray carefully about the ward that we wished to work on. Specific wards had never been mentioned and as our course progressed, I began to feel slightly uneasy. I knew exactly where I wanted to be and believed implicitly that 2B was where God wanted me, for why else would I have been put there in the first place? In spite of my strong convictions, I did wonder if Michael might object because of my link with 2B. I was thus dreading decision time.

There was a lovely sense of unity in our group. We always began with a time of prayer and listened to St Luke's account of Jesus commissioning the twelve apostles, sending them out to preach the kingdom of God and to heal. (Luke 9 verses 1-6.R.S.V) Verse 2 from Luke chapter 10 inspired us all:

'The harvest is plentiful, but the labourers are few, pray therefore the Lord of the harvest to send out labourers into his harvest.'

Considering that I was the newcomer, I soon felt comfortable within the group. I did not participate as much. However when I did say something, I sensed that I was making a worthwhile contribution. Having up to now, always been the most timid person in any group situation: for me to actually volunteer anything was something short of miraculous! Needless to say, Michael occasionally (so kindly) chose to put me on the spot! Perhaps, he had recognised my tendency to lazily leave it to everyone else.

On Wednesday 20th October, Michael informed us that he had received replies from eight managers, accepting his offer of a ward pastoral visitor. He stated that as there were nine of us, he only needed one more response and then we were all in business. He would tell us the ward at the close of our session. The meeting was a continuation of visiting and communication skills. In pairs, we had to practise listening to each other, to try and ascertain the mood conveyed. Very little of the session mattered. I was full of foreboding. What on earth was I going to do if 2B had not replied?

Would I have to go and speak to them? I recognised that I was going to have to be totally honest with Michael about my strong calling. The meeting dragged on interminably and then Michael was infuriatingly slow in his long-winded account of the special commissioning service. Sick with anxiety, I prayed fervently that I would hear what I longed for.

Finally, he read out the names of the eight ward managers. With a sinking heart I realised that Karen Woulds' name was not included. Michael looking directly at me, said quietly, 'I'm sorry Heather, I've not heard from 2B.' I immediately sensed that he was on my wavelength and that my fears about his possible disapproval were groundless. Stunned, I just sat in utter disbelief. I sensed total support from everyone: for they all appeared so concerned, as if they too were sharing my dismay. I blurted out how I believed that God had called me to that ward and concluded by describing my eventful overnight stay in June.

One or two people tried to make helpful comments. Knowing how busy staff were, it was quite possible that the letter was still waiting to be read. Someone else pointed out that God might want me on another ward. What I had started on 2B, could be continued somewhere else. This unpalatable idea had of course occurred to me, numerous times. Now it had become a possible outcome. It was unbearable to contemplate.

Michael decided that without mentioning my name; he would have a tactful word with Karen, to discover if she was at all interested in the scheme. He concluded the meeting with specific prayers for this new venture. He prayed for us all individually and I was the last to be mentioned. Afterwards, Peter remarked that he could read the disappointment in my face. He promised to pray for me. Michael reassured me that all was not lost and I was not to despair. Nonetheless, I drove home with a heavy heart. Mum could tell immediately that something was wrong. I off-loaded to her and felt a great deal better.

The following morning I prayed in great detail about the problem and I shed a few tears. As I prayed for the strength to accept the probability of a different ward: somehow I could not believe that it would turn out like that. Having committed it all to God, I did feel less troubled. All of a sudden, the vivid recollection of how close God had been to me on 2B absorbed my entire being. I felt completely inspired: acknowledging that God was well aware of how special a place 2B had become to me. He knew my deepest feelings and longings exactly.

John naturally shared my concern and he too tried to make suggestions as to the best way of tackling the issue. He lightened the matter by joking '2B or not to be, that is the question?' I had to laugh! Why was I being put through it again? As the anniversary of my admission to hospital drew nearer, I knew that I had to keep it in perspective. I told myself, 'This is nothing to what we were facing a year ago.' Yet quite honestly, it mattered so much. In spite of praying to accept the outcome, I could not envisage going willingly to another ward.

The following Sunday I was on chapel rota. Michael informed me of his conversation with Karen. Apparently, she had not had time to consider the matter fully but would give him her answer early in the week.

Monday 25th October, knowing it was crunch time, I spent ages that morning in prayer. I tried to pray unselfishly; asking that Karen would realise how much it would benefit her patients, to have a pastoral visitor: someone who would have plenty of time to sit, listen and be alongside the patients. As I read my Daily Light, one verse really spoke to me, *'If two of you shall agree on earth as touching anything that they shall ask, it shall be done for them of my father which is in heaven.'* Matthew 18 verse 19. Authorised K.J.V. Immediately recalled Peter's words that he would be praying for me and I was sure that the others were as well. How marvellous it would be: if at our next meeting on 27th October, (which would be one year exactly since my admission onto 2B) that I should hear some positive news from Karen. Towards the end of my quiet time I impulsively thought, I must phone Val Wilkinson and ask her to pray for me. No sooner had I thought this, than I knew that there was no need. God was fully in the picture. I had committed it all to Him. He had to do the rest. There was nothing more for me to do. I felt totally at peace.

Before 5 o' clock I was in absolute chaos in the kitchen. A friend had called unexpectedly mid-afternoon and I was behind with the meal preparations. Charlotte came through from the lounge and handed me the phone. An unfamiliar voice said, 'Hello.' Quite puzzled, I then realised that it was Michael. I beat a hasty retreat upstairs to be alone. 'I don't suppose you really want to hear from me as I've not made things easy for you,' remarked Michael. I remember thinking in some surprise, *I'm not blaming you, it's not your fault.* Immediately my defence mechanism stepped in because I stated, 'You've got some bad news for me!' Michael sounding extremely serious replied, 'It depends how you look at it.' There was a long pause... and then a gleeful chuckle, 'You're in business kid!' He told me that after Karen had given him her answer; he had explained his reasons for being concerned. She was very pleased to hear that I was to be the ward's pastoral visitor and thought that I would be well suited for the role.

The next minute I was literally jumping for joy around the lounge. In embarrassment, Charlotte and Thomas promptly closed the curtains. They thought that I had gone stark raving mad. Waiting for John's return home from work was unbearable! As soon as I saw him I said laughingly, '2B or not to be that is the question?' I then dissolved into hysterical laughter. My elation could not be contained. I was bubbling over with joy. What a stark contrast to the sombre mood of a year ago.

That night I visited Judy Williams, a friend from our ex-Bishop's Course Group. It was a long while since we had talked and I had so much to tell her. Judy was the person who had experienced the same thoughts as I had: believing that my tumour would in fact bring about a change in Charlotte. As I now understood it: the change that had most certainly occurred had been in me. Judy admitted that I was far more relaxed and less wound up about Charlotte than I used to be.

On Wednesday 27th October, before our training course began, I now felt it appropriate to visit 2B. Alison Brown, Tracey Holland and Rachel Frecklington were at the nurses' station. They were very pleased to see me. I had only been chatting to Tracey a few moments when the surgeon, accompanied by two junior doctors arrived. I reminded him that it was a year since my major operation. Tracey queried what I was doing at the hospital. I mentioned the training course, telling her that she would find out later. I then visited Jo Townend. As a celebration she had brought me flowers, liqueur chocolates and a card: on which she had written that she thought that I would do a great deal of good on 2B.

Consequently after all this excitement, I was the last to arrive for the meeting. A Macmillan nurse spoke on caring for the terminally ill. It was a sombre subject. Afterwards when she had left, I shared my good news. They all looked so relieved and it was extremely touching to see their concern. Michael asked if I would share with the group the significance of the day for me. In our closing prayers, Michael gave thanks to God for my healing and for bringing us all to the hospital for this new ministry.

When the group had dispersed, Michael and I went to the chapel where we discussed the past year's developments. He assured me that just as good things had come out of my illness; God would continue to do really great things through me, in the work that He had chosen for me. After a brief time of prayer Michael gave me a blessing. It was a truly beautiful end to such an eventful year. By the time I arrived home at almost 11 o'clock (having left home at 6pm): Mum had begun to think that they had kept me in!

Chapter 36

The Commissioning

As the commissioning service drew nearer, I became very jittery. I felt quite scared about this new undertaking. We were all allowed to invite a few guests and there was to be a buffet afterwards. There would of course be various representatives present from hospital management. It was to be a celebrated occasion.

I rang Neil Russell and updated him on how things were developing for me. He was really pleased to hear my news but unfortunately was unable to attend the service. In the end, my special guests were: John, Mum, nurse Jo Townend and Val Wilkinson. The children declined. There were friends from church whom I would have liked to invite but decided it would be tactful to merely invite a churchwarden from St. Mary's and St. Michael's. Nevil Cooper could not attend but I was delighted that Charles Hawkesworth could.

Michael had mentioned that he would be involving one or two of us in the service. I thought how much it would mean for me to do a reading. John advised me to wait to be asked. Still the desire persisted and so I decided to ring up and ask Michael outright. By then he had already sorted out the New Testament reading and the Gospel but agreed to include a short Old Testament reading for me. I was overjoyed with the choice of Scripture. It was very familiar to me, from the prophet Isaiah. It spoke of the miraculous things God would do in order to save his people:

'Strengthen the weak hands, and make firm the feeble knees. Say to those who are of a fearful heart, "Be strong, fear not! Behold, your God will come with vengeance, with the recompense of God. He will come and save you."

Then the eyes of the blind shall be opened, and the ears of the deaf unstopped; then shall the lame man leap like a hart, and the tongue of the dumb sing for joy. For waters shall break forth in the wilderness, and streams in the desert.'

Isaiah chapter 35. verses 3-6 R.S.V.

The reading seemed so appropriate for me and I was thrilled that the word tongue was included. Yes, I could certainly sing for joy, albeit out of tune! Most marvellously, major surgery resulting in the reconstruction of my tongue had not permanently marred the quality of my life, or of my diction.

On Wednesday 8th December, I sat with the eight others who were to be commissioned as pastoral visitors. I was focusing intently on the personal significance of the evening. I recalled how special the chapel had become: primarily the corner where John and I had so often sat; to light our candle and to pray. Throughout that grim November, John and I had gained so much strength and comfort here. What precious moments it held for both of us.

In the midst of my anguish I had trusted God. I had clung to the belief that as incredible as it had seemed at the actual time: there was a deep underlying purpose for my cancer and bringing me into hospital. Naturally, it had not been easy to accept such a positive outlook and to see beyond the initial horror. God certainly had not been kidding me. Quite amazing blessings had been mine since surgery. How humbling to understand the purpose that God had now in store for me at the hospital: this wonderful place of healing. I now refer to my life as 'pre-op.' and 'post-op.' The experience of having cancer, having brought about such a remarkable and well needed transformation.

I prayed to be enabled to keep my emotions in check, so as not to mar the occasion. Sitting there before the service, I marvelled at the awesome, frequently strange and disturbing manner in which God works in our lives. Tonight I was feeling incredibly strong and so positive. I knew that I looked good and I felt wonderful. Whereas this time last year I was still enduring the nightmare (8th December 1992 was actually the night before my final operation to remove the metal arch bar from my mouth). All in all, it had been a dramatic catalogue of events to live through in little more than a year.

A tiny part of me began to wish that I had not pestered Michael to allow me to do a reading, but then I always did feel nervous before reading in church. It had to be. There was no better way of thanking God for the restoration of my clear voice. It would go well.

As I assembled a glass of water and my service sheets underneath my chair: in my mind's eye flashed the image of a jigsaw where all the pieces except one were in situ. It was a most overwhelming sense of revelation. The events of the past few years and notably those of last year, resembled the fragments of a puzzle: which at long last had been sorted and were finally being put into their rightful position. God had made sense out of the mess! Here in the chapel at Pilgrim Hospital, the final piece was about to be placed.

EPILOGUE

The Lost Chain

In May 1994, I realised that I had mislaid my gold neck-chain. After accidentally breaking the cross and chain, which I had been wearing continuously since surgery: I had taken to wearing this piece of expensive jewellery. I had earned twenty-five pounds doing a translation from French into English, for a Lincoln public house about the Napoleonic Wars. This fee had gone towards the cost of buying the chain, which in the early eighties had cost eighty pounds: far more than we would have paid otherwise.

I believed that I had most probably left it rather carelessly amongst the jumble on my dressing table. Charlotte, having borrowed jewellery before without permission, denied all knowledge of it. John of course, was exasperated at my typical scattiness. He expected me to tear the house apart in a thorough search. I searched our bedroom and Charlotte's. I even checked underneath our bed, in case the chain had dropped onto the floor. All the dressing table drawers were emptied and the back of the unit carefully scrutinised. Nothing! It was very puzzling.

Strangely enough I did not respond frantically to the loss of something I was so fond of, as I would have done pre-op. I was irritated at its disappearance, peeved that I had been irresponsible in not putting it away properly. Doubtless the chain had been vacuumed up and by now was lost forever. Apparently, I was so unconcerned, that I did not even bother to check the dust bag. I had far more important things to occupy me. I put it down to a very costly error of judgement.

Monday, 18th July 1994 was to be a very sad day for me. The chapel, situated on the first floor of Pilgrim Hospital was to be closed. Since hospitalisation, I had continued to make use of a quiet corner of the chapel, where a small table and candles were located. I always lit a candle and spent time in prayer, before and after pastoral visiting and clinic appointments. That morning, I did my pastoral visiting on 2B and lunched with Val Wilkinson in the hospital restaurant. The chapel meant a great deal to her too.

In addition to the chaplaincy team, there were many others at this thanksgiving service. Val and I sat either side of Morgan Woolsey; whom I had first met while she was a patient on 2A. By now, Morgan attended the fellowship group at our home that Val, John and I had begun earlier that year. Before the service began, I had tried to prepare myself for this sombre occasion. I had spent a final few minutes in prayer and had lit my last candle.

It was a beautiful service. In his sermon the Revd. Arthur Jolly, the Free Church Chaplain at Pilgrim, spoke of the need to give thanks for the good that God had done in this very special place and to believe that He would continue this in our new chapel. We had to go forward to an even better future. We had to move on. It was most inspirational. I listened, trying hard to accept such a worthy and positive viewpoint: in spite of the sorrow that was engulfing me in having to leave this sanctuary; where John and I had drawn so close to God and to one another. The comforting thought struck me, that all my loved ones had been to this place of worship and here was I now amongst some very dear friends; whom I had only got to know since surgery. I then recalled how Charlotte had never visited the chapel. That I regretted so much.

Earnestly focusing on the prayers, I realised that I was in danger of becoming slightly tearful. Trying hard not to sniff too loudly, I dabbed at my nose. Not only were my eyes moist but so was my nose! In consternation, I discovered that I had a nosebleed. Praying frantically that I could control it and avoid spoiling the service, I applied a tissue. Fortunately Morgan and a lady sitting behind me spotted my plight and plied me with extra tissues. I had to remain sitting for part of one hymn but thankfully the nosebleed only lasted a few minutes. I think that I had become so wound up beforehand that stress had caused it. To experience the slight discomfort and possible embarrassment of a nosebleed was inconsequential to how I appeared when I first attended a hospital service: complete with muscle pedicle. I have often suspected that God has a weird sense of humour!

After school that afternoon, Charlotte was in a pleasant mood. She actually enquired whether I had enjoyed a good day and queried what I had been doing. I mentioned that I had attended the closing down service of the chapel and how sad I was about it. Consciously keeping my voice extremely casual, I felt led to say, 'Of course, you never did go in there did you.' Her next words were to knock me for six! Charlotte admitted that during a visit, she had left the ward and out of curiosity had followed the signs for the chapel. There she had lit a candle for me. She had wanted to keep it a secret. How thankful I was then for its closure: for if it had not occurred, I might not have learnt of her visit. Charlotte was flabbergasted by my exuberant reaction to what she had divulged. My joy was indescribable. Discovering this meant so much to me: far more than if I were to find that lost chain.

Weeks later I was vacuuming our bedroom. I went on my knees, all of a sudden prompted to look beneath the bed again, though convinced that I had probably sucked my chain up long ago. As I peered underneath, the thought struck me how wonderful it would be; if like the parable in the Bible, I were to find it.
The Parable of the Lost Coin:
'Or what woman, having ten silver coins, if she loses one coin, does not light a lamp and sweep the house and seek diligently until she finds it? And when she has found it, she calls together her friends and neighbours saying, "Rejoice with me, for I have found the coin which I had lost."' Luke chapter 15 verses 8-10 R.S.V.

Deciding that my dressing table could do with a quick dust, I hastily pushed the clutter to one side. I bent down to attach the brush attachment and then turned round. There before my astonished eyes, like a tiny golden snake, lay a crumpled gold chain. It lay where two thin prayer books had been propped against the back wall of the unit. It had obviously been sandwiched between them.

I am convinced that God used this incident, to demonstrate how relationships are far more precious than possessions. In this instance the loss of the chain was purely temporary. The joy of its rediscovery, was nothing compared to the joy of the revelation that Charlotte too, had made her offering in the hospital chapel.

Tuesday 26th July 1994

After a hectic shopping spree at Lincoln, we all settled down that night to watch a video of 'The Hiding Place.' I had already read the book, based on Corrie ten Boom's account of her experiences in Ravensbrück concentration camp. During my stay in hospital, a friend had given me a book of daily meditations by the same author, so I was well acquainted with this remarkable Dutch lady's story.

Ever since becoming a mother; I have found it emotionally more distressing to observe suffering of any kind. I would deliberately avoid viewing harrowing scenes. Tonight was to be different. All the same, before the film had even begun, Thomas joked, 'Mum, you'd better not watch it, you'll only cry!'

The 'black and white' production made in 1975, did not appear as visually disturbing as I had imagined. In sharp contrast to the ghastly concentration camp conditions, Corrie and her sister Betsie displayed the most amazing Christian witness and love. On one occasion Betsie was asked how she could remain so faithful and so thankful in the midst of unspeakable horrors. She responded by saying that although they were in this suffering world; they were also in God's kingdom and spiritually could be uplifted from the present grimness, into something far more precious. I could certainly identify with Betsie's words: God can lift us above our immediate distress. I knew that this had happened to me during my days in Pilgrim *(See Chapter 25)*.

Later on Betsie referred to them being in a pit. She went on to say that no pit is too deep; for God is there alongside. He shares the experience with us and does bring us out. At the mention of the word **pit**, an overpowering realisation that I had been in my own very deep pit, engulfed me. That word spoke volumes. It was as if the full horror of what I had been through had been kept from me, up until tonight. Now the true nature of what I had been up against really impacted and intense emotions were finally liberated.

Afterwards, I retreated to my bedroom. Thomas had been quite right; I was upset but not for the usual reasons. Something far more profound had been triggered off. My heart-rending sobbing seemed to go on for a very long time… all the anguish of the cancer…

surgery... hospitalisation... and the dreadful trauma of my post-op. recovery. At some point Thomas appeared. It was now no longer a joking matter but one of great concern. He went away to fetch Charlotte. I did explain a little to her. John of course, swiftly followed and I managed the briefest explanation. He was probably as shocked as I was by this unexpected outpouring of grief. What a relief that it occurred one year and seven months after my time in hospital; when mercifully I was well-adapted into my new post-op. way of life. I am thankful that it took place in the privacy of my own home, with only my nearest and dearest as witnesses. This dramatic release of suppressed emotion, was a most crucial part of my inner healing.

APPENDICES

Appendix 1

28.10.92   **Major Surgery**

Hemiglossectomy:

- Skin incision made along right clavicle (collar bone) for approximately 7 cm.
- Mandible (lower jaw-bone) split at its point to allow access to tongue.
- Excision of approximately 1/2 the tongue.
  In my case, 1/3 excised: a tumour, 18mm. in diameter (category - Squamous Carcinoma Moderately Differentiated) on right lateral border and surrounding tissue margin; along with segment extending downwards to root of tongue.
- Adjacent floor of mouth, along with tissues of upper part of neck on right, also excised.
- Frozen section of suspect right lymph node and thyroid gland sent to Pathology Laboratory.
- With the removal of a small tumour from the tongue or oral cavity, it is often adequate to suture together the edges of the wound.
- However in more extensive surgery (in my case, to ensure a clear outcome and to allow the post-op. tongue the greatest degree of mobility) a flap of tissue is used in the reconstruction.
- A flap is a mass of tissue, partially removed from its normal site, used to repair the defect and to prevent food and drink being channelled directly into the laryngeal outlet instead of the oropharynx. The flap adds an appropriate amount of bulk, while maintaining as far as possible, suitable contours in the oral cavity. Therefore difficulties with rehabilitation of swallowing and articulation are lessened.
- Different types of flap are in common use for Reconstructive Head and Neck Surgery:
- cutaneous (skin) myocutaneous (muscle and skin) and muscle.

- Until a few years ago, the majority of flaps used were pedicled flaps.
- (With advances in microvascular surgery, the free flap is now frequently used).
- A pedicled flap is transposed tissue, which is still attached to its blood supply and original position in the body.
- The Pectoralis Major Myocutaneous Flap is commonly used in this repair.
- To gain access to right pectoralis major muscle, skin incision was made 5 cm. from right axilla (armpit) across upper margin of right breast down towards the mid-line and continued approximately 5 cm. along the inframammary fold. Right breast then elevated from underlying muscle.
- Flap of muscle and skin (obtained from chest wall), along with their associated artery and vein, tunnelled underneath upper chest and brought out as chunky sausage shape (pedicle) from right clavicle incision.
- Pedicle threaded under broken jaw and attached to grafted tissues used in repair of tongue.
- Underneath part of tongue reconstructed using fat (from between skin and muscle of chest) and skin flap.
- The pedicle is used not to repair defect (in my case) but to provide a channel for vital blood supply to the fat and skin.
- Flap sewn into place still attached to chest.
- Jaw wired together.
- Skin on donor site closed.

Pharyngostomy:

- Incision made in left side of neck.
- Pharyngostomy tube inserted.
- Tube then passed into pharynx (throat), down oesophagus (gullet) and into stomach for enteral nutrition.

Insertion of Metal Arch Bar:

- Insertion of metal arch bar in mouth to secure broken jaw and to give best possible jaw alignment and correct bite.
- Final procedure (approx. 25 minutes) performed by Miss Evans, the Locum Associate Specialist from Oral Department.

Appendix 2

11.11.92   **Minor Surgery**

Tracheostomy:

- Incision made into 3rd and 4th cartilage rings of trachea (windpipe).
- Tracheostomy tube inserted to maintain airway during surgery.

Pedicle removal:

- Pedicle divided from chest and jaw line.
- Duration of op. approx. 40 minutes.

Appendix 3

9.12.92

Removal of metal arch bar:

- Removal of Metal Arch Bar by Mr. Glendinning - under local anaesthetic and sedation.

Postscript

13.02.02

Hemithyroidectomy:

- Removal of large multinodular goitre (right lobe of thyroid) from neck.

05.03.02

- Thyroid cancer diagnosed.
- Further treatment to follow…